About the

J.D. Gilbert lives in London, England. University of Cambridge include modern history of Japan. After his studies, he worked as a manager of a historic house and art gallery whilst trying to 'make it big' in the music industry with his rock band. He then moved into the field of education where he has worked for the past two decades. He has practised Nichiren Buddhism with the SGI for twenty years.

Praise for The Evolving Buddha

"So many people say that if they were to take up a religion, it would be Buddhism. For them, and for the thousands of existing practitioners, here is a beautifully written book on the Nichiren tradition as practised within the SGI movement which, for the first time, places the core teachings and practice within a larger jigsaw of human understanding, history and science.

Each chapter is purposeful, brings in relevant research, and de-mystifies prevailing issues like distrust of organised religions. Each chapter is peppered with accounts of the author's experiences which keep the text grounded and give it a very human touch.

Consistently asking the questions the reader wants answered, it promotes a questioning approach consistent with freedom of thought."

Jim Cowan, author, *The Britain Potential* and editor, *Buddhism of the Sun*

"Buddhism teaches a timely message of the unity of all humanity and the cosmos. In contrast, as a religious tradition it has fractured along a thousand lines over two millennia. Political, cultural, and institutional factors which led to rigid dogmatism are to blame. In *The Evolving Buddha* author J.D. Gilbert offers an alternative: an empowering practice that adapts to changing times and circumstances. After all, the Buddha denied permanence, a stance that should apply to any doctrines expounded in his name.

From the Mahayana reform movement that produced the scripture the Lotus Sutra, to the Japanese priest Nichiren who strove to return Buddhism to its humanistic origins, up to today's global peace-oriented lay society Soka Gakkai, Gilbert outlines a progressive vision of what Buddhism is and can be. His narrative is both scholarly and personal, providing many access points for an array of readers, whether curious or sceptical. He also contributes to a growing body of Soka Gakkai-specific literature written from the perspective of those steeped in the Western cultural tradition.

J.D. Gilbert has found a path of heartfelt engagement within Soka Gakkai while retaining a sharp and penetrating gaze on its deeper message. I highly recommend the book for seekers of all stripes who are open to a new or better understanding of a life-changing modern iteration of the Buddha's teachings."

J.M. Walsh, author, *Dial In: Soka Buddhism on the Religious Spectrum*

"Having just finished reading *The Evolving Buddha*, I do not think I have ever read anything that has impressed and inspired me more. The book is a must-read for anyone who wants to learn for themselves about a dynamic and ever-evolving form of Buddhism. It is of great interest to those who have a concern for the teaching and learning of others and the happiness of all human beings.

The Evolving Buddha is an impressive and inspiring work, thoroughly well researched and documented. J.D. Gilbert succeeds in managing with three different styles of detailed presentation; scientific expositions, philosophical argument and profound personal experience."

José Cavilla, Former Dean and Head of Faculty of Education, Garnett College, University of London

J.D GILBERT

THE
EVOLVING
BUDDHA

New Perspectives and Dynamic
Change in Nichiren Buddhism
(SGI)

All Rights Reserved

Copyright © 2021 J.D. Gilbert

J.D. Gilbert has asserted his right under the Copyright, Designs and Patents Act 1988 to be identified as the author of this work.

Cover design by Flyfisher

Cover image by Christos Georghiou from © iStock

Chapter icon created by kareemov from Noun Project and page break icon by Stevie Biffen from Noun Project.

The book cover design is copyright to J.D. Gilbert

First published in 2021 by Gojyo Books

The book is sold subject to the condition that it shall not, by way of trade or otherwise, be lent, resold, hired out, or otherwise circulated without the author's prior consent in any form of binding or cover other than that in which it is published and without a similar condition, including this condition, being imposed on the subsequent purchaser.

ISBN-13: 979-8-57913-374-8

Dedicated to my mentor, Daisaku Ikeda

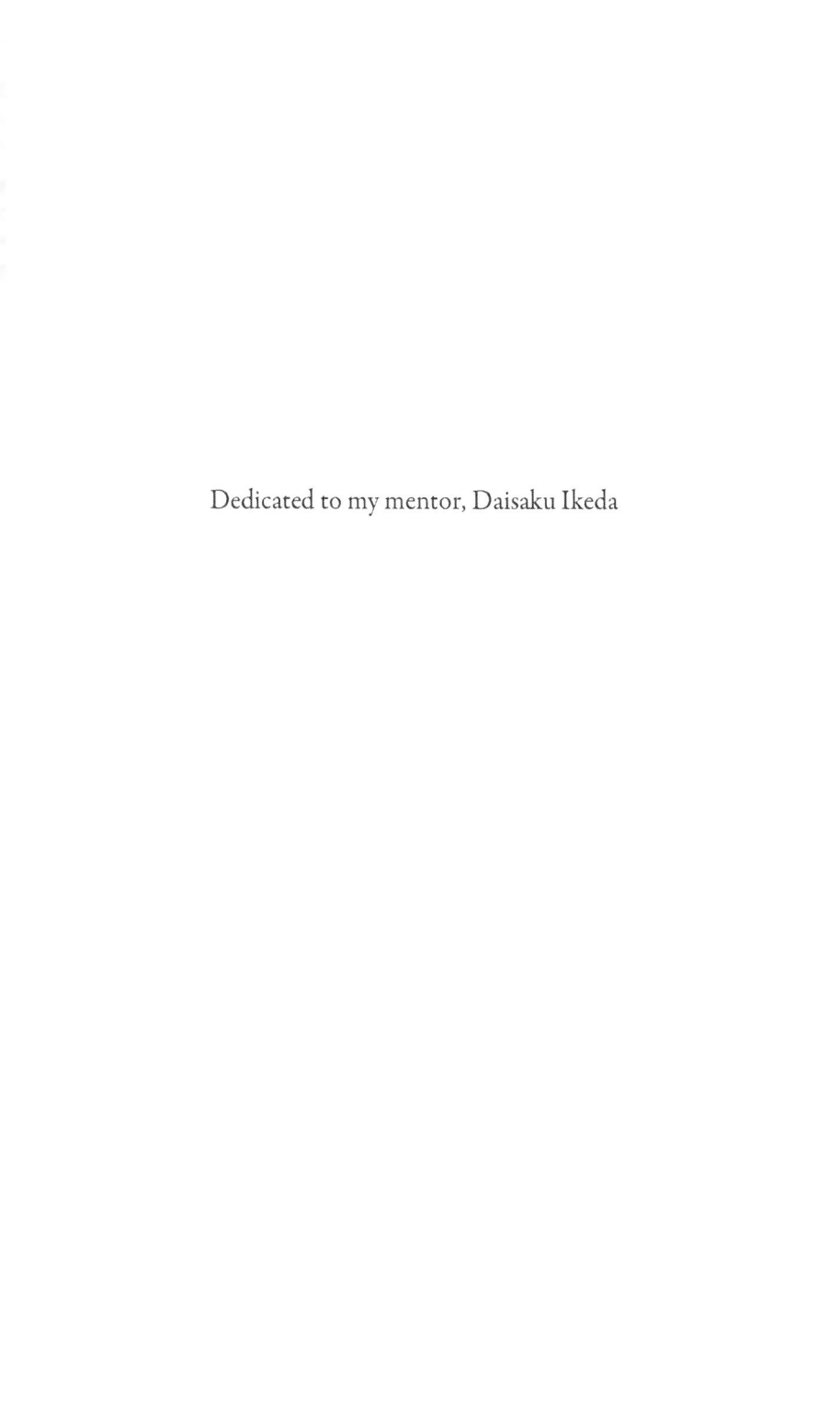

Acknowledgements

Many thanks to Fleur Clackson who first encouraged me to write the book after a chance meeting at the SGI South London National Centre, Brixton. Thanks to Barbara and John Krol, Pepe Cavilla, Paul Robison and Vania Adams who gave their time to edit and respond to my draft. Their help and input was invaluable in readying the manuscript for publication.

Thanks to Joan Anderson and Yuki Kawanaka at the SGI Publications Department in Tokyo for assisting so considerately my submission to use quotes from Daisaku Ikeda and Nichiren and to the Publications Committee for giving permission in this regard. To Mick Walsh and Jim Cowan, many thanks for your encouragement and input - two pioneer leaders for kosen rufu from either side of the Atlantic whose experience, breadth of knowledge and open mindedness are inspirational.

Thanks to all the authors who graciously gave me permission to quote from their works and for their enriching contribution to our understanding of Nichiren Buddhism and life in general. Gratitude to Sue Grossey for her advice in bringing the book to publication and Mike Heritage for such a beautiful cover design. Thank you to my mentor, Daisaku Ikeda for the impact he has had on my life and the world. Finally, thanks to my wife and children for giving me the support, space and time to complete this work and to all the friends who encouraged me in creating this book.

CONTENTS

Introduction	1
Chapter One The Lotus Sutra – The King of Sutras	15
Chapter Two Nichiren – The Ordinary Buddha	39
Chapter Three Nam-myoho-renge-kyo – The Roar of the Lion	73
Part 1 – How Does Chanting Work?	73
Part 2 – New Scientific Horizons	91
Part 3 – The Science of Chanting	110
Chapter Four The Gohonzon – Entering the Treasure Tower	123
Chapter Five The Soka Gakkai and SGI – The Value Creators	149
Part 1 – Why Do I Need an Organisation?	149
Part 2 – Our Collective Conditioning	166
Part 3 – Why Choose SGI?	184

Chapter Six
Daisaku Ikeda – The Bond of Mentor and Disciple   201
Part 1 – Why Have a Mentor?   201
Part 2 – Ikeda's Philosophy   221
Part 3 – On Persecutions   232

Conclusion   247

Glossary   260

Timeline   274

Selected Bibliography   281

Notes   288

Abbreviations

Quotations from Nichiren Daishonin in this book are taken from *The Writings of Nichiren Daishonin* published by Soka Gakkai in 1999 and are given the initials WND followed by the volume and page number.

Quotations from The Lotus Sutra in this book are taken from Burton Watson's translation published by Colombia Press in 1993 and are given the initials LS followed by the page number.

All other quotations are endnoted with full details of the book in the Bibliography at the back of the book.

INTRODUCTION

2000 was the year when everything changed. At the age of 25, I was living in a rented shared house in a suburb of London, England. I had experienced a stable middle class upbringing and had studied history at Cambridge University. Although my mother was an upbeat and generally positive figure, my father, despite being an intelligent and good-hearted man, was sadly dogged by severe depression throughout his adult life. After a major breakdown when I was around 3 years old, he was put on long term lithium medication. I successfully completed my university education, though my heart held ambition was to make it in the music industry.

It was in the summer of the year 2000, however, when my world began to implode. At the end of the previous year, my father committed suicide and a month later, my long term girlfriend of 5 years left me. Already prone to anxiety, I began to feel increasingly desperate.

I had previously gone on a number of personal development courses which had helped with my self-awareness and low moods. I resolved to spend over £1000 to attend this particular organisation's week long training course in the Blue Ridge Mountains in the United States. Instead of 'sorting my head out' as I had hoped, the intense activities sent me over the edge psychologically. In one of the sessions where the participants were supposed to vent their anger in a darkened room, I became disturbed by the attentions of one of the other participants.

I came out of the course a nervous wreck, with 3 days ahead of me in New York sightseeing, staying with a friend. Whilst my friend was at work, I wandered the streets of Manhattan in a daze, my hands trembling just as my father's had near to the end of his life. I ventured into a Hare Krishna centre to talk to one of the monks, but left dissatisfied with his talk of the material world being entirely an illusion. I returned to England in a far worse state than I had left, but equally open to anything that would return me to at least the equilibrium I had before my visit to America.

It was in early August of that summer that I walked into the SGI Buddhist centre on Richmond Green to ask about meditation. When the receptionist told me that they didn't meditate but chanted, I promptly told him that wasn't for me and headed out of the door. In one of those moments where one's life is changed forever, a woman was walking through the door as I exited. She stopped me and asked what I was doing there. When I explained, she told me she held chanting sessions at her place with lots of young people and I was welcome. I gave it a go.

After my first try at chanting, I tidied my room for the first time in 6 months. It certainly seemed to have given me some energy. I was encouraged to test it with goal setting in terms of relationships and my music career and, as a result, positive

INTRODUCTION

openings manifested. I started to go to SGI discussion meetings and chanted with others. My life opened up and, most importantly, after about 5-6 months of chanting, my anxiety was fully dispelled and I began to feel happier than I ever had before.

After 8 months of Buddhist chanting, morning and evening for about 10-20 minutes at a time, I decided to become an SGI member and receive my own calligraphic scroll (Gohonzon) to chant to. I soon took on responsibility supporting other young men with their chanting and helping organise Buddhist activities.

Meanwhile, I moved away from a music career to train to become a teacher and I used the Buddhist chanting to regularly reinvigorate myself in the arduous struggles in the classroom. In the UK, primary school teaching is now considered the most psychologically stressful career one can have in terms of the number of mental health referrals from those in the profession. Dropout rate is high, with half of teachers quitting in the first five years of their career. My chances did not look great considering my family history and track record, including moving from jobs every two years at the most. However, I have now been a teacher for 20 years, and in the last 7 have been a Deputy Head Teacher at a school I absolutely love. I am certain chanting gave me the tools and the resilience not to give up in the hardest of times. In addition, I have a wonderful loving family and even my mother now chants having seen such a change in me.

THE EVOLVING BUDDHA

What will you find in this book?

Buddhism is a mystery to many – conjuring in the mind a mixture of exotic and oriental imagery. Buddhism for those who have examined it, is a wonderful, awe inspiring, eye popping, life challenging, reality facing revelation of what life can offer. Buddhism is a precious jewel for anyone to take. It is a soul searching, human centred, roller coaster ride which enriches our everyday interactions. This book was conceived to help on that journey.

There are many, many, many books on Buddhism out there, a considerable number of which are aimed at the 'introductory market': the Buddhism in a nutshell crowd. I feel that market is more than fully saturated and filled with doubtlessly invaluable offerings. This is not an introductory book. It won't teach you about the basic principles through a well-crafted modern novel (For that, I recommend *The Buddha, Geoff and Me* by Edward Canfor-Dumas) or explain how it can be applied in everyday life (*The Buddha in Your Mirror* by Martin, Morino and Hochswender fits the bill for this) or give you a more in-depth summary of the philosophical underpinnings of Buddhism (Try *The Buddha in Daily Life* by Richard Causton).

Instead, this book is a declaration, an illustration of how humanity works and as a result how Buddhism really works. It is an exploration of the organic and evolving dynamic that is Buddhism and, more specifically in this case, the life enhancing and humanistic teaching of Nichiren Buddhism as espoused by the SGI (Soka Gakkai International), one of the big three Buddhisms in its geographical spread and reach (alongside Zen

INTRODUCTION

and Tibetan), the biggest form of Buddhism in such diverse countries as Brazil, Italy and Japan. I hope it will be of interest to not only those currently practising Buddhism but also those intrigued by the subject.

Nichiren Buddhism, or Soka Gakkai Nichiren Buddhism in this form, has its roots in 13th century Japan where it was founded by a monk, Nichiren in the tumultuous age of the Kamakura Shogunate. Nichiren saw in the egalitarian and life affirming teachings of the Lotus Sutra the path to enlightenment. The Soka Gakkai (which means 'Value Creating Society), a lay Buddhist movement, interpreted Nichiren's teachings for the modern era, resulting in explosive expansion after the Second World War in Japan and later around the world. From being almost solely practised in Japan before 1960, it has spread to 192 countries and territories in little over 50 years. This is in part because of the flexibility of the teaching to adapt to local customs and cultures without being trapped in a particularly Japanese mindset. More importantly though, the logic and practicality of the philosophy and, most importantly, the beneficial effects of its primary practice of chanting the phrase Nam-myoho-renge-kyo have been the key to its success.

My motivation for writing this book

I gave the initial brief overview of my experience with Buddhism, in part, to introduce why I came to write this book. By way of further explanation, let us move forward 10 years to 2010/11 when a health crisis shook my Buddhist practice. At this time, to alleviate the insomnia which was a symptom of my condition, I began to practise mindfulness meditation and meditated for an hour a day for almost 2 years (I also continued to chant, if less than before and attend SGI discussion meetings during this time). I found the meditation initially helpful and did gain many positive experiences from it.

During that period, I dabbled in all sorts of meditative practices and explored different organisations, including the Quakers, Insight Meditation, Thich Nhat Hanh's Community of Interbeing and Yogananda's Self Realizing Fellowship, to name but a few. Although I saw benefits in all these groups, none of them quite inspired me the way SGI meetings had. Furthermore, the meditation was not ultimately helping me with my health problem and insomnia. Eventually, I received the right medical treatment to resolve the issues and almost immediately had a realisation. I wanted to reengage with the chanting and SGI activities more fully. Since then I have not looked back, yet one further incident would provoke me to go deeper in my Buddhist practice and ultimately to write this book.

SGI is a lay movement organised on a grass roots local level by volunteers, ordinary SGI members with a minimal paid leadership in each country to centrally administer the running of things on a national level. This has been the case since its inception in 1930 but up until 1991 SGI was also affiliated to an older traditional form of Japanese temple based Buddhism, Nichiren Shoshu. In 1991, Nichiren Shoshu excommunicated some 10 million lay members of SGI worldwide, hoping that this would result in the end of SGI. This did not take place and SGI continued to prosper independent of an organised priesthood as a fully lay movement. The differences and

INTRODUCTION

divisions that caused this split have been examined in a number of independent books, most notably in the Oxford University press book *A Time to Chant* by Bryan Wilson and Karel Dobbelaere (see Appendix especially in this publication) and in Clark Strand's *Waking the Buddha*. Recriminations and accusations flew both ways in the years following the split. However, both Wilson/Dobbelaere and Strand see the separation as a far more inevitable development for SGI, an outward looking, egalitarian and progressive movement in contrast to the priestly caste of Nichiren Shoshu, authoritarian, conservative, traditional and hierarchical. The contrast in these two approaches will be key in understanding the logic behind this book, and the split will be looked at again at times in the chapters that follow.

My own experience of this split came not in 1991 (well before I started practising), but in 2016 when two members of SGI whom I knew, chose to move across to Nichiren Shoshu. This came as an initial surprise to me. Why would they leave this wonderful organisation? Ostensibly, the reason was SGI's decision to move away from worshipping what was known as the Dai-Gohonzon – a supposed super mandala (devotional object) bestowed on all humanity. SGI gave a valid explanation that all mandala Gohonzons have the same beneficial effect, but for these two members, attached to this traditional concept, it was not enough. The issues surrounding the Dai-Gohonzon will be looked at more fully in a chapter of the book.

I had a clear understanding from an SGI perspective of the merits of our lay movement and the pitfalls of a traditionalist priestly hierarchy. Studying the inspirational, humanistic and open minded writings of my Buddhist teacher, Daisaku Ikeda, founding president of SGI, had given me an essential grounding. I had no need to hear the inflammatory protestations of the priests whose jealousy and ire towards SGI had continued unabated. And yet, I wanted to hear another voice, an impartial voice beyond any partisan lines. I did not search for that voice on the internet, knowing full well the unchecked and spurious statements found there on every topic, including SGI Buddhism. Anti-religious, anti-SGI, anti-Japanese, the haters and the distortion of facts proliferate on the World Wide Web. To see the wood for the trees, the falsities from the facts, is not an easy task.

Instead, I turned to verifiable sources and a system which although not fool proof or open to bias, involves a process of verification and checking. Academic research and books must undergo a series of reviews, revisions and resubmissions before finally being accepted or rejected for publication. As I studied SGI, Nichiren and Nichiren Shoshu from the perspective of Oxford University, Princeton University, the University of Hawaii, Kyoto University and Leuven Catholic University, my Buddhist faith in SGI was reconfirmed, my understanding of the development of Buddhism given greater clarity.

I began to take an interest in reading more widely about SGI Buddhism whilst continuing to study Ikeda and Nichiren's writings. I delved into what is becoming a rich literary heritage developed by ordinary SGI members and non-SGI writers, including those of other religions, outside of official publications – a heritage which offers insights and information that can, again, enrich one's practice.

INTRODUCTION

The book's purpose

An early idea for this book was to call it 'Buddhism Revealed', to offer SGI members and the general public concepts, facts and ideas that are not at the forefront in SGI publications. However, this seemed a limited purpose; the sharing of titbits gleaned from these books, the sense it was an exposé of something hidden. This initial idea developed further after reading the works of J.M. Walsh, a member of SGI-USA and, although not a professional academic, a scholarly master of Nichiren Buddhism who has advocated what I am going to describe as a 'universalist approach' to SGI Buddhism by illustrating the interconnections between all religions. Unequivocally taking SGI President Daisaku Ikeda as his mentor, he has broadened his study of Buddhism to suggest progressive changes in outlook and perspective without any sense of creating a breakaway movement. The latter point is extremely important because Ikeda's broad and all-encompassing approach to Buddhism has meant that, internationally, members of SGI have already been free to hold such a progressive and inclusive attitude to their Buddhist practice which can accommodate a range of views, centring on essential core principles based on faith, practice and study, and the centrality of the dignity of life. It should be noted that faith in SGI Buddhism is not faith in an external deity but faith in one's potential combined with an open mind, a flexible spirit and a willingness to engage with Buddhist principles.

This book aims to illuminate a universalist approach in SGI, re-clarifying and supporting it with some well researched evidence in some key areas to show how the principles of

THE EVOLVING BUDDHA

Nichiren Buddhism have evolved and are still evolving. I am indebted to a number of scholars in sharing their findings and make no claims other than this book is a synthesis and summation of current research in a number of Buddhist related topics, supplemented with my own personal experiences of practice.

A universalist approach

What does this universalist approach mean? It means seeing all religions as human-made, as something that has organically developed and grown from people's wisdom and interactions. It means that religion, whilst retaining its spiritual essence and core principles, can be improved and developed over time, depending on the society and historical context it is being practised in. A universalist approach rejects absolute dogma or the fundamentalist viewpoint of the primacy and unchallenged superiority of a particular religion. It is open to criticism and analysis, but is willing to state the validity and efficacy of its particular practice. It is respectful of others' beliefs and philosophies, seeing the similarities, not just the differences between them and the ultimate commonalities of all human spirituality.

I suggest a universalist approach is absolutely vital at a time when across the world we see entrenched and restrictive viewpoints which demonise the other, suppress freedom of expression and thought through religious dogma and precedent and threaten people who differ in their opinion. Such authoritarian, conservative and fundamentalist viewpoints are seen in every major world religion and political system. Daisaku

INTRODUCTION

Ikeda's greatness is to no small extent attributable to his leadership in moving SGI away from a fundamentalist viewpoint as sole provider of truth/salvation, to the all-encompassing broad spirited movement we have today. My purpose is to further clarify Ikeda's approach through the lens of some of the research that has come to light in recent years. The late Shin Yatomi, the former Study Chief of SGI-USA very much contributed to this process in his incisive book, *Buddhism in a New Light* which made a clarion call for the prioritisation of universal values over dogma and authority.

Yet tradition, precedent and history have a hold on us, and rightly so. If, at regular intervals, we changed everything we believed and held dear, it would lead to chaos. Human conditioning is there for an evolutionary reason, something we will examine in a later chapter. However, that hold can make religions believe they are the possessors of a pure and unsullied truth handed down in perfect holy scriptures that cannot be questioned or analysed. It can mean these holy words or objects can be used as weapons to oppress people in terms of authority, sexuality, gender, race and independence of thought. Such a mindset can refuse to accept the scientific evidence railed in front of it, or the suffering human being who needs compassion above all rules. Religious self-righteous dogma, in Buddhist terms, is what Nichiren termed 'the devil king of the sixth heaven', a mythic metaphor for the tendency in human beings to control others for their own ends.

In this book, I want to look at some of the long held traditional concepts in Nichiren Buddhism which have had value in the historical context of their time, but can be re-examined under the light of modern understanding. Such concepts may have even inspired the innovative and universal practice of chanting Nam-myoho-renge-kyo. However, such concepts can become a sham, a half-hearted gesture once greater understanding is applied. Taking a universalist approach, we do not need to feel let down or devalued as SGI Buddhists when certain historic absolutes dissolve. In fact, we can be liberated to see the absolute value of our Buddhist practice, unfettered by uncertainty and unresolved doubt.

I must, however, make it clear that this book is not an official SGI publication. I have held a variety of responsibilities in SGI at different levels, but this book is my own personal journey in study, and reflects my individual views, not those of SGI as a whole. I am nonetheless grateful to Soka Gakkai for giving me permission to quote from Nichiren and Ikeda's writings.

In the first chapter, we will look at the origins of the Lotus Sutra, the teaching which Nichiren considered the source of his innovative philosophy and practice. The second chapter will look at Nichiren's identity and its implications to attaining enlightenment. In the third chapter, we will consider the key element of practice, chanting Nam-myoho-renge-kyo. What *is* the Mystic Law it encapsulates and can science give us the answer? The fourth chapter examines the mandala (devotional object) – the Gohonzon, how it evolved along with Nichiren's own spiritual journey and its ultimate meaning. In the fifth chapter we focus on the Soka Gakkai and SGI – how they have developed, and the science behind being part of a community. In the sixth chapter, we meet Daisaku Ikeda and see what he stands for, how his thought has evolved and why he has been

INTRODUCTION

persecuted. We will also look into the logic behind the mentor and disciple relationship.

Above all, we can see that Buddhism, in fact, all human endeavour, is not fixed in its content. It is constantly changing, adapting to the times and new understanding of what makes us human. Nichiren Buddhism and SGI are evolving sometimes subtly, sometimes dramatically, and this realisation in itself can be liberating - can be enlightening. As we take on the challenges of a world changing more rapidly than ever, now is the time to embrace the Evolving Buddha.

CHAPTER ONE

THE LOTUS SUTRA

THE KING OF SUTRAS

"The Lotus Sutra is the king of sutras, true and correct in both word and principle. Its words are the ultimate reality, and this reality is the Mystic Law (myoho). It is called the Mystic Law because it reveals the principle of the mutually inclusive relationship of a single moment of life and all phenomena. That is why this sutra is the wisdom of all Buddhas."

On Attaining Buddhahood in This Lifetime (WND 1, p3)

The lady who introduced me to Nichiren Buddhism is a special person, not just in how she transformed my life but in her unique character. For the purposes of the book I will call her Tina. Tina is a fearless battler who knows her mind and is not afraid to put people straight. In England we use the term Marmite, a popular food spread to describe things you either love or loathe. Tina is a bit like Marmite. Her compassion and charisma made her many friends and me adore her, but she would not back down in a debate or pander to social niceties. Her independent mind and passion for practising Buddhism greatly inspired me. At Tina's rented flat near to where I lived, there would always be a panoply of people: young, old, English, Japanese, Italian, Hungarian, Buddhist and non-Buddhist. Tina is Hungarian by birth but brought up in England. After the tragic loss of one of her children and a difficult divorce, she began a search to find deeper meaning in her life, which first brought her to the Spiritualist church and then finally to Nichiren Buddhism, which she has practised ever since.

When SGI-UK decided to initiate a country-wide dialogue initiative called the 'mini meeting campaign', encouraging SGI members to connect with friends, family and colleagues, Tina took things one step further and stood at Speakers' Corner in Hyde Park, London, a traditional venue for free speech and spoke to over a hundred people about Nichiren Buddhism. SGI leaders did not feel this was quite the spirit of individual and personal dialogue, but many years later the head office at Taplow received a letter from an Israeli man in Tel Aviv, who had been in the crowd and had begun to practise Buddhism from then on with great effects in his life.

A while after I had begun chanting, Tina said she had a present for me. Coming to my place to chant one day, she handed me a typed manuscript. At first glance, I thought she had written a book or a play but, in fact, this was the Lotus Sutra. Tina had typed it out for me, but this was not the first time she had done this. She had also previously hand written an entire copy of the sutra (sutra means Buddhist scripture).

THE LOTUS SUTRA

Sutra-copying is considered meritorious in East Asian Buddhism, as an expression of devotional practice. Although Tina's decision may seem a little eccentric and not something that contemporary Nichiren Buddhists are encouraged to do, Nichiren does refer to the copying of passages of the Lotus Sutra in a number of his writings. Tina was unique in this act of piety, and this would be my first introduction to the Buddhist writing which underpins the basis of Nichiren and SGI Buddhist practice.

A fantastical realm

The Lotus Sutra is one of the most influential of all Buddhist texts. Its story is portrayed in truly epic proportions on a vast cosmic canvas. Rich and fantastical imagery abound including a multitude of Buddhas and Bodhisattvas with transcendental powers, mythical creatures, bejewelled towers, fearsome demons and heavenly beings. Beyond this cast of exotic characters we find allegorical stories providing Buddhist teachings: burning houses, ornate carriages, magically conjured cities and precious jewels.

Central to this multiplicity of imagery is the magnificent 'Ceremony in the Air' and its treasure tower. In the eleventh chapter of the Lotus Sutra, a gigantic tower covered in precious objects and jewels erupts from the earth. Seated within the tower is Many Treasures Buddha who promises to appear wherever the Lotus Sutra is preached. Heavenly offerings rain down in approval and Shakyamuni Buddha uses his transcendental powers to bring forth a multitude of Buddhas and Bodhisattvas, raising them up in the air to see the treasure tower opened and revealed.

THE EVOLVING BUDDHA

Hidden meaning

Behind the mind-boggling imagery is the profundity of the Lotus Sutra's message. There is more to the text than a surface reading would engender from a narrative that verges on science fiction. The Lotus Sutra has been meditated upon, contemplated, unpicked, reinterpreted and read for its deeper meaning for hundreds of years, over successive generations of Buddhist sages and practitioners. For example, Nichiren saw the treasure tower in metaphorical terms, as representative of the preciousness of our own lives and of our inherent potential to reveal the most wonderful of states, Buddhahood. In a letter to a loyal follower he writes:

"Abutsu-bo is therefore the treasure tower itself and the treasure tower is Abutsu-bo himself. No other knowledge is purposeful…You may think you offered gifts to the treasure tower of the Thus Come One Many Treasures, but that is not so. You offered them to yourself." (WND 1, p299)

Nichiren placed primary importance on the Lotus Sutra as the source of his teachings and practice. Its supremacy historically and philosophically was the basis for the development of his unique, empowering and egalitarian form of Buddhism. In the modern era, SGI study and the writings of SGI President Daisaku Ikeda consistently cross reference the sutra. In his multi-volume work, *The Wisdom of the Lotus Sutra*, Ikeda engaged in dialogue with notable authorities from the Soka Gakkai Study Department to examine in great detail each chapter of the Lotus Sutra.

THE LOTUS SUTRA

A new perspective

And yet, there is a challenge that lies behind our perspective of the Lotus Sutra in the modern age. Contemporary research conclusively points to there being no direct link from the words of the Lotus Sutra to Shakyamuni Buddha – Siddhartha Gautama, the historical Buddha. All Buddhist sutras begin with the phrase, 'This is what I heard', acknowledging that the following text would be a faithful record of Shakyamuni's utterances by his close disciple Ananda. On further investigation, in the case of the Lotus Sutra, the possibility that Ananda heard these words from Shakyamuni is highly implausible.

In fact, the Lotus Sutra is thought to have been composed in stages between 50 and 200 CE (Common Era), most probably in the Central Asian Kushan Empire, 500 to 700 years after the Buddha's passing. The Lotus Sutra is a Mahayanan text, which means literally Great Vehicle, in comparison to the Theravadan texts which purport to be of earlier origin. Does this change of perspective on the origins of the Lotus Sutra put Nichiren and SGI's philosophical basis on shaky ground? In this chapter, I will suggest that it does not. Can SGI's practice be called Buddhist if it originated from a source other than the thoughts of Shakyamuni Buddha? I will state absolutely that it can. However, to steer us onto a new basis extracted from the origin myths of the Lotus Sutra, we must first look into the long established beliefs surrounding it and importantly Nichiren's view.

THE EVOLVING BUDDHA

Nichiren's view of the Lotus Sutra

Nichiren was an unrivalled scholar with an intellect of the highest calibre. His surviving written works portray an impressive breadth of knowledge of contemporary religious texts and the associated analysis. He acknowledged contradictions and errors in some of the Buddhist sutras and commentaries, but he worked under the conventions of his time. It is not a disparagement on his greatness to recast his understanding in a new light, and will not mean that one must reject the deeper meaning that he found in the Lotus Sutra.

Nichiren made his first vow as a youth having entered temple life at 12 years old. He vowed to become the wisest person in Japan to repay his debts of gratitude to his parents and society. From this point, his spiritual journey of study and reflection began, later taking him to the major centres of learning in the country and finally to declare the supremacy of the Lotus Sutra and the practice of chanting Nam-myoho-renge-kyo on 28th April 1253. This mantra can be literally translated as 'I offer devotion to the wonderful law of the Lotus Sutra' but also has multiple other meanings.

Nichiren argued that the Lotus Sutra held the key to a fully Buddhist practice which could empower all people to realise their greatest potential – their Buddhahood in an age of strife and chaos. His reasoning had two defined features. One involved categorisation of the Buddhist teachings by drawing on proof from within the sutra itself, on commentaries and other supporting sutras. We could note this reasoning as 'documentary'. The second reason was based on Nichiren's deeper reading of the text, drawing forth the profound philosophical teaching which it embodied.

In his treatise written whilst in exile on Sado island, off the coast of Japan and entitled 'The Opening of the Eyes', Nichiren used a critical method of evaluating Buddhist teachings called the fivefold comparison. This begins with a comparison of Buddhist and non-Buddhist teachings, then Mahayana and Therevada (Hinayana, as Mahayanans described it, meaning the lesser vehicle), then true Mahayana, to provisional Mahayana (in other words the Lotus Sutra compared to pre-Lotus Sutra teachings). The next two levels go further in unpicking the essential practice within the Lotus Sutra. What must be noted is, that Nichiren often referred to the Lotus Sutra's pre-eminence in the third comparison, by citing the following words from the Immeasurable Meanings Sutra (which is considered a prelude to the Lotus Sutra), "In these more than forty years, I have not yet revealed the truth." The Lotus Sutra itself emphasizes its supremacy to other sutras, stating for example, "it is the foremost among all that is preached by the Thus Come One (Buddha)" (LS p207) and "among all that is preached, it is the most profound." Many other sutras make similar claims, which is why Nichiren placed special emphasis on the quote from the Immeasurable Meanings Sutra. This was based on a historical understanding of the era which he considered himself to be in, based on a Buddhist chronology, a chronology which is still referred to in SGI today.

THE EVOLVING BUDDHA

The selection of the time

Nichiren believed that he was propagating his teaching in the fifth five hundred year period after the Buddha's passing, 'The Latter Day of the Law', which was regarded as a muddied age rife with conflict and confusion as predicted in the Lotus Sutra itself. This would be a time when Shakyamuni entrusted to his disciples, "(you) must spread it widely (kosen rufu) throughout Jampudvipa (the known world) and never allow it to be cut off."(LS p288)

Nichiren believed the Buddha had lived between 1029 and 949 Before Common Era (BCE) based on Chinese chronologies. This meant that the fifth five hundred year period, the Latter Day of the Law, had started around 1052. However it is generally recognised from modern research that the Buddha passed away approximately in 400 BCE[1]. This would mean the Latter Day began in 1600 or so, long after Nichiren's passing. Nichiren's powerful sense of mission was greatly defined by his sense of historical moment supported by the evidence at the time. In SGI meetings, the chronology based on the Lotus Sutra still abounds. Does it matter that Nichiren's chronology may have been faulty based on what we know now? Perhaps we need to see the concept of the Latter Day of the Law, or 'mappo' as it was traditionally referred to, in broader terms.

Nichiren's urgent resolve to liberate humanity from suffering, was based on the idea of an era of conflict and chaos and yet, irrelevant of any chronological framework, the period he lived in abounded with tragedy and darkness. In his 1260 masterwork, "On Establishing the Correct Teaching for the

Peace of the Land", he describes the disastrous state of 13th century Japanese society replete with warfare, famine, earthquakes and epidemics.

"Oxen and horses lie dead in the streets, and the bones of the stricken crowd the highways. Over half the population has already been carried off by death, and there is hardly a single person who does not grieve." (WND1, p6)

Although the Latter Day of the Law was defined as a 500 year period (which we would currently be in, based on the new chronology), it is more broadly seen in SGI as a continuing era that exists in the environmental, social and political challenges we see today. Just as Nichiren saw in 1260, SGI today sees a spiritual and philosophical change in humanity's outlook and basis as the key to improving the external tribulations in society. Quite when an era began, is ultimately irrelevant to the reality that degeneracy and suffering exist, and to how society can be fundamentally changed for the better.

Profound meaning

It would have been a very empty kind of Buddhism if Nichiren had aimed to validate his position by historical documentary proof alone. In fact, Nichiren often cited three proofs to justify the ultimate value of his teaching, "In judging the relative merit of Buddhist doctrines, I, Nichiren, believe that the best standards are those of reason and documentary proof. And even more valuable than reason and documentary proof is the proof of actual fact." (WND 1, p599)

Actual proof has been an axiom of faith for SGI members, who have proven the efficacy of faith, practice and study in

Nichiren Buddhism through transformative experiences in their own lives. A cursory glance at any of the SGI publications, in any country across the world, will highlight the importance of personal experience as a test of the value of chanting Nam-myoho-renge-kyo. For Nichiren, the Lotus Sutra's importance lay not in merely the documentary proof we have discussed thus far, but in how it actualised a complete philosophical basis for the revelation of Buddhahood, the highest life state, for ordinary people.

The Lotus Sutra was supreme on this basis, but this did not come from a surface reading of the colourful stories and imagery. It came from a deeper reading of the text, which drew upon Nichiren's predecessors' own insights on the profound meaning lying beneath the cosmic interplay of fantastical characters. This is why SGI members are not actively encouraged to, at least initially, read the Lotus Sutra or focus on it as a primary text. This is because relying only on the Lotus Sutra would most likely lead us to interpret it from our own limited perspective and at a superficial level. Nichiren's deep understanding of the Lotus Sutra came from his own profound contemplative, sometimes described as 'bodily', reading of the text, which in turn was inspired and indebted to great masters prior to him, Dengyo, Miao-Lo and T'ien-t'ai.

Nichiren did not suggest the Lotus Sutra was perfect or absolute in and of itself. He revered it because of two outstanding principles which he elicited from it and which he considered could relieve all suffering, transform society and realise the Buddha state in ordinary people's lives.

The first of these he found residing in the second chapter of the sutra, 'The Expedient Means' chapter. T'ien-T'ai, a

Chinese Buddhist sage, had previously drawn forth from the Lotus Sutra the concept of *ichinen sanzen*, 'Three Thousand Realms in a Single Moment of Life.' In essence, this was a framework based on life, the individual, the environment, causal factors and ten key life states that indicate we all have incredible potential in each life moment to respond in a huge multitude of ways. The ten life states (also known as the Ten Worlds), states of being ranging from hell, hunger and anger to rapture, learning and realisation, were importantly mutually interconnected to one another to allow the individual to draw from any one of them the state of Buddhahood, which is a condition of compassion, courage, life-force and wisdom. Although this concept was crucial to Nichiren's philosophy, it was still in what he called the theoretical part of the Lotus Sutra and was only made real in the essential later section of the Lotus Sutra within the 16th chapter.

During this 16th chapter, 'The Life Span' chapter, Shakyamuni Buddha reveals that he did not attain Buddhahood under the Bodhi tree in India in his present lifetime, but reached Buddhahood an infinite length of time before in previous lifetimes. Nichiren was clear, though many have misinterpreted him, that this did not mean Shakyamuni attained enlightenment at a fixed point however far in the past, but that the state of Buddhahood, along with the other nine life states, are eternally abiding features of existence. With this clarification in the 16th chapter, ordinary people could reveal their greatest self in the life moment. It is these two chapters, the 2nd and 16th that SGI members recite morning and evening, known as gongyo, before they begin their core practice of chanting Nam-myoho-renge-kyo. We will consider Nichiren's understanding of the Lotus Sutra later in the chapter, but for now let us fast forward to our modern age and the current research on the Lotus Sutra's origins.

Our modern understanding

It is still common in SGI meetings for lecturers to refer to the Lotus Sutra as the penultimate teaching produced by Shakyamuni Buddha and his highest creed – his final masterpiece after 40 years of instruction. And yet a cursory glance at the evidence paints a very different picture. Before looking at the research, let us consider one point which is patently obvious when one reads the sutra; the stories are fantastical and imaginary. How could Shakyamuni extend his tongue across the universe? How could heavenly gods suddenly appear as a giant jewelled stupa broke from the earth? For the faithful in the first millennium of the Common Era, these powerful images may have seemed a true record of the past, yet to even a child in our current world, they are clearly works of fiction created to illustrate a point.

Daisaku Ikeda affirms in *The Wisdom of the Lotus Sutra*, that events described in the sutra are not factual, but that they represent aspects of an enlightened life.[2] It is also acknowledged that when they speak of the stories as if they are real, Ikeda and the Study Department members do so only for the sake of convenience. Nichiren too, saw the Lotus Sutra in allegorical terms, something we will return to.

The oldest surviving version of the Lotus Sutra dates from 286 CE and is a Chinese translation of the original Sanskrit.

Evidence of earlier Sanskrit forms exist from the great Mahayana sage, Nagarjuna, who mentions it extensively in approximately the second to early third century CE. In Ikeda's early work *Buddhism, the First Millennium*, he acknowledges studies that indicate the Lotus Sutra could not have come into existence any earlier than the first century BCE[3]. In both this work and in the 1990s' *The Wisdom of the Lotus Sutra*, Ikeda affirms his belief in a direct connection between Shakyamuni and the Mahayana sutras, but he sees further academic research as appropriate and that, regardless of the outcome of historical research, the profound essence of the Lotus Sutra could not be tarnished[4]. J.M. Walsh, a member of SGI-USA, has written two books that tackle this subject in detail with a meticulous scholarly approach. I am indebted to him in sifting through the current research on the origins of the Lotus Sutra and acknowledge his role in much that I convey in this chapter.

Who created the Lotus Sutra?

The Mahayana movement, which the Lotus Sutra is a fruit of, has often been described as a lay movement of ordinary Buddhist practitioners, living in everyday society, who began to stand up against an increasingly dogmatic and atrophying monastic order which controlled not only the religious order but access to the teachings and ultimately the attainment of Buddhahood. This story certainly has powerful resonance for SGI members, who in their own reformation/renaissance threw off the shackles of priestly dominance and dogma. However, the idea that lay believers were instrumental in the development of Mahayana is mainly supported by scholars in

Japan, whereas elsewhere in the world it is met with scepticism[5].

It seems most likely that the sutra was the work of members of the monastic order working within the existing system. Nagarjuna, mentioned earlier, who was a highly significant figure in uncovering, reformulating and propounding the Mahayana movement, was a monk. The Mahayana sutras including the Lotus, have many descriptions of visionary experiences that most likely derived from the deep meditative experiences which were more readily available at the time to a trained monastic.

The creation of the early Mahayana literature does not seem to have been as a result of an organised movement, and could have been initially produced as practice aids in a particular monastic community that were later recomposed as sutras. These works were mapping out new innovative territory but were not distinct from the main Buddhist community at the time. Only with the work of Nagarjuna and others were these works assembled, codified and possibly recomposed leading to, as their popularity grew, a Mahayana movement.

Certainly, the Lotus Sutra reflects a sense of heightened tensions between Early Buddhist monks and Mahayanists, lay or monastic. In the second chapter, 5000 arrogant Early Buddhist monks, nuns and lay believers leave the assembly where they had gathered to hear the Buddha. The Lotus Sutra's thirteenth chapter describes three powerful enemies who will persecute those who uphold the Lotus Sutra. They include proud and boastful monks, forest dwelling monks greedy for profit and support, and white robed laymen respected and revered by the world. In chapter 10 of the Lotus Sutra, we find the passage often quoted by Nichiren,

"Since hatred and jealousy toward this sutra abound even when the Thus Come One (Buddha) is in the world, how much more will this be so after his passing?"(LS, p164)

Where did the Lotus Sutra come from?

Modern scholars place the birthplace of the Lotus Sutra in the kingdoms of Gandhara and Bactria between modern day Afghanistan and Pakistan. These territories had, for many centuries, a tradition of Zoroastrian worship, the first monotheistic (or dualistic involving a fight between good versus evil), non-tribal religion. This is a time far before the development and spread of Islam to these lands. Gandhara and Bactria also came under Greco-Macedonian influence, ruled by the successors of Alexander the Great. In the second century BCE, Buddhism was being actively propagated in the area.

J.M. Walsh suggests an interplay between Zoroastrianism and nascent Mahayana ideas. For example, the mythical saviour Buddha of the future, Maitreya, who features in Mahayana texts, resembles Saoshyant the future savior of Zoroastrianism[6]. The religions of the fertile crescent – Judaism, Christianity and Islam would also be influenced in their development by a saviour concept first derived from Zoroastrianism. Around this period, Greek craftsmen in Gandhara also began to create beautiful lifelike images of the Buddha.

The formalisation of Mahayana took many years, but seems to have fully developed once the Kushan dynasty took control of Gandhara and Bactria in the first century CE. At the time when Mahayana sutras written in Sanskrit make their appearance, Kusha was thriving and expanding its empire south to more traditional established Buddhist areas, encouraging a flow of texts and monastics. The late Shin Yatomi, study department chief of SGI-USA and a posthumous master professor of the Soka Gakkai study department, referred to the Lotus Sutra, according to scholars, as having been composed in Kusha between the first and third centuries CE[7].

Is knowing this a problem for Buddhists?

So, if we take the current consensus that the Lotus Sutra was created in a Himalayan kingdom independent of Shakyamuni many centuries after his passing, does this provide an existential threat to Nichiren Buddhists and the SGI? Certainly for followers of the Nichiren Shoshu priesthood, I would suggest it does. They stress an unbroken lineage, through successive high priests to Nichiren and on down to Shakyamuni as author of the Lotus Sutra. A pure unbroken line passing the heritage of faith is key to their exclusivist sense of superiority and their often purported claim to be 'True Buddhism'.

SGI still, at times, refers to its own lineage. In fact, SGI-UK at the time of writing this have begun to include a lineage of Buddhism on the inside cover of their monthly magazine, the *Art of Living*. Likewise the main international website sokaglobal.org has Buddhist lineage as one of its tabs. However, SGI can hardly claim to have an unbroken lineage, at least in a continuous chronological sense.

The Soka Gakkai was founded relatively recently in 1930 and, since the split with the priesthood, has shone a light on the actual historical reality of the transference from one

Nichiren Shoshu high priest to another over the centuries in the book *The Untold Story of the Fuji School*. Evidence of child high priests and successional disputes make it clear a pure unbroken lineage is a myth. In fact, SGI's approach to a lineage is emphasised as a spiritual inheritance embodied in the appropriate actions of their three founding presidents, Makiguchi, Toda and Ikeda in the modern era. No reference is made to the individual who actively introduced Makiguchi to this Buddhist practice. Likewise, if the Lotus Sutra embodied the most profound Buddhist teachings, could it lay claim to have inherited the spirit of the Buddha without having a direct connection to him? The aforementioned SGI-UK publication, the *Art of Living*, states, "The Lotus Sutra contains the essence of Shakyamuni's teachings," which is suitably open language not to directly attribute the sutra to the Buddha.

Nichiren's progressive approach

How we view the Lotus Sutra is intrinsic to this approach, and Nichiren's own view of the sutra can point the way. As discussed earlier in terms of the treasure tower, Nichiren did not take the Lotus Sutra as a literal dogmatic text that could not be questioned. He saw it most importantly as embodying profound life teachings. Another example is the story of the dragon king's daughter, found in the 'Devadatta', 12th chapter of the Lotus Sutra. In 'The Opening of the Eyes', Nichiren writes,

"When the dragon king's daughter attained Buddhahood, this does not simply mean that one person did so. It reveals the fact that all women will attain Buddhahood." (WND 1, p268)

In other writings, Nichiren acknowledged no one had ever seen a dragon and he clearly wants to draw a universal principle of female empowerment from this story.

Furthermore, Nichiren did not finish with propounding the superiority of the Lotus Sutra compared to other sutras. He divided it into a theoretical and essential part and placed the 16th chapter above all other chapters, as the pre-eminent teaching. In 'The Blessings of the Lotus Sutra', he writes, "Bear in mind that the 28 chapters of the Lotus Sutra contain only a few passages elucidating the truth but a great many words of praise." (WND 1, p673)

The process of extracting deeper meaning from the Lotus Sutra did not finish there, for in a number of writings, he considered the Lotus Sutra, based on what is appropriate for the era, to have fulfilled its purpose and to have no further practical use on a literal level.

"Now in the Latter Day of the Law, both the Lotus Sutra and the other sutras are of no use. Only Nam-myoho-renge-kyo (has the power of benefit to lead to enlightenment)" (WND 1, p902)

The chanting of Nam-myoho-renge-kyo therefore supersedes the Lotus Sutra entirely. As Daisaku Ikeda writes,

"From the perspective of the implicit meaning of the Lotus Sutra taught by Nichiren Daishonin, Nam-myoho-renge-kyo is the essential teaching, while the Lotus Sutra as a whole...is the theoretical teaching. Nam-myoho-renge-kyo is the essential teaching because it is the great law to be propagated in the Latter Day."[8]

We begin to see in Nichiren's teaching a blueprint for a progressive and developmental approach to the sutra. This process did not begin with Nichiren, for T'ien-t'ai's theory of *ichinen sanzen*, three thousand realms in a single moment of life, in the 6th century CE drew out a new, deeper understanding of the sutra which Nichiren would in turn draw upon. Prior to T'ien-t'ai, Kumarajiva's preeminent Chinese translation of the text, allowed T'ien-t'ai to develop his theory, as only in Kumarajiva's Lotus Sutra translation does one find the ten factors that are key to *ichinen sanzen* and are recited in SGI gongyo recitation three times. In other translations in Chinese, Tibetan and in existing Sanskrit manuscripts, a different or shorter list of factors is subscribed to. T'ien-t'ai was also influenced by Nagarjuna's teachings in developing his philosophy.[9]

Multiple Lotus Sutras

At this point we can step back to see that the evolving meaning of the Lotus Sutra points to, in a sense, 'multiple Lotus Sutras' rather than just one text.

In his book, *Waking the Buddha*, Clark Strand beautifully takes this concept further than even Nichiren and SGI have so far. Strand is a Buddhist writer and former Zen monk who stands outside of any specific religious tradition. His eloquence on the SGI movement is all the more powerful in the fact that he is an impartial witness rather than an SGI member. In his chapter, 'Even to the fiftieth person,' he interviews SGI General Director, Masaaki Masaki. Masaki clarifies to Strand that it was a mistake to suppose there was only one Lotus Sutra, and that second Soka Gakkai President Toda taught about the Lotus Sutra of Shakyamuni, the Lotus Sutra of T'ien-t'ai and the Lotus Sutra of Nichiren. Masaki states, "The essence of the various Lotus Sutras is of course the same... but the way in which the sutra needs to be presented depends on the conditions of the age and the capacity of the people who read it."[10] But Strand then develops Toda's theory further, "My feeling is that there is a contemporary expression of the Lotus Sutra based on these and that this is what the three presidents of the Soka Gakkai have appeared in the world to teach."[11]

With Toda's doctrine that 'the Buddha is life itself' and Ikeda's central philosophy based on the dignity of life, we have new contemporary expressions of the Lotus Sutra's core message. Strand takes this message even further, referring to new Lotus Sutras always developing to ensure the message remains alive. A new sutra is born when it travels heart to heart, reigniting its meaning in that society. Strand sees the spirit of human revolution as taught by Daisaku Ikeda, empowering individuals based on the common human value of the dignity of life, as this era's full manifestation of a new Lotus Sutra. In recent years, Ikeda's novelised account of the development of the Soka Gakkai has been described as a sutra for our age, something which resonates with Strand's message, a message which Strand believes will resonate across religions and cultures, transcending the confines of Buddhism.[12]

The Lotus Sutra's message is therefore not confined to one text. It is an evolving expression of the incredible potential in human life and therefore does it matter whether it was created by the historical Buddha or, as most likely is the case, was a synthesis of wisdom generated by wise and empowered individual practitioners of Buddhism many centuries later? Its recasting and regeneration through the millennia points to a different focus, on its underlying humanistic values.

THE LOTUS SUTRA

Can any texts be attributed to the Buddha with certainty?

In fact, the questions surrounding the origins of the Lotus Sutra can be easily applied to any other work of the Buddhist canon attributed to Shakyamuni, including the Pali texts which are the scriptures of the Theravadan branch of Early Buddhism. Theravada is the only surviving school of a multitude of 18 Early Buddhist schools and it claims that the Pali canon directly reflects the words of the Buddha. Theravadan Buddhists often claim that, as a result, they represent the true Buddha's teachings and they cast doubt on the provenance of the Mahayana teachings as a later distortion of Shakyamuni's message. I experienced this first hand in a talk I gave when, during the Question and Answer session, a Theravadan practitioner in the audience questioned my talk and me even being a Buddhist on this basis.

Modern research, however paints a far less clear picture of the original source of the Pali texts, in a similar vein to the origins of Mahayana, though admittedly further back in history. At the time of Shakyamuni Buddha's life, there were no scripts with which to write down his teachings. Early Buddhist texts were passed down through oral tradition, and the Pali canon was finally written down in the first century BCE, three to four hundred years after the Buddha's passing[13]. As a result, even the Pali texts cannot be directly attributed to the Buddha with any certainty. Indeed, schools of Buddhism such as Theravada or even monastic communities of any kind, do not seem to have existed in the early years of Buddhism's founding.

In the early 300s BCE, Megasthenes, a Seleucid ambassador, visited south and central Asia and described Buddhists approximately 100 years after Shakyamuni's death. As a dated, independent source, Megasthenes' record is important and describes a variety of itinerant practitioners living in forests, visiting and begging in villages and staying in donors' houses in towns[14]. There is no sign of an organised monastic community, which makes it likely that the Pali canon developed its emphasis on monastic rules and references later, as the Early Buddhist schools formed and consolidated the Buddhist community, perhaps in response to competing developments in Hinduism which became more sophisticated and systematized between 250 CE and 100 CE. Some scholars also suggest that karma and reincarnation were not inherent parts of the Buddha's original message, and were inserted into the Pali texts as they gained stronger influence in society due to Hinduism's development in this period.

A melting pot of ideas

It is perhaps wiser to see Buddhism in all its elements, as a growing and developing entity throughout its history rather than the ideas of one man in 5th century BCE India. Buddhism developed not in isolation, but in a time and place where a melting pot of ideas, philosophies and religions were not merely existing side by side or competing against each other, but were actively influencing each other. J.M. Walsh's writings, based on the scholarly references he cites, describe a religious silk road in central Asia where influences between Buddhism, Zoroastrianism, Greek philosophy and Hinduism can be readily seen. For example, the Buddhist lord of the dead, King Yama, whom Nichiren refers to, is known as Yima in

Zoroastrianism and is also presented as the teacher in an ancient Hindu text the Kath Upanishad[15]. In his masterwork *Dial In*, Walsh paints a picture of the deep interconnections between all major religions at the source of their ideas.

From a Buddhist perspective, all religions are human-made, so this evolving interactive process should not come as too much of a shock. In fact, as it points at commonalities and change, the message of universal common ground in our shared humanity can come to the fore over dogmatic differences. I hope that by illustrating the organic process of creation and development that the Lotus Sutra has undergone, we can see a broader, all-encompassing approach to the Buddha's teaching, and in turn, Nichiren's and SGI's message of the preciousness and dignity of every human life. This is the key message of the Lotus Sutra however it was created.

CHAPTER TWO

NICHIREN

THE ORDINARY BUDDHA

"If Nichiren's compassion is truly great and encompassing, Nam-myoho-renge-kyo will spread for ten thousand years and more, for all eternity."

On Repaying Debts of Gratitude (WND 1, p736)

At the foot of Mount Kiyosumi, surrounded by Japanese pines, stands Seicho-ji temple. Commanding views of the Pacific Ocean in the distance, the temple retains a sense of isolation and timelessness in rural Chiba despite its relative proximity to the conurbation of Tokyo beyond the peninsula where it is located. Cutting through from the north, we took a single track road, interspersed with 'Beware of the Monkeys' signs, for the final stage of our journey there, on a cloudy August day. The dense foliage and rugged terrain gave a sense that much was still the same from the last thousand years.

Nestled in a valley, the temple was deserted with the number of visitors we came across countable on one hand, a far cry from the throngs who visit SGI's Hall of the Great Vow in Shinanomachi, Tokyo. Although none of the original buildings from Nichiren's time remain, the layout and traditional constructions make imagining the life of the young Nichiren on the grounds easy. Currently owned and run by Nichiren Shu, the sect of Buddhism based on Mount Minobu, Nichiren's hut where he resided has been rebuilt on the edge of the site against a cliff. The grave of his master, Dozen-bo still stands – a pile of aged, smooth, oval stones. We asked a priest where the Gohonzon was, the sacred scroll created by Nichiren to chant to, but he told us there was no Gohonzon there, the object not having the importance to Minobu believers it does for other followers of Nichiren Buddhism. Instead, Nammyoho-renge-kyo is inscribed on stones and plaques around the site.

The young Nichiren

It was here at Seicho-ji where the young Nichiren was educated, tonsured as a monk and where he returned to proclaim his teaching. A prophet, master, rebel, prisoner, Buddha. Nichiren's profound impact on the world continues to grow with the global expansion of the SGI movement. Born in 1222 C.E., in the fishing village of Kominato in what was then known as Awa province, Nichiren was 11 years old by Western numbering when he was sent to study at the local temple of Seicho-ji. A full record of Nichiren's life is not within the scope of this chapter but suffice to say Nichiren chose the religious life at Seicho-ji and took on his first great vow to become the wisest person in Japan in order to repay his debts of gratitude to his parents and the people and fundamentally relieve the prevalent sufferings of his society. In so doing, he left the confines of his temple to travel extensively to the major centres of learning in Japan, returning in 1253 to announce his conclusions on the 28th April of that year. In proclaiming the practice of chanting Nam-myoho-renge-kyo (daimoku) and rejecting the major forms of Buddhism prevailing at the time, Nichiren would undoubtedly have caused a stir.

As an exclusive practice to reveal one's enlightened life in the moment, Nichiren's advocation of the daimoku was revolutionary. It is worth noting that the phrase Nam-myoho-renge-kyo may not have been invoked regularly or with any focus prior to Nichiren but that Nichiren did not invent the daimoku. Nam(u)-myoho-renge-kyo existed before Nichiren and was one Japanese transliteration of the Chinese title of the Lotus Sutra with the Nam(u) meaning respect or devotion to, attached to the start of it. The earliest authenticated use of the daimoku phrase has been found in a written prayer on the occasion of a memorial service for deceased parents in 881 CE.[1] Nichiren believed that his predecessors Dengyo and T'ien-t'ai knew of Nam-myoho-renge-kyo but that the time was not right to propagate it.

In any event, Nichiren's declaration was a radical departure in the history of religion which would have a major impact on the world. Tradition describes how the outrage engendered by Nichiren's announcement meant he had to flee almost immediately from Tojo Kagenobu, the local steward who was incensed by the criticisms of the established Buddhist schools. More recent historical research suggests that Nichiren may not have had to leave until the winter of 1254, perhaps a year later and that his presence gradually polarized the community in Seicho-ji into those who supported Nichiren's new position and those who held to the beliefs and traditions of the Tendai Buddhism practised at the temple at that time.[2] The historian, Takagi has also suggested Kagenobu's ire at Nichiren, which was clear from the source materials, derived not merely from the Lotus centred practice Nichiren advocated but because he had supported the local landowner, a nun called Nagoe-no-ama against the competing claims of Kagenobu as the Shogunate-appointed overlord.[3] This conflict would culminate in 1264 at Komatsubara, when Nichiren returned home again, and Kagenobu and a band of men ambushed him, severely injuring Nichiren and killing two of his followers.

An outsider all his life

The persecution by Kagenobu was, however, incidental to the power of the Shogunate government who Nichiren came into direct conflict with, resulting in two perilous exiles and a near execution. From birth, Nichiren was an outsider. According to Nichiren he was born to a poor fishing family though some academics conjecture his father may have had higher social standing in the past and fallen from grace. Nichiren may even have been adopted, a suggestion supported by the types of words he used in his writings to refer to his mother. It is, however, worth noting theories may have been created by later disciples trying to provide Nichiren with a noble background to further validate his status. Regardless, he would most likely have had a strong regional accent from the Kanto area where he grew up, in contrast to the refined way of speaking promoted in Kamakura and Kyoto by the upper echelons of society. In fact in 1269, Nichiren wrote to a disciple studying in Kyoto encouraging him to "use your own provincial speech" rather than adapt to the manners of the court nobility.[4]

The Imperial aristocracy were also dominant in positions of authority within the Buddhist orders and viewed the Kanto region where Nichiren came from as a provincial backwater. It is therefore likely that, during Nichiren's years of studying at the major centres of Buddhist learning, he would have been able to access the libraries and texts but not the aristocratic factions who dominated the higher ranks of the clergy. The tradition that he may have been a disciple of Shunpan, the senior Tendai scholar on Mount Hei, is unlikely and not supported by Nichiren's writings, though he may have attended his lectures. Takagi suggests that this rejection in his student days may have inspired his axiom 'rely on the law not upon persons' which Nichiren took from the Nirvana Sutra.[5]

Without privilege or vested interests, Nichiren could place a critical eye on the practices and beliefs of his day to ascertain the cause of the problems and suffering plaguing society. In rejecting the practice of praying to the otherworldly Buddha, Amida to realise a release from suffering in a paradise after death, Nichiren put himself on a collision course with the *Bakufu*, the Shogun-led government of the day. Unable to receive an official hearing, Nichiren became more adversarial in the face of the persecutions that assailed him and, as sanctions and suppressions flowed, Nichiren and his followers became more marginalised in the eyes of society. This, in turn, conversely helped Nichiren to define his philosophy in opposition to the religious and political authorities of the day, summarised by his declaration,

"Even if it seems that, because I was born in the ruler's domain, I follow him in my actions, I will never follow him in my heart." (WND 1, p579)

With his unremitting passion and courage to elucidate the Buddhist law, Nichiren saw himself and his followers, who at their peak in his lifetime, may have only numbered a couple of thousand, not as a rejected minority, but as Jacqueline Stone describes, on "center stage of their historical moment," liberated and joyfully empowered.[6]

An experience inspired by Nichiren's example

Nichiren's fearless resolve in the face of rejection and persecution from the authorities is a timeless example of how to respond to oppression and injustice. Taking inspiration from his struggles, I have been able to muster courage and to face some challenging times in my life with a fighting spirit.

One example, which has had a major impact on my circumstances, was when I was purchasing our family home. Early on in my Buddhist practice, I had been encouraged to set ten year determinations. What did I want mine and others' lives to be like in a decade's time? These were tangible goals which included buying a house in my local neighbourhood in London. This specific resolution seemed particularly outlandish as I was then in my first year of teaching on a relatively low salary. House prices in London had skyrocketed since the late 1990s and my local area was expensive. With encouragement that 'nothing is impossible', I set this determination along with a number of other aspirations for myself and for the happiness of others on New Year's Eve and chanted that night towards them.

In the intervening ten years, this ambition was not always at the forefront of my mind. Life's ups and downs made it seem impossible at times. And yet, give or take a couple of months, ten years to the date of setting that goal, my family and I successfully purchased a beautiful, spacious house in my local area. We had chanted that the place would not only be a wonderful family home but would create value by being used to host local Buddhist meetings for our community. The elderly lady who was selling the house had chosen our offer above a larger one put forward by a property developer because she wanted to see a family move into her home.

In the UK, the process of finalising the buying and selling of a property is quite protracted. Signing of contracts and completion of the deal usually happens just before moving in and vendors and purchasers can pull out, or agreements can be cancelled at the last minute.

Everything was going smoothly towards our purchase and we were near to moving in. I was busy at work when the bank we had arranged the finance with, one of the largest in the country, called me. I presumed it was for some tiresome customer survey and so I did not get round to calling them back for two weeks. When I did finally call, the news was bad. The operative told me that my mortgage offer had been cancelled. Despite my pleading, she refused to explain the reason why. Did I have a black mark on my credit score? Was there something in my past which had come to light that had affected their decision? The woman on the other end of the phone would not explain, stating that it was company policy not to give a reason when a mortgage offer was withdrawn. Protestations to her manager and her manager's manager led to the same response.

I felt powerless and wronged, a blank wall of indifference staring me in the face. How could I get another mortgage deal if I did not know why I had been suddenly rejected for this one? The black mark of this rejection would have to be shared, if it had not been already, and the likelihood of receiving another offer in the few days before we were meant to purchase the property was nigh on impossible.

I began to chant at first in the pits of despair, the bleakness of the situation overwhelming me, but after sometime, the energy and hope that chanting can provide began to reinvigorate me. I would fight this but I needed help and guidance.

Buddhist guidance to take on the bank

A senior Buddhist leader, Barry, appeared in my mind. Barry had been chanting Nam-myoho-renge-kyo and practising Buddhism since the 1970s. When he was a teenager, as a joke, a friend had pushed him off the top diving board of his local swimming pool paralysing him from the waist down. This had not stopped him becoming a highly successful advertising executive and family man. He had swum in the Paralympics, recorded a hit record for Manchester United football team, and above all, had a wealth of Buddhist wisdom to share.

Still unnerved, I called Barry who invited me to his home immediately. After explaining the situation and chanting together, Barry gave me clear, practical advice. To win in this struggle, I had to go on the offensive just as Nichiren had, to take on the bank with every ounce of energy I had. He told me to write a letter, not longer than one page, stating the issue and outlining what I would do if they would not tell me the reason for dropping my mortgage or reinstate it. Going to the newspapers and the financial authorities would be my recourse. Once prepared, Barry told me to send the letter to every possible person in the bank that I could.

I returned to my flat that Friday night empowered and with direction. Over that weekend I devoted myself to alternating between chanting and sending out the letter. At first, it was difficult finding any emails for the bank as they had consciously avoided publishing them but after some online research and looking at their annual reports, I discovered the company employee list and how they configured their emails.

I literally deluged the company with my letter, like an aerial bombing raid of emails. The executive board, the non-executive board, the mortgage services department, the customer relations team – name a department in that bank and pretty much every employee and manager received my letter that weekend. By Sunday night, I had sent hundreds of emails and even engaged my local Member of Parliament to get in touch with his contacts at the bank.

At around lunchtime on the Monday morning, I received a call. It was the softly spoken Head of Mortgage Services from this major national bank. He started humbly apologising for how I had been treated and reiterated their policy of not explaining their change in mortgage decisions. However, on this occasion, he had authorised to make an exception. It transpired, after talking it through with him, that the system had highlighted my mortgage as potential fraud because the lady we were buying from had never got around to officially putting the house in her name after her husband had died over twenty years previously. Not only that, the house had never been sold before, having always been in the same family. The computer had seen the original price from the 1920s of a few hundred pounds and flagged a potential fraud.

Once I had clarified these points with him, the mortgage was reinstated, the sale took place and we successfully moved in. The Head of Mortgage Services later wrote to me that as a result of the case he would review how all customers were treated in such situations. In standing up in this situation, I potentially helped many others in the future. Many people, I imagine, would have just accepted the bank's decision faced with a wall of corporate indifference and just given up. Although my troubles do not compare to the scale of what Nichiren faced, the fact that I was able to challenge it was in no small part down to being part of a tradition trail blazed by Nichiren of challenging injustice and authority through faith.

Practising Buddhism does not mean life will be problem free nor will everything go your way. However, it can provide a dauntless spirit and the strength to challenge whatever we encounter. Like Nichiren, the Buddhist practitioner can feel energised and even happy in the middle of adversity. Rather than lamenting our fate, Buddhism can provide the strength to rejoice, as Nichiren did when he stated, "I, Nichiren, am the richest man in all of present-day Japan." (WND 1, p268) He said this despite, at that time in February 1272, being in exile on snow-bound Sado Island, in a draughty, dilapidated hut facing a paupers' graveyard where dead bodies were left discarded.

NICHIREN

How do we know what Nichiren was like?

Nichiren's confidence in his mission and assured vision for the future has been passed down to us thanks to the preservation of a great many of his writings. Unlike Shakyamuni, Christ or Mohammed, we have the good fortune of a primary source material written by the sage himself. Nichiren's writings vary from lengthy treatises to government officials to warm, compassionate epistles to his followers filled with gratitude and encouragement. Nichiren's wisdom, humanity and unstinting concern for his disciples is amply evident to the modern reader. Interestingly for a historian rather than a practising Buddhist, no contemporary references to Nichiren in secondary sources, such as government papers, survive. Nichiren is our sole source from when he was alive in understanding the story of his life.

Nichiren holds a preeminent place in SGI Buddhism as the founder of its practice and philosophy and as teaching master who fully revealed what can be achieved and how to respond in the direst of circumstances – a life filled with joy, compassion, spirit and boundless freedom despite everything that he experienced. That Nichiren should be referred to as an eternal mentor of Buddhist faith is clear, the primacy of his role unquestioned.

And yet, the status afforded him in various Nichiren schools differs and a traditional viewpoint derived from Nichikan, the 26th Abbot of Taiseki-ji has gradually been moved away from, though still has influence especially in Japan. In this chapter, we will examine the concept of Nichiren as Eternal Original Buddha and the developments away from this established doctrine. In so doing, I hope to unpick our understanding of what a Buddha and Buddhahood really are and to consider how this topic enhances our appreciation of the universalist approach to SGI Buddhism in the way we regard Nichiren.

The concept of an Eternal Original Buddha

For many SGI members practising in the West, the idea of Nichiren being a timeless eternal Buddha removed from his identity as a human being may seem quite an alien concept. Certainly culturally in the West, through SGI President Daisaku Ikeda's guidance and our own cultural norms the idea has been relegated to an irrelevance, a non-issue. In the month I am writing this, I attended a large meeting at SGI-UK's Grand Culture Centre, Taplow Court where a national women's leader emphasized in no uncertain terms that we are all equal to Nichiren Daishonin and all equal to the three founding presidents in potentiality and inherent worth. Ideas of Nichiren as an original or true Buddha are consigned to the mists of time during the days of association with Nichiren Shoshu before 1991.

And yet, the traditional view of Nichiren as a special, eternal, Buddha of beginningless time still appears at times in SGI study material, even if in reality SGI's emphasis and conception of this idea have radically transformed. To summarise, Nichiren Shoshu priesthood teaching is constructed on the basis of the 'Doctrine of Nichiren as Eternal Original Buddha' which Nichikan clarified and fully defined in the 18th century C.E. Nichikan asserted that Nichiren is a primordial Buddha from the beginning of eternity, was superior to Shakyamuni Buddha, and that in fact, Shakyamuni in the remote past had previously practised the law to attain enlightenment under the eternal primordial Buddha, who was Nichiren, later to be reborn in the 13th century to propagate the teaching in the Latter Day of the Law. For Nichikan and by dint the current Shoshu priesthood, the idea of Nichiren casting off his transient identity and revealing his true self when he survived his attempted execution by the authorities at Tatsunokuchi beach in 1271 was not the occasion when he fully revealed the universal state of Buddhahood per se but specifically the moment he revealed his special exalted identity as this unique primordial Buddha. We will examine this event later in the chapter.

It is worth noting that Nichikan actually advocated two objects to worship. The first was the Gohonzon based on the Dai-Gohonzon, a devotional scroll claimed to be inscribed by Nichiren for all humanity and the fulfilment of his life's purpose. But the second was 'the imaginary statue of Nichiren himself' in the form of a fashioned statue representing the law equals the person. It was only in the mid-20th century under the 59th High Priest Nichiko Hori that this latter doctrine was discarded. Founding Soka Gakkai Presidents Makiguchi and Toda however rejected it from the outset and excluded this element of founder worship from the Soka Gakkai's liturgy and ritual.[7]

An assertion of power

The concept of Nichiren as a special original Buddha has also been used to assert authority and hierarchy in Nichiren Shoshu. For example, it claims to give the Dai-Gohonzon supposed special power based on the idea of the 'oneness of the Buddha and the law' purportedly embodied in it, which values

THE EVOLVING BUDDHA

Nichiren's status as original Buddha as much as the universal law. According to the priesthood, the Dai-Gohonzon's special status therefore derives from the special Buddhahood or 'secret enlightenment of the true Buddha' which Nichiren is said to have revealed and imbued in this particular mandala. Furthermore, the concept is taken further in relation to the High Priest's authority and identity. According to Nichiren Shoshu, as Nichiren's sole ordained emissary in the present, the High Priest has become, in recent times, considered by his followers to be the 'True Buddha' himself. The Dai-Gohonzon ceased to have any special exalted status for SGI in 2014. We will consider in further detail the evidence related to the authenticity of the Dai-Gohonzon and the claims related to it in chapter 4.

With Nichiren transformed into an object of worship, a transcendent or even deified being who brings salvation, the priesthood has been able to take the role as mediator between the follower and the salvation offered by the Buddha. The outcome is a top down hierarchical system which subverts Nichiren's message and debases ordinary practitioners. In a shocking revelation of how the lay followers of Nichiren Shoshu perceive themselves, a Mrs Uchida wrote in the lay publication Hokkeko, "His Holiness (the High Priest) is the only person who has inherited from the Honourable Daishonin, the Dharma body comprising the 'Oneness of the Buddha and the Law' in a pure form. Consequently, the relationship between priests and lay people should be understood in the form of master and slave, or as upper and lower."[8] Behind this distortion and self-abasement is the concept of Nichiren as a special original Buddha.

NICHIREN

A delicate shift

The SGI movement in practice and approach is very far removed from such statements. However the clear rejection of this status for Nichiren has been even more subtle than the rejection of the Dai-Gohonzon, perhaps because as a less tangible issue it has naturally changed at grassroots level without the need for doctrinal debate. In an SGI publication of June 2016, Nichiren is described in the following terms: "The treasure of the Buddha from the perspective of time without beginning is Nichiren Daishonin, the Buddha of beginningless time or eternal Buddha, who revealed in his own life as an ordinary person the fundamental law for attaining Buddhahood."[9] A delicate shift can be noted here. Nichiren is afforded the special status of the eternal Buddha and yet he revealed it as an ordinary person and what he revealed was a 'fundamental law' accessible to all.

The scholar Yukio Matsudo has examined this issue based on Nichiren's writings. He considers the view of Nichiren as a special primordial Buddha as nothing but 'founder worship' and a hagiographic deification of Nichiren himself. Nichiren fully manifested his Buddhahood but revealed in his own life nothing other than the "mystic principle that is originally inherent in all living beings," in other words, the universal essence of enlightenment, the world of Buddhahood. Conversely, Nichiren held up as the only eternal original Buddha creates a "dogmatic, exclusivistic and fundamentalist understanding of Nichiren"[10], and he ceases to be an ordinary person. Instead, Matsudo suggests Nichiren was a pioneer opening up the Buddha way to all ordinary people and that the eternal is only found in the present moment when we reveal our Buddhahood.

Nichiren's own view of himself

In supporting this approach, most crucially, Nichiren never claimed himself to be an original, eternal Buddha. Traditional Nichiren Shoshu analysis has claimed that Nichiren implied this status indirectly. For example in his major thesis, 'The Opening of the Eyes', he describes himself as the pillar, sun, moon, mirror and eyes of the ruling clan, and father and mother to the ruling clan. These may link to the concept of the sovereign, parent and teacher who would deserve reverence according to Nichiren but there is absolutely no implication that they link to a special Buddha from the eternal past. Nichiren unquestionably considered his importance to the peace and future of Japan to be essential but that he had some special status as a Buddha does in no way come across. The only time Nichiren does purportedly refer to himself in such exalted cosmic terms is in transfer documents notably the 'One Hundred and Six Comparisons' and 'The Mystic Principle of the Original Cause'. Modern scholars including some at Soka University, consider these writings, which do not feature in the English translations to be inauthentic creations from a later time.

  This case is supported by the work of Professor Miyata of Soka University who confirms from his research that the doctrine of Nichiren as Original Buddha was unknown to Nichiren, Nikko Shonin - his disciple and to Nikko's disciples. It only emerged in the late 14th century under the 6th High

Priest Nichiji and was given clear articulation by the 9th High Priest Nichiu (1402-82). Nikko considered himself a disciple of Nichiren and that Nichiren was a Buddha for our times, but this is far from considering him the Eternal Original Buddha.[11]

Where does the idea of an original Buddha come from?

The concept of a primordial Buddha or 'Adi-Buddha' comes originally from Vajrayana Buddhism. The concept could well have entered Nichiren Shoshu by way of the Japanese Shingon sect or esoteric Tendai teachings which had already incorporated this belief, often viewing the Buddha Mahavairocana as their first and primordial Buddha.

In addition, Nichiren Shoshu has traditionally interpreted Nichiren's references to 'Lord Shakyamuni of True Buddhism' or the 'Eternal Buddha Shakyamuni' as meaning Nichiren – quite a leap of interpretation when Nichiren never refers to himself in these references. Matsudo argues through examination of Nichiren Daishonin's writings that the Buddha Shakyamuni who attained enlightenment in the remotest past is viewed by the Daishonin as the revelation of the eternal existence of the great universal law of Buddhahood. In other words, the eternal Shakyamuni, Nam-myoho-renge-kyo, the state of Buddhahood, the Mystic Law are all one and the same and all accessible to all humanity. The law is therefore primary not the person.

In 'The Object of Devotion for Observing the Mind' Nichiren writes, "Shakyamunis's practices and virtues he consequently attained, these two laws of cause and effect are all contained within the five characters of Myoho-renge-kyo. If we believe in these five characters, we will naturally be granted the same benefits which he has." (WND 1, p364) This is the cause of all Buddhas and must be activated within an ordinary human being. As a result any Buddhas who are no longer also an ordinary person are not of this world, such as Amida, Mahavairocana, Maitreya and even Shakyamuni in a deified form (the latter having assumed this status in the Minobu school of Nichiren Shu.) There are not two separate types of Buddhas, one mystical and supernatural and one mundane. Only in the ordinary human being can Buddhahood be revealed.

What is a Buddha according to Ikeda?

Daisaku Ikeda, President of SGI has advocated this approach and most clearly expressed it in his dialogues from the 1990s, *The Wisdom of the Lotus Sutra*, "Majestic Buddhas are but illusions that have nothing to do with reality. The only actual Buddhas are ordinary people who each moment bring forth the eternal life force of time without beginning. There is no Buddha existing apart from the people. A Buddha set above the people is a fake, an expedient means." [12]

Ikeda also confirms the meaning of the eternal Buddha as "the very life of the universe that continues to function ceaselessly."[13] Ikeda directly relates the term 'remotest past' to not a finite moment in the far distant past but eternity in the moment. Thus, every time we chant to the Gohonzon we can live that eternal moment, "Each day we start anew from time without beginning, the starting point of life."[14] The true reality of life is this original source which is Nam-myoho-renge-kyo. Ikeda offers a humanised way of perceiving the eternal Buddha as ultimate truth revealed within ourselves.

NICHIREN

Original Enlightenment

This correlation between ordinary people and the eternal cosmic law is not to be confused with the medieval Tendai Buddhist concept of 'Original Enlightenment'. In 'Original Enlightenment' theory, ordinary people are inherently Buddhas just as they are without the need for any practice or action. All phenomena are just as they manifest, expressions of the true reality. Nichiren undoubtedly drew on this tradition and vocabulary from the Tendai school as he enrolled and trained as a Tendai monk. However, his emphasis on practice to reveal inherent Buddhahood and his challenge to the authorities of his day, starkly contrast with original enlightenment thought, which has been considered to encourage passive acceptance of the social reality by merely acknowledging that we are all already Buddhas.

An awareness of original enlightenment thought is relevant to Nichiren Buddhism for two main reasons. First, it allows practitioners within SGI to be on their guard against a similarly passive view that we are all Buddhas without the need for practice creeping in to cultural trends and terminology. Secondly, the debate in academic circles surrounding the validity of some of Nichiren's writings has been driven by a sectarian passion to remove Nichiren from any association with original enlightenment and therefore individuate him from the Tendai school of Buddhism. This move was spearheaded by Yorin Asai, an academic from Rissho University, which is affliliated with Nichiren Shu, the Minobu school of Nichiren Buddhism. Asai rejected as later forgeries any writings by Nichiren that implied any reference to original enlightenment thought in a sectarian attempt to assert Nichiren Shu's independence from the rival school of Tendai Buddhism. His approach became academic orthodoxy for many years. More recent scholarship, including Jacqueline Stone of Princeton University, has challenged this approach; the rejection of certain texts and its underlying motive. Unimpeachable writings that Asai could not question, such as the 'Object of Devotion for observing the Mind' and 'On Establishing the Correct Teaching for the Peace of the Land', clearly contain elements of original enlightenment thought.

And yet, Nichiren creates a totally new paradigm whilst incorporating an appreciation of the universal capacity for Buddhahood. It must be revealed through an individual's faith, practice and study, and when the individual reveals their Buddhahood so too will their environment. Nichiren writes in 'On Establishing the Correct Teaching..', in the moment those who embrace faith in the Lotus Sutra, "The threefold world will all become the Buddha land" and " the regions in the ten directions will all become the treasure realms."(WND 1, p25)

There seems not a little irony that it was a scholar from a Nichiren school who unfairly attacked Nichiren's writings to advance the school's sectarian ambitions. Regardless, it should be acknowledged that some works, most notably transfer documents which, again, had a sectarian motive behind their creation, may be later forgeries. However, Nichiren's treatises and writings to his followers taken as a whole offer a consistent richness of thought. As the practical philosophy embodied in the SGI, they have offered profound life changing inspiration to Buddhist practitioners over the years.

This is none more the case than with the *Ongi Kuden*, 'The Record of the Orally Transmitted Teachings.' As a secondary source material, it is considered to be notes taken by Nikko Shonin from Nichiren's lectures on the Lotus Sutra. In that sense, it may not be the exact words that the Daishonin used. Moreover, Rissho University again have taken particular aim at the *Ongi Kuden,* claiming it to be a later forgery because of its use of original enlightenment style language and because the first verified version that has so far been discovered comes from the 16th century. In the SGI translation by Burton Watson, it is readily acknowledged that the earliest known version dates from a copy made in 1539 by a priest from the Eight Chapters branch of Nichiren schools.

Regardless of its origins, the *Ongi Kuden* stands as philosophically consistent with Nichiren's teachings, emphasising our inherent Buddha nature and the practice of chanting the daimoku to reveal it. The possibility that it is a rearrangement of Nichiren's lectures by his or later disciples remains, but it has been pointed out that Shakyamuni and Christ left no autographed writings at all yet should every Sutra or scriptural teaching of Jesus be rejected out of hand as pious forgeries rather than examined for their philosophical worth?[15] To reject the *Ongi Kuden* would be to lose such beautiful expressions of SGI philosophy as "Cherry, Peach, Plum and Damson", the evocative metaphor of our own uniqueness and value, just as each fruit has its own unique qualities and taste. In addition, there exist hundreds of smaller fragments of Nichiren's writings in which the meaning is indecipherable. If they were complete, would we have other teachings to supplement our practice? Nichiren Buddhism has developed based on the writings that have survived through the centuries, and we have the great good fortune that so many have.

A master of metaphor

Above all, Daisaku Ikeda has made the most valuable contribution in revealing the heart of Nichiren's teachings for the modern era. It must also be acknowledged that all words are always open to a variety of interpretations. Trying to take every word of Nichiren literally is the mistake of fundamentalists. Who in this modern era believes in the range of spirits and Gods who Nichiren refers to in what could be considered literal terms? Perhaps Nichiren himself did not believe they actually existed, but much of his audience certainly did and he wrote to them accordingly. Nichiren's references to fantastical creatures and events such as the Kalakula insect which swelled in strong winds or the golden mountain that glitters more brightly when scraped by the boar must be taken as metaphors for the challenges we experience in daily life. Ultimately, Nichiren set his own standard in how to evaluate and interpret his philosophy and writings. In 'The Hero of the World' written to Shijo Kingo in troubled times, he writes, "Buddhism is reason. Reason will win over your lord." (WND 1, p839) Based on the standard of reason, which will change as society, science and culture develop, Nichiren's writings will need to be revisited and revitalised in each era, something Daisaku Ikeda has led in modern times.

NICHIREN

How did Nichiren change?

Returning to Nichiren's identity as a human being who fully revealed his most enlightened aspect rather than an inherent special cosmic Buddha, it is of value to look at the development of his thought and life to see that, just as the Lotus Sutra and the Gohonzon underwent a process of development and refinement, so too did Nichiren as a teacher.

Looking back on his life, Nichiren described how as a young acolyte at Seicho-ji, he prayed to the statue of Bodhisattva Space Treasury (*Kokuzo*) and had a 'jewel of wisdom' bestowed on him. Although it might traditionally be considered Nichiren gained his first enlightenment at this point, he acknowledged that despite the insight he acquired, his understanding gradually developed in his teens as he studied the various sects in Japan, first at Seicho-ji and later around the country. In 'Refuting Ryokan and the Others', he describes his studies of all the different schools but states, "I found it difficult to resolve my doubts." (WND 2, p1050). By 1242, at the age of 21, Nichiren's nascent philosophy was taking shape. His earliest authentic writings date from this year and not only focus on the Lotus Sutra as an important teaching but emphasize "the Mystic Law is characterized by the fact that the Ten Worlds are mutually contained in each other...what the Lotus Sutra intends to teach is that the ordinary person is in truth a Buddha, because he is endowed with the Ten Worlds."[16]

By 1253, Nichiren was able to confidently declare his teaching and this is evidenced in his 1258 writing, 'The Meaning of the Sacred Teachings of the Buddha's lifetime' in which he declares the Lotus Sutra to be the Buddha's ultimate teaching and purpose whilst also identifying the daimoku with the wonderful law and with the concept of three thousand realms in a single moment of life. In 1260, in 'On Reciting the Daimoku of the Lotus Sutra' he writes,

"The two characters of Myo-ho of the daimoku contain within them the heart of the Lotus Sutra... Therefore, the merit of chanting the five characters of Myoho-renge-kyo is great and immense." (WND 2 p229)

A new self-understanding

Nichiren's essential practice and philosophy were in place from the 1250s, but Nichiren's own sense of mission and identity were still to develop. His first exile to the Izu peninsula (1261-63), gave Nichiren a sense he was living the persecutions predicted in the Lotus Sutra and as a result he was now practising "twenty-four hours each day and night" (1262, The Four Debts of Gratitude) (WND 1, p43) It can be argued however, that Nichiren at this point considered himself to be a reformist Tendai monk rather than the creator of a new school. On returning from exile, he began to lead monthly lectures on the 24th of the month, the day of T'ien-t'ai's death on the latter's 'Great Concentration and Insight'.[17]

The Tatsunokuchi persecution of September 12th 1271, when he was taken to the shore to be executed, is traditionally seen as the moment when Nichiren cast off his transient nature to fully reveal his Buddhahood. It was undoubtedly considered by Nichiren himself to be a defining point of his life and a transition to a radically new self-understanding that he was without doubt the votary of the Lotus Sutra for his time. In 'The Opening of the Eyes' written during his first winter in exile on the inhospitable Sado Island as a final testament to his followers in the event of his death, he writes:

"On the twelfth day of the ninth month of last year (1271) between the hours of the rat and the ox (11pm-3am), this person named Nichiren was beheaded. It is his soul that has come to this island of Sado." (WND 1, p269)

Concerning this point as a new departure for his teachings, he later writes, "As for my teachings, regard those before my exile to the province of Sado as equivalent to the Buddha's pre-Lotus Sutra teachings." (WND 1, p 896) In an essential sense, Nichiren's philosophy did not majorly change. Faith in key chapters of the Lotus Sutra and the chanting of daimoku were extolled before Sado. What really changed, Stone suggests, is Nichiren's realisation of his mission as the leader of the Bodhisattvas of the Earth, Jogyo or Superior Practices, who according to the Lotus Sutra, was entrusted by Shakyamuni to spread the Lotus Sutra in a later age.[18] In April 1273 on Sado he writes in 'The Object of Devotion for Observing the Mind', "Now in the beginning of the Latter Day of the Law,...the Bodhisattvas of the Earth have appeared in this world for the first time solely in order to bring the medicine of the five characters of Myoho-renge-kyo to ignorant people." (WND 1, p 375)

Nichiren was no longer a self-perceived Tendai monk initiating a new teaching to reform existing schools, particularly Tendai, but the creator of a universal philosophy distinct from any that had come before. The Gohonzon was developed on Sado, as were the doctrinal foundations to

THE EVOLVING BUDDHA

Nichiren's teaching, such as the Three Great Secret Laws – the daimoku, the object of devotion (Gohonzon) and ordination platform or place of practice. Nichiren, never knowing when his life might end in the severe conditions of exile on Sado, poured his life fully into developing his thought and, in effect, established a new religion.

After his exile

Nichiren, of course did survive and his final years were spent from May 1274 until just before his death in September 1282 secluded at Mount Minobu on the upper reaches of the Fuji river. This was by no means a hermetic life, as Nichiren gradually gathered disciples who resided with him at his new abode and he continually encouraged the growing community of believers across the country through letters whilst further clarify his teaching. Interestingly, although Nichiren later wrote that he had decided from the outset to retire to the mountains following the Chinese precedent that one should do so if one has admonished a ruler three times and not been heeded, a letter to Toki Jonin in May 1274 announces Nichiren's intention to become a solitary wayfarer instead.[19]

A large proportion of Nichiren's preserved writings come from his time at Minobu. As an ordinary human being who had manifested the life state of Buddhahood, he was not removed from the reality of the ten life states and the natural sufferings of aging and sickness. On 20th January 1282, in the depths of the winter of what would be his final year, he wrote to his loyal disciple Nanjo Tokimitsu assuring him of his father and younger brother's attainment of Buddhahood, yet acknowledging his own suffering and limitations.

"My clothes are thin, my food supplies exhausted. Nights I am no better off than the cold-suffering bird, and in the daytime I think constantly of going down to the village. The sound of voices reciting the sutra has ceased, my religious meditations grow thin and I grieve to think that, should I falter in my practice in this present existence, I must go on suffering…But with these gifts of yours my life has been restored." (The Beginning of Spring, WND 2, p982)

Fully revealing his Buddhahood

Nichiren's unaffected humanity and unvarnished honesty regarding his life condition at the time are refreshingly honest. These are the words not of a special cosmic Buddha but of an ordinary human being who did incredible things and achieved a momentous life but who still suffered like the rest of us. Nichiren is the eternal mentor with respect to the Buddhist teachings for members of SGI. One can even describe him as the Buddha of the Latter Day of the Law in that he fully revealed his Buddhahood in the most trying of circumstances, providing us with the example of his extraordinary life, profound practice and encouragement based on great compassion and deep understanding of life. But above all, he remains a human being, equal to us in value and ultimately in respect.

THE EVOLVING BUDDHA

What is Buddhahood?

In this chapter, we have looked at the humanity of Nichiren but we have also acknowledged his revelation of Buddhahood, something open to all practitioners of Nichiren Buddhism. But what is Buddhahood actually and how does one know when it is being revealed? Tatsunokuchi was a big revelatory moment for Nichiren. Likewise, second Soka Gakkai President Josei Toda experienced profound awakening experiences in prison during World War Two. And yet, on the contrary, Nichiren Daishonin's Buddhism is not about aspiring for these momentous, revelatory 'see the light' moments but an ongoing, more subtle revelation of the state of Buddhahood within our lives, filled with compassion, life force, courage and wisdom for all, not the awakening of one particular gifted individual.

The Buddha nature, strictly speaking, refers to one's potential for revealing the manifest state of Buddhahood. The Buddha nature concept was first expressed in the Nirvana Sutra which was probably compiled around 300-350 C.E. Shin Yatomi, the late Study Department Leader of SGI-USA, describes how the Nirvana Sutra uses the metaphor of yoghurt and milk to exemplify the Buddha nature. The Buddha nature is like yoghurt and people's lives are like the milk. The sutra states, "I say that yoghurt exists (in milk) because it comes from milk." In other words, Buddhahood exists within ordinary people but requires cultivation just as it is required to turn milk to yoghurt.[20]

For Nichiren, we activate our Buddhahood in any given moment immediately by chanting Nam-myoho-renge-kyo. This was Nichiren's abiding and central tenet. In this sense, revealing our Buddhahood does not require some revelatory, awakening experience. It is simply us at our very best, connected with ourselves and our environment, exuding compassion and vitality. In the daily guidance book *For Today and Tomorrow*, Daisaku Ikeda is quoted on July 5th stating,

"What does attaining Buddhahood mean for us? It does not mean that one day we suddenly turn into a Buddha or become magically enlightened. In a sense attaining Buddhahood means that we have securely entered the path, or orbit, of Buddhahood inherent in the cosmos. Rather than a final static destination at which we arrive and remain, achieving enlightenment means firmly establishing the faith needed to keep advancing along the path of absolute happiness limitlessly, without end."[21]

Ikeda has never referenced himself having any overwhelming awakening experiences such as his mentor Toda had and I consider that all for the good. Extreme awakening experiences are undoubtedly valid, real and beneficial for the individual involved. However, they are rare and provoked generally by dire circumstances such as that of the popular new age writer Eckhart Tolle whose awakening manifested from essentially a nervous mental breakdown. These kind of experiences place enlightenment outside the remit of our ordinary lives. Nichiren through his teaching of immediate enlightenment and Ikeda through his writings, such as *The New Human Revolution* embody a radically different paradigm of Buddhahood not placed on an exclusive pedestal for the rare few, but a Buddhahood found in all life and in our mundane ordinary existences.

THE EVOLVING BUDDHA

Respect for our own Buddha nature

Shin Yatomi does however emphasise that one's approach to chanting is important and that if we have a dependent, passive or weak mindset towards prayer, the results will be less satisfactory. He sees our belief and respect for the Gohonzon must be in tandem with an equal faith and respect for our own lives. The Buddha nature within us is ultimately the fundamental object of respect which is embodied in the Gohonzon. Yatomi rejects any form of self-disparagement as counter-productive and contrary to the spirit of Buddhist prayer and faith.[22]

Nichiren makes it clear Myoho-renge-kyo is the Buddha nature of all living beings and uses the metaphor of a caged bird to illustrate how Buddhahood manifests.

"When we revere Myoho-renge-kyo inherent in our life as the object of devotion, the Buddha nature within us is summoned forth and manifested by our chanting of Nam-myoho-renge-kyo. To illustrate, when a caged bird sings, birds who are flying in the sky gather around, the bird in the cage strives to get out. When with our mouths we chant the Mystic Law, our Buddha nature, being summoned, will invariably emerge." (WND 1, p887)

The birds flying in the sky represent the Buddhahood inherent in the universe whilst the singing of the caged bird is our Buddhahood activated. The synchronicity one experiences from Buddhist practice can also be related to this fusion with external Buddhahood in our environment. The cage may represent our ignorance or ordinary humanity manifested in the ten life states, yet we do not need to leave the cage of our ordinary existence to experience the joyful flight and song of our own Buddha nature.

Who are the Bodhisattvas of the Earth?

Our identity as Buddhas is manifested in seeing the universal Buddha nature in oneself and others and working to awaken it in all people. This self-conception as ordinary people manifesting as Buddhas goes in parallel in SGI philosophy with the idea of SGI members as Bodhisattvas of the Earth. The concept of Nichiren as an original Buddha has diminished in emphasis in SGI culture. However, the teaching that those who practice and share this teaching with others have a profound karmic relationship to it, based on a fundamental identity as Bodhisattvas of the Earth, has developed in recent years. It has come to greater prominence since the split with the priesthood and is frequently referred to in Ikeda's writings. The Nichiren Shoshu priesthood consider only Nichiren to be a Bodhisattva of the Earth and that the laity and priests are the followers of the Bodhisattvas of the Earth, marking a further fundamental difference with SGI. Nichiren writes, "If you are of the same mind as Nichiren you must be a Bodhisattva of the Earth." (WND 1, p385)

The Bodhisattvas of the Earth feature in the Lotus Sutra appearing in the 15th chapter, pledging to propagate the teaching of the Lotus Sutra in a future muddied and evil age. Unlike heavenly bodhisattvas described elsewhere in the sutra, they dwell on the earth and literally emerge from it. Dignified and inherently enlightened, they are described as Shakyamuni's original disciples. The concept of Soka Gakkai members as the Bodhisattvas of the Earth was an essential aspect of Josei Toda's philosophy for the spread of Nichiren Buddhism after the Second World War and was furthered by Daisaku Ikeda, his successor, across the world. Nichiren's statements regarding his own status without doubt clarify his mission as a votary of the Lotus Sutra, yet he is not always clear regarding his role as a Bodhisattva of the Earth. In encouraging his disciples he is more explicit, stating that there are no Bodhisattvas of the Earth apart from him and his followers[23] and that if one can chant Nam-myoho-renge-kyo one must surely be a Bodhisattva of the Earth (WND 1, p 385) However, conceiving ourselves as these beings from the remote past can be a conceptual challenge if not unpicked.

Recalling our examination of the Lotus Sutra in chapter 1, the first aspect to understand is that the emergence of the Bodhisattvas of the Earth was not an actual event that happened somewhere in the past. It was an allegory for the workings of our own lives. Nichiren writes in 'The Object of Devotion for Observing the Mind' how the Lotus Sutra is a metaphor for our life conditions and writes regarding Shakyamuni of the Life Span Chapter,

"He was speaking of the world of bodhisattva within ourselves. The bodhisattvas,... who emerged from beneath the earth, are the followers of the Shakyamuni Buddha present in our lives." (WND 1 p365-6)

As a result, our identity as Bodhisattvas of the Earth is less a fixed karmic inheritance than a state which can be activated when we chant, but most importantly, when we also share the commitment to spread the teaching in a similar vein to the pledge that the Bodhisattvas of the Earth made to Shakyamuni in the Lotus Sutra. Being a Bodhisattva of the Earth in SGI is therefore not an automatic entitlement but a conviction and a choice based on a shared sense of purpose with Nichiren and the three presidents of the Soka Gakkai. In so doing, we manifest the expansive life state of Bodhisattva and Buddha in our own lives and join in our own ceremony in the air when chanting in front of the Gohonzon. Being a Bodhisattva of the Earth is an active choice which involves commitment, not a fixed status we are automatically endowed with.

The decline in religious sentiment in the West seems to only be increasing, with the majority of young adults in 12 European countries having no faith. A wide variety of reasons can be attributable to this trend, but one factor could be considered the irrational contradictions within a religion which just do not wash for the majority of the populace in a scientific age. For example, even in those who do practise Christianity in the UK, a quarter profess to not believing in Jesus' resurrection from death. There will always be some wonder and mystery regarding the universe. Its mechanics may be fully fathomed, but the big Why?, the reason for existence in the first place, may forever be unanswerable. Yet religion, whilst delving and communing with this mystery, must keep an eye on unverified claims that in the present age just seem daft. Nichiren as a cosmic eternal Buddha could be put into this category. Nichiren embraced a unique mission and fused with the eternal Buddha nature of the cosmos but the inspiring part to his story is, so can we.

CHAPTER THREE

NAM-MYOHO-RENGE-KYO

THE ROAR OF THE LION

"When once we chant Myoho-renge-kyo, with just this single sound we summon forth and manifest the Buddha nature of all Buddhas; all existences... This blessing is immeasurable and boundless."

Those Initially Aspiring to the Way (WND 1, p887)

PART 1 - HOW DOES CHANTING WORK?

According to tradition, early in the morning of April 28th 1253, Nichiren climbed to the top of the hill at Kasagamori adjacent to his lodgings in his home temple of Seicho-ji. The spot affords a magnificent view of the cedar clad hills rolling towards the Pacific Ocean and as the sun began to rise, the 32 year old Nichiren chanted Nam-myoho-renge-kyo for the first time. Although the details of this moment have not been retained in his writings, Nichiren did state, "I, Nichiren at the beginning of the summer in the fifth year of the Kencho era (1253) began chanting them (Nam-myoho-renge-kyo)." (WND 2, p652)

If you happen to have the opportunity to visit Seicho-ji, you will find a fine modern statue of Nichiren placed on a man-made promontory. Look closer at the foot of this cliff and you will find a far more ancient statue of Nichiren which marks the more realistic position of the first daimoku (invocation of Nam-myoho-renge-kyo). My own experience at Kasagamori was perhaps not quite as profound as that first invocation for as I chanted the daimoku across the hills of southern Chiba, my 8 year old daughter was screaming at the bottom of the hill about how bored she was!

A universal chant

That spring, Nichiren set into motion a revolutionary practice and interpretation of Buddhism. This simple method of chanting the phrase Nam-myoho-renge-kyo has impacted on millions of lives improving not only their inner well-being but transforming their situations for the better. The independent pan-Buddhist writer, Clark Strand in his book *Waking the Buddha*, tested a single question: "Did Buddhism have a teaching that was so universal it could pass quickly from person to person without getting stopped in its tracks, leaping across national, ethnic, economic and even religious boundaries?"[1] Strand concludes that the SGI has such a teaching in its central focus on the dignity of life, but I would answer that the chanting of the daimoku has likewise transcended these boundaries across the world. The incredible diversity of SGI is testament to this effect, and at its foundation is the chanting.

NAM-MYOHO-RENGE-KYO

J. M. Walsh, the scholar, author and SGI-USA member, posits that there is a certain linguistic logic to the phrase which makes it universal. The Nam of the daimoku is Sanskrit and Myoho-renge-kyo is a Japanese phonetically derived version of the ancient Chinese title of the Lotus Sutra. Unlike Chinese, Japanese is non-tonal, so that meaning is not derived from the pitch, making it far easier to chant. Likewise the phonemes in Nam-myoho-renge-kyo are associated with nearly all languages. By contrast, Sanskrit recitations require highly accurate pronunciation which involve trainee Hindu priests spending years to learn to pronounce correctly.[2] The universality of Nam-myoho-renge-kyo has, therefore, a practical basis which means a Bolivian, an Eskimo and a Ugandan can all pronounce it without too much difficulty.

Furthermore, the British biologist Rupert Sheldrake has looked at the universal significance of chanting and singing to all life. Sheldrake illustrates the fundamental aspect of the use of vibration and sound by citing Charles Darwin's descriptions of the animal kingdom. Not only does he refer to more obvious examples such as frogs and birds but also many insects, including spiders, which produce rhythmic sounds, usually by rubbing together special structures on their legs. In fact, from the specific rhythms of woodpeckers, to singing mice and the calls of gibbons, sound and rhythm are an elemental part of the natural world. Sheldrake considers the chanting of mantras as a way in which a group can enter into "a literal resonance with each other" and "into a resonance with those who have chanted the same chants before." He also looks at the mechanics of chanting. Vowels create a continuous flow of air with the mouth open while consonants generally block or obstruct the flow of air (though notably 'n' and 'm' just divert the air through the nose). The vowel sounds are elemental in a chant in creating a specific pattern of vibration. Nam-myoho-renge-kyo is notable in incorporating four different key vibrational vowel sounds, ee, eh, ah and oh plus mm and nn which also have specific vibrational effects.[3]

It is worth discussing at this point that the Nam is fully pronounced in writing as Namu. Some Nichiren sects still pronounce the u. One SGI member I knew, got very caught up with the existence of this u sound and would pronounce it in a way that meant he was out of rhythm with others chanting with him. This resulted in him and his partner stopping chanting altogether in the end. On this issue, it is first of all important to clarify that Nichiren often refers to Myoho-renge-kyo, the title of the Lotus Sutra, as the key fundamental law and the phrase to be chanted as in the quote at the beginning of this chapter. The Nam or Namu is a relational marker, a sign of respect towards the Mystic Law, Myoho-renge-kyo. I like to use the metaphor of a swimming pool. The Nam is the diving board into the swimming pool of the law of life, Myoho-renge-kyo. In that sense the use of Nam is acceptable as it does not form part of the essential phrase itself. Secondly, a Japanese final vowel sound such as an u is often unvoiced, and this explains how Namu naturally and unquestionably became Nam in the chanting of the daimoku. Finally, if you have tried chanting Namu-myoho-renge-kyo, you will find it does not flow on the 3/3 rhythm which makes Nam-myoho-renge-kyo so natural and after some practice, effortless. The quality and quantity of daimoku are therefore impeded by trying to emphasise the u.

NAM-MYOHO-RENGE-KYO

Actual proof

However easy, natural or elemental the phrase is to chant, it would be meaningless if it did not result in tangible benefit. "Even more valuable than reason and documentary proof is the proof of actual fact," (WND 1, p599) as Nichiren states.

In my 20 or so years of practice, I have experienced countless times when chanting has been proven to me. Some based on the positive causes that have derived from the wisdom, energy and positivity which the chanting in the morning produced, others in which the synchronicity of events has been beyond my belief to happen in the normal course of events.

On its broadest level I can see how the trajectory of my life before chanting – prone to anxiety, depression and the transitional nature of my work- has transformed to a positive, centred and fundamentally happy life with a career I thoroughly enjoy. On a more specific level, here is an example from my work for the purposes of illustration.

After one year of practising Buddhism, I decided to retrain as a primary school teacher. Prior to this, I had been working in administrative jobs and trying to make it in the music industry. In a newly qualified teacher's first year in the job, there are a number of hurdles to overcome and objectives one must fulfil in order to become a properly registered teacher. The year was extremely challenging for me, as I was in sole charge of a class of 7 year olds for the first time. In my first week in the job, I went out on the Friday night with some friends and was physically unable to speak due to the exhaustion. My morning daimoku sustained me through those very difficult first few weeks, giving me the courage, hope and life force to cope with the role.

THE EVOLVING BUDDHA

A series of observations of my teaching would take place in order for me to become a fully qualified teacher. The first one by a visiting outside professional did not go well. It was therefore essential that my second observation went well to pass the year. I planned an ambitious maths lesson and of course chanted copiously for it to go well. On the morning of the observation, I began to prepare the resources for the lesson which would begin at 9 am. It became apparent to me very soon that I should have prepared these the night before and did not have enough time to cut out and create all the items which were crucial for the success of the lesson. Chanting quietly, I frantically began what seemed like an impossible task, my heart sinking at the thought of the inspector walking in to a half ready lesson in ten minutes time. At that precise moment two heads appeared around the edge of the classroom door, two older children asking if I had any jobs to do. This was of course precisely what I needed, but was all the more incredible because the school had a very strict policy that children were not allowed to enter the school before lessons started at 9am. I had never before, nor would ever after, have any children offering to do jobs for me before school. Suffice to say, between the three of us, the resources were prepared, the lesson was a success and my teaching career was saved!

The incredible synchronicity of this experience has been repeated on a number of occasions in different circumstances to me, something which did not occur before I had started chanting. This has brought me to the conviction that something more than a general good feeling resulting from chanting, leading to more positive action and therefore more positive results, is at work here. In his book, *The Buddha in Daily Life*, Richard Causton dedicates 127 pages to the meaning of Nam-myoho-renge-kyo. We will not be looking at the multiple layers of significance of the phrase, interesting as that may be. Instead we will be considering the question that nags in every Nichiren practitioner's head – how does the chanting actually work?

A scientific age

In other chapters, we look at research that can provide an evolving perspective on aspects of Nichiren Buddhism. The chanting of Nam-myoho-renge-kyo, however, is a timeless and unchanging crux at the heart of the practice, but our understanding of chanting, how it functions and the science behind it, is evolving. This chapter will look at the developments and studies within and outside SGI that can bring us closer to understanding what happens when we chant.

We live in a scientific and knowledge-based society. Scientific innovation has transformed human life in the last 150 years, in many ways for the better, and as a result, science underpins the way we understand our world and our place in it. It is therefore only natural that we look to pointers in science which might explain the anecdotal evidence of the actual proof of chanting. SGI President Daisaku Ikeda has stated, "President Toda predicted that 200 years later everyone would finally understand the significance of our efforts. He also said, 'As science progresses, the validity and correctness of Buddhism will be increasingly borne out'."[4]

THE EVOLVING BUDDHA

Buddhist explanations of chanting

We will look at how this statement from Toda is increasingly coming to fruition. Before we do so, let us examine how the chanting of Nam-myoho-renge-kyo has been explained within the tradition starting with Nichiren. In his copious writings, there are many expositions of the functioning of the daimoku:

"What is most important is that, by chanting Nam-myoho-renge-kyo alone, you can attain Buddhahood. It will no doubt depend on the strength of your faith. To have faith is the basis of Buddhism." (WND 1, p832)

We reveal this highest life state in the act of chanting but equally, our openness, receptivity and focus, in other words faith, have an impact on the outcome. Nichiren also, in many of his writings, clarifies that the phrase is 'our life itself':

"The entity of Myoho-renge-kyo in all its splendour-just what is this entity? If we hope to answer this we must say that it is the eight-petalled white lotus that is the true nature of our own lives. Since this is so then the essential nature of our own lives is Myoho-renge-kyo." (WND 2, p80)

So the daimoku not only reveals a life state within us but is itself the most essential aspect of our life. This all-encompassing element of the phrase is fully explained by Nichiren in his writing 'The Entity of the Mystic Law' that "all beings and their environments are themselves entities of Myoho-renge-kyo." (WND p417) and that this phrase physically embodies the Mystic Law of life, the true aspect of all things. The writer J.M. Walsh points out that Nichiren repeatedly refers to the Mystic Law transcending individual minds. For example, Nichiren instructs a follower to chant to the Gohonzon with the prayer that all the Buddhas of the universe will take possession of his body to assist him. Walsh writes, "Read with the understanding that the eternal Buddha, the Dharma realm, the Lotus Sutra, Nam-myoho-renge-kyo and our own lives are one, we can grasp that Nichiren is referring to the workings of a universal and compassionate Buddha consciousness within our lives."[5]

So how has the concept of a universal, all-encompassing law embodied in Nam-myoho-renge-kyo, been developed in the modern era, most notably by the presidents of the Soka Gakkai? Daisaku Ikeda and Josei Toda before him, have reclarified and elucidated this principle in accessible modern terms. In his novelised account of the growth of the Soka Gakkai, Ikeda writes, "Simply put Nam-myoho-renge-kyo is the fundamental law of the entire universe, the ultimate force that moves everything."[6] Ikeda has also expounded the fusion with the greater self as a way of explanation.

"This greater, cosmic self is related to the unifying and integrating 'self' that Jung perceived in the depths of the ego. It is also similar to Ralph Waldo Emerson's 'universal beauty', to which every part and particle is equally related; the eternal One."[7]

A fusion with the entire universe is further illustrated in the following well known passage:

"Gongyo and daimoku are a ceremony in which our lives commune with the universe. During gongyo through our faith in the Gohonzon, we vigorously infuse the microcosm of our individual existence with the life force of the macrocosm, of the entire universe. If we do this regularly each morning and evening, our life force is strengthened."[8]

Ikeda also illustrates this point with modern analogies, most notably of radio waves:

"The air around us is filled with radio waves of various frequencies. While these are invisible, a television set can collect them and turn them into visual images. The practice of chanting daimoku to the Gohonzon aligns the rhythm of our own lives with the world of Buddhahood in the universe. It tunes our lives, so to speak, so that we can manifest the power of Buddhahood in our very beings."[9]

Chanting making a difference

Open any SGI magazine from around the world and you will be drawn to the personal experiences of countless individuals who share how chanting and Buddhist practice has made a powerful difference in their lives. An emphasis on material change as well as spiritual change, is synonymous with the Soka Gakkai's interpretation of Nichiren Buddhism, for which it has faced criticism in the past. On a philosophical basis, SGI Buddhism sees no fundamental separation between the material/physical and the unseen/spiritual. In that sense material benefit and value created from it, resulting from the chanting, are not surprising. Furthermore, Nichiren himself was very much focused on worldly concerns. His career-defining salvo at the authorities of the day entitled 'On Establishing the Correct Teaching for the Peace of the Land' (1260) is an epistle to solve the famines, disputes and disasters which were afflicting 13th century Japan. Distrust of material benefit may come in part from the separation of the spiritual and material rooted in Christian belief systems. In addition,

Clark Strand considers that the criticism often comes from upper middle class Buddhists of European descent, who have rarely had to worry about money or material security, and points out to them the "hypocrisy of criticizing others for wanting the very things that they already have and therefore take for granted…Today when met with comments like 'they chant for money', I answer that while financial security is certainly an issue for some, we shouldn't let that distract us from the fact that SGI members also chant for the happiness of friends and family, for human rights and human dignity and for equal treatment of …minorities."[10]

My chanting has certainly changed in its focus over the years. At age 25, I had a long list of material aspirations, whilst at 45 my chanting is primarily directed towards my family, friends and fellow members and creating value in my environment. One of the very first determinations I chanted about was to have a girlfriend, having been dumped by my long term girlfriend more than a year prior to starting practising. Just over a week after I began chanting regularly, I went to a party at my previous boss's house and a girl asked me out on a date. Due to the fact that this had never happened before (or since!) I felt this was my first taste of actual proof. At the time it felt almost like magic, but on reflection I can see that I went to that party in a very different life state than I would have without the chanting. Instead of the mildly depressed and anxious person I had been, I was energetic and gregarious, dancing away, and I am sure it was this positive change which drew a positive response in my environment.

THE EVOLVING BUDDHA

Religion and Science

Overall, Nichiren and Ikeda's explanations of the workings of chanting focus on a fusion between the individual and a greater entity or Mystic Law which could equally be termed a universal consciousness or spiritual force. Explanations based on material brain changes or physical health benefits, which have been the basis of mindfulness' evidential claims in recent years, are not the prime focus of SGI practice. So is there a similar evidential basis for the concept of a universal consciousness, a Mystic Law? A growing body of academics and researchers would state there is, and in examining this question we see Toda's prediction of a scientific basis to Buddhist philosophy being gradually fulfilled.

Such questions are important because, as we mentioned earlier, we live in a scientific age. The historian Arnold Toynbee states in his dialogue with Ikeda, that he sees the gradual recession of Christianity in the West has been filled with "three other religions: 1) the belief in the inevitability of progress through systematic application of science and technology, 2) nationalism and 3) communism."[11] Of these three, I would suggest that a materialist, scientific belief system is the most all-pervading in the world today and in many ways quite rightly so, as its evidential basis and clear progressive impact on our lives supersede the unquantifiable superstition of past ages.

Religion and science could be considered to serve different purposes, and many presume that there is contradiction between them. Science looks at truth based on observable phenomena, whilst religion and perhaps most explicitly Buddhism asks, 'does it create well-being and a most meaningful and value-creating life?' Science takes observable data and explains what things and processes do, the structure and tendency of things but not ultimately what they are, their intrinsic nature. The fact that an electron, a pineapple, a human being exist, is still a wonderful mystery. A mystery which an underlying principle such as a Mystic Law explains in terms different to materialist science. Despite this difference in purpose from the outset, SGI Buddhism has embraced science as an important co-existing aspect of life, if not the only answer. Tsunesaburo Makiguchi, the founder of the Soka Gakkai stated, "I could find no contradiction between science, philosophy, which is the basis of modern society, and the teaching of the Lotus Sutra."[12]

Recent scientific studies may be taking us even nearer to substantiating, in scientific terms, the amazing benefits of chanting and in so doing show us more clearly a universal aspect to Buddhist practice and philosophy – a middle way which accommodates scientific knowledge and religious intuition.

The renowned scientist, Stephen Hawking, is famed for his search for a 'Theory of Everything'. Indeed, the Oscar winning film of his life is titled just that. Yet Hawking pointed out that even if an elegant equation could be found, the question of what 'breathes fire' into the equation to create a living universe would still be unanswered.[13] In other words, however much we understand the mechanics of the universe, why is there anything at all? Is there a force, a dynamic, a ground of being on a non-physical level which manifests the universe? In Buddhist terms, is there a dharma – a Mystic Law?

THE EVOLVING BUDDHA

Is understanding consciousness the answer?

Many philosophers and more recently academics have looked at consciousness as the key to validating the mechanism or evidential law that underlies the universe. Consciousness is our inner awareness, beyond the froth of our everyday thoughts, which knows we exist. A functional approach to consciousness which sees it merely as the result of brain mechanics, has been widely recognized to be insufficient in explaining it. By examining a brain, scientists have been unable to prove why it should be conscious. This has led to a number of scientists and leading academics including Peter Fenwick of King's College, London University and Steve Taylor of Leeds Beckett University to suggest that there is an increasing body of evidence to prove that consciousness lies outside the brain, and that it is potentially fused or connected to a universal consciousness, which one might call a Mystic Law.

Around ten years ago, the Centre for Applied Buddhism at the SGI-UK Headquarters, Taplow Court, invited Susan Blackmore, lecturer and writer on consciousness and Zen Buddhist practitioner, to give a talk. Blackmore began to give a series of examples relating to how illusory our perceptions are, how we lack free will and that ultimately consciousness may be nothing but the correlates of our brain activity, the idea that we are looking out on a world which is a theatrical mirage produced by neural activity. At the time I was impressed. It seemed a rational way of looking at things. One of the young women serving tea at the event was not so convinced. "I don't agree with her," she told me. "Despite our circumstances dictating our range of choices, I still have choice. I chose this

Buddhism." Her words made me reflect and I kept revisiting this point. Are we mere automatons, machines with the appearance of awareness and choice or is there more? The sense of that final point of consciousness, that deep awareness I felt, kept nagging at me. After all, I am still thinking!

What Blackmore was propounding, was the reductionist or materialist position on consciousness. Whether we are aware of it or not, a scientific materialism underpins our belief systems in the West. The astounding breakthroughs in understanding derived from Newton's laws of physics and Darwin's explanation of evolution, increasingly brought science to the fore and a view of the universe not as divinely planned but as a great machine. Matter was seen as the primary reality of the universe and anything including life itself could only be explained in material terms.

As the English academic, author and lecturer/researcher in psychology, Steve Taylor has illustrated in his book *Spiritual Science*, reductionism/ materialism has become a belief system like any other belief system including those of religions, to the extent that materialist scientists will discount valid scientific evidence which runs counter to their views of a material-based universe.[14] Taylor suggests it can also be a worldview that is bleak and barren, seeing ourselves as separate from one another with life being fundamentally purposeless and meaningless. Does a materialist outlook contribute to the hedonistic mindset of most of humanity and the wilful destruction of the environment? Perhaps.

In the last thirty years, neuroscience, the study of the workings of the brain, has grown vastly in its prominence as new imaging technology allows us to study the brain in ever more complexity. And yet, neuroscientists would admit that the entire endeavour has brought them no closer to understanding the mystery of consciousness. The neuroscientist, Antonio Damasio wrote in an article for *Scientific American*:

"One question towers above all others in the life sciences. How does the set of processes we call mind emerge from the activity of the organ we call brain?"[15]

Taylor has pointed out that even the research aimed at mapping different states of mind to areas of activity of the brain, is not generalizable and varies from person to person, so is far from finding a source of consciousness within the grey matter itself.[16] Ikeda considered the source of consciousness in his work *Life – An Enigma, a Precious Jewel* noting,

"Though much of the activity involved in consciousness takes place in the brain, consciousness is not necessarily confined to the brain. It is impossible to pick out a place in the body and say, 'This is where consciousness resides.'...In some respects, the workings of consciousness, mind and spirit are as mysterious in real life as in dreams."[17]

If consciousness is extended outside the brain, then the endless endeavours of the neuroscientific community will never reap a solution. Because of the non-physical quality of consciousness, a growing body of evidence is challenging the materialist conception of it. This movement of leading researchers and academics has been called pan-psychism, pan-spiritism or the intrinsic consciousness movement. In contrast, Peter Fenwick has termed the materialist view as "scientific fundamentalism", a belief that the understanding of material properties of the world is sufficient to explain everything.[18] Regarding consciousness, Daniel Dennet's neurophilosophy characterizes this latter position. Dennet believes nothing is required to explain wider states of consciousness than neural activity in the brain. And yet, nothing near an explanation of how consciousness arises via the brain has been found. However, from a materialist point of view, considering evidence that consciousness has a non-material quality outside the brain, goes against the basis of their beliefs and thus credible findings and reasonable hypotheses are rejected out of hand and their proponents are pilloried.

Scientific breakthroughs have met resistance throughout history when they challenge conventional thinking of the time. Benjamin Franklin was laughed out of the Royal Society when he brought up the subject of lightning conductors and when Stevenson proposed using locomotives on the Liverpool to Manchester railway for the first time, learned men gave evidence it was impossible to travel over 12 miles per hour.

Steve Taylor suggests that the brain does not produce consciousness "but rather it acts as a kind of receiver, which transmits and canalizes universal consciousness (or spirit force which is equivalent to it)".[19] This universal consciousness acts more like a field than a localized point, transcending matter but interacting with it, the human brain being one of the most highly evolved receivers of it. Evidence of such a theory could lead to an understanding of chanting's connection, influence and results linked to this universal consciousness field.

This also links with the Buddhist concept of the three truths, ke – the truth of temporary existence or ever changing phenomena, ku – the truth of non-substantiality or unmanifest potential in life and chu – the truth of the middle way, true entity of being, the all-pervading essence of the universe, Nam-myoho-renge-kyo. Evidence for such a theory could lead to a greater understanding of chanting's connection to and impact on this universal consciousness field. So let us look at the science which points towards the credibility of Taylor's paradigm and the likelihood of a 'wonderful law' of the Universe, as the Orally Transmitted Teachings of Nichiren often call it.

NAM-MYOHO-RENGE-KYO

PART 2 - NEW SCIENTIFIC HORIZONS

Quantum weirdness

The first area of research and scientific discovery which points to a shift in understanding regarding the existence of a universal consciousness, is the field of quantum physics. From a theoretical basis in the early 20th century, quantum principles have been proven conclusively over the last fifty years in the laboratory. Quantum physics has shown that the world emerges from a deeply interconnected fabric and experiments have shown testable connections between phenomena separated in space and time. It has elucidated that the fundamental particles of matter are not made of solid stuff but are patterns of potential and vibration and are impacted by the observer. Explaining quantum physics is not within the scope of this book, but looking at a few interesting experimental outcomes may help contribute to our understanding of the universe and how chanting can interact with seemingly separate individuals.

Action at a distance or quantum entanglement refers to particles interacting with each other at a distance. Experiments have worked with photons that once having interacted with one another, no matter how far apart they are moved from each other, work in a highly correlated and harmonious fashion. American researchers in 2015 found the odds against the correlations being caused by chance as 1 in 170 million and Chinese scientists were able in 2017 to show with a satellite, the linked harmony of entangled particles 870 miles away from each other.[20] If one accepts the Big Bang theory of the universe, then all matter was at its outset connected together in a tightly packed fragment before expanding across space. In that sense it was entangled and interacted from the very beginning, like the photons in the experiments. Could this set up a non-local interconnectedness, a non-separation between any particles in the universe?

Further photon experiments have brought up another surprising conclusion which runs counter to a traditional view of how matter works. The double slit experiment involves beaming a light towards two tiny slits with a detector screen. Standard science would expect the light photons to act like particles and produce a cluster of points on the detector screen. Instead, however, the light acts like a wave, creating an interference pattern which scientists have concluded show the photons travelling through the slits not as defined matter, but as a cloud of potential in wave form. However, if a detector screen is put on the slits, the light acts as a normal particle and clusters of impact points appear on the far screen. Incredibly, the way the observers observed the photons impacted on their behaviour and nature.[21] Pascual Jordon stated, "Observations not only disturb what has to be measured, they produce it."[22]

Adrian Nelson, an author and psychologist, sees quantum physics not only as challenging the view that science can remove the subjective observer from its verifiable evidence, but also as creating a mystery which sees consciousness having an impact on our environment. As a result, it offers the possibility of consciousness working on a non-local level. Some quantum scientists reject any interpretation of the results of quantum science, claiming that the results just 'are' and that with our limited perceptions we cannot fully ever explain quantum weirdness. This may be the case, but all science inherently gets interpreted by humans because it is only humans who create tests and observe phenomena. In contrast, many quantum scientists have come to conclusions approaching those of Adrian Nelson's, including the founding fathers of quantum mechanics such as Max Plank.

Quantum biology is a new and burgeoning science which seeks to explain some of the mysteries and hitherto unexplained workings of nature via quantum physics. Photosynthesis, the navigation of migrating birds and the process of tadpoles metamorphosing into frogs has been finally explained through theories of entanglement and potentiality found in quantum effects. Thus, these mysterious properties are not confined to the very tiny sub atomic levels in which quantum mechanics was first proven, but function within the macrocosmic world, including ourselves.

Testing psychic phenomena

The next area worth considering in relation to consciousness, is the study of psychic phenomena or psi research, as it is now commonly referred to. This is a somewhat controversial field, because it has been traditionally categorised together with many un-credible and quite plainly superstitious beliefs in the paranormal such as hauntings, witchcraft, fairies and the like. Steve Taylor makes an important distinction between these soft paranormal phenomena, which are highly questionable and lack any meaningful evidence, and 'hard' paranormal phenomena where a rigorous, testable, evidential basis has been established over the last few decades through scientific enquiry. This category includes telepathy, precognition, remote viewing and remote influence (also called psychokinesis- the ability to influence physical systems with mental intention).

This is a challenging area which materialist scientists reject out of hand, since these hard psi phenomena not only contradict, but are thoroughly inexplicable when considered from the perspective of a purely materialist world view. In response to the challenge psi researchers have experienced, contemporary psi experiments have been carried out with stringent scientific methods even more rigorously than in many other areas of scientific study, in order to counter claims of flawed methodology. Ikeda has also considered these kind of experiments and observed, "Experiments in extrasensory perception offer definite indications of how human beings can influence each other in the purely spiritual realm."[23]

In 2008, the psychologist Dean Radin conducted experiments using photons in a similar way to the quantum system experiments we have discussed earlier[24]. However, this time Radin wanted to see what the influence of consciousness or mind could have on a quantum system. A photon was directed to travel down two possible pathways. When the path was not resolved by observed measurement as we saw earlier, a wave pattern was produced. If one pathway was blocked a particle signature was produced showing the photon took that route as a particle.

Radin then arranged that participants in an electromagnetically shielded chamber direct their attention to 'observe', in their mind, the path of the photon. Radin found a marked increase in the photons taking one path and being registered as a particle rather than diffusing as a wave. Particularly with experienced meditators involved (who perhaps had greater skill at focusing attention), he calculated the odds against chance of the results occurring, to be 107,000 to 1. With control trials where no attention took place, there was no significant reduction of the interference pattern. In later experiments, Radin trialled 5000 participants all around the world and the findings seemed to indicate that, even from thousands of miles away, the individuals could influence the quantum system. Such results point to a role for consciousness beyond the brain and unbounded by space.[25]

Human telepathy, the ability to transmit words, emotions or images to another person's mind by means other than the known senses, is not a facility we may encounter on a day-to-day basis and is at best, a weak phenomenon. And yet, scientists have been able to pick up communication or connection between minds, particularly with pairs who shared an emotional bond. Experiments on twins and bonded pairs from the 1960s to the present, have shown how a stimulus such as a flashing light that affects the brain activity of the receiving participant, also affects the other participant in terms of their brain activity, even when they are a distance away in a dimly lit, electromagnetically shielded room.[26]

Ganzfeld telepathy experiments attempt to produce a particularly receptive mental state for participants by blocking sensory input from the outside and relaxing the individuals to a dreamlike state between waking and sleeping. The second participant is then taken to an isolated area at least 50 feet away and shown a clip of four randomly selected images. The sender is asked to mentally project specifically one of the images to the receiver in the relaxed state as a target image. Afterwards, the receiver is shown 4 images and ranks them in order of what came to her mind. Only if the correct image is ranked 1st is the session a 'hit'.[27] If random chance was at play over time, the hit rate would be 25%, a 1 in 4 chance, and yet over the thousands of times this experiment has been conducted in multiple studies, the hit rate is 32-35%, a highly notable statistical difference from a scientific perspective, since the odds against chance of this happening are calculated at one in 29 quintillion.[28] Again, rigorous controls and checks have been in place to assure sceptics of these results.

Rather than seeing this evidence as the sending of remote signals between brains, could this be similar to the way entangled particles correlate? No information is 'sent' between them but they are entering complementary states fused to a greater field. Dean Radin has stated,

"Quantum mechanics reminds us that the universe is ultimately a holistic, tightly integrated web, and thus it is not out of the question that no signals need to pass between brains... From a holistic perspective all brains are already connected to everything from the get-go, and not just through space. Through time too."[29]

If, in ultimate reality, we are part of the greater self -a wider consciousness, the separation between human minds is not fundamental and the ability to enter mental spaces of others on occasion, is therefore a possibility. In citing similar experiments from some time earlier, Ikeda has stated, "It seems to me significant that the inner influences of our life-forces on other lives, so long postulated by Buddhism, is now being examined and demonstrated by non-Buddhist para-psychologists."[30]

NAM-MYOHO-RENGE-KYO

What can death tell us about a consciousness?

The next area of study in this developing perspective does not involve refined experiments and must gain its evidence from personal anecdotal sources. This is because it deals with the most sensitive of subjects, the death of a human being. And yet, a body of research in this field has led a number of senior academics to the conclusion that it provides likely proof of a universal consciousness. One of the leaders in this field is Peter Fenwick, a Neuropsychologist and Senior Lecturer at King's College, University of London. Fenwick has carefully collated, over many decades, accounts of near death experiences, death bed visions and death bed coincidences.[31]

Near death experiences are highly lucid visons and experiences, which take place during a state of temporary brain death, such as when a patient suffers a cardiac arrest, and in which all monitoring devices assert that the brain is completely shut down. From the research, around 10% of patients experience lucid visions, often of a compassionate, brilliant light and feelings of peace, joy or bliss. These are common to all cultures and despite some cultural variations, these common elements crop up regardless of age, gender and even religious faith or lack of it. About one third of the experiences are also preceded by an out-of-body experience, some of which have accurately described what was happening in the hospital room when the patient was fully unconscious. Fenwick has also studied deathbed visions, in which the dying describe how they meet visions of dead relatives and, again, the journey to a terrain of light, love and compassion; and deathbed coincidences which seem to involve a drive on the part of the dying person to reach out and connect with people emotionally close to them, irrespective of the distance involved, to reassure and say goodbye to them. These can take the form of lucid dreams by the relatives of those who are near to the moment of death but can also occur when awake.

Fenwick's research has not led him to a belief in a particular after-life or a spirit world, but it has resulted in him concluding that there is a likelihood of a greater field of consciousness. If consciousness can occur in the absence of brain activity then how can consciousness derive solely from the brain? No single satisfactory explanation based on brain science has been advanced. Fenwick also rejects the possibility of coincidence regarding premonitions experienced by relatives, due to the sheer quantity of evidence he has accumulated, often when the death was not expected at all. Again, a wider field of connection beyond the self is seen as the most likely explanation.

Near death experiences have been looked at by SGI President Ikeda in his dialogue with astronomer and mathematician, Professor Chandra Wickramasinghe, *Space and Eternal Life*. Wickramasinghe tells Ikeda that near death experiences "may eventually provide us with insight into life, consciousness and mind." Ikeda states "At the very least, this phenomenon can be said to suggest the possibility that, rather than all of the body and mind's functions being extinguished at death, they continue to exist in some form," and "that ultimately neither psychological, pharmacological nor neurological interpretations suffice to satisfactorily explain the import of near-death experiences." Wickramasinghe then affirms "... the data does indeed appear consistent with the hypothesis of a consciousness that leaves the body and has an independent identity and existence after death."[32] These words very much echo Fenwick's conclusions of mind as a field, but he does stress "it is important to remember that any theory which tries to explain non-local mind does not displace current neuroscience but leaves it as a valuable basis on which consciousness acts through and within the brain."[33]

Awakening experiences

The final area of study which may shed some light on the possibility of a universal consciousness, is the research on transcendent or awakening experiences. The author, Emily Esfahani-Smith defines such experiences as follows:

"The word 'transcend' means 'to go beyond' or 'to climb'. A transcendent, or mystical experience is one in which we feel we have risen above the everyday world to experience a higher reality."[34]

Common features of such experiences are heightened awareness, positive emotional states such as love and compassion, and a sense of greater connection to people, nature or even the whole world. It is in this last facet in which, to a greater or lesser extent, our sense of self diminishes and our fusion with a greater whole manifests, that we viscerally experience an awareness which points to a greater consciousness beyond the confines of our limited ego.

Steve Taylor describes three key triggers of awakening/ transcendent experiences: contact with nature; spiritual practice and psychological turmoil. Within awakening experiences there is also a range of degrees of intensity, from low-level experiences of simply heightened awareness and feeling more alive, to medium intensity experiences of a sense of interconnection, to high intensity experiences in which we feel fused with the essence of the universe or our sense of limited self dissolves. Taylor claims these experiences are not uncommon, with a 2008 study finding 80% of 487 respondents having had some form of awakening or spiritual experience.[35] These experiences transcend all religions and are equally experienced by the non-religious. They again point, from an experiential basis, towards an inherent fusion with something beyond the microcosm of the individual, a fusion with the great life or law of the universe.

Josei Toda's awakening

Second Soka Gakkai President Josei Toda's enlightenment in prison echoes a high intensity transcendent experience derived from spiritual practice. In early March 1944, Toda had been chanting 10,000 daimoku a day and re-reading again and again the Lotus Sutra. Dwelling on a passage from the introductory Immeasurable Meanings Sutra, which provides 34 negations of what a Buddha is not (neither self nor others, neither square nor round etc..), he came to an impasse as to his understanding of the inherent meaning of these lines. Toda returned to chanting. Daisaku Ikeda relays in Volume 4 of his novel *The Human Revolution* what happened next:

"..filled with a boundless rapture he began to walk. It was a tiny cell. He clumped up and down it, his emaciated shoulders braced, his fists tightly clenched. He thought: Buddha is life itself and an expression of life! It does not exist outside ourselves but does exist within our life. No, it exists outside our life too. It is one reality of the life of the universe!

He wanted to proclaim it – to everyone and anyone! The small cell seemed to expand endlessly in that instant."[36]

Toda, in fact, had two awakening experiences, and it was the second one in which he experienced himself as a participant in the Lotus Sutra's ceremony in the air, that further solidified his sense of supreme mission as a Bodhisattva of the Earth, a practitioner who the Buddha entrusts the propagation of the Lotus Sutra. The wonder of these experiences goes far beyond that prison cell in 1944 for they were the profound catalyst, the source of the energy and inspiration for the incredible growth of the Soka Gakkai after World War Two. My life and all SGI members' lives would be very different without the awakening experiences of Josei Toda.

Toda's transcendent encounters were on the high intensity range of Taylor's scale. Toda later described the fusion as follows, "It is like lying on your back in a wide open space looking up at the sky with arms and legs outstretched. All that you wish for immediately appears. No matter how much you may give away there is always more. It is never exhausted."[37]

At the beginning of the 20th century, the writer William James catalogued such awakenings as 'peak experiences' that can profoundly result in deep personal change. The chanting of Nam-myoho-renge-kyo afforded Toda this world changing transcendent experience, and his tireless struggle to share Nichiren Buddhism was founded on a desire, similar to Shakyamuni and Nichiren, to empower ordinary people to experience a similar fusion with the universe and an elevated life state.

THE EVOLVING BUDDHA

What the chanting of the daimoku affords is a grounded, vital and centring spiritual practice which allows participants to experience transcendent awakening across the scale from low intensity to occasional higher intensity states depending on application, time and effort. It is notable that although Toda's enlightenment in prison as a peak high intensity experience is central to SGI's history and development, Toda's successor, Daisaku Ikeda does not claim a similar moment of full awakening. Instead, through Ikeda's example described in his novels *The New Human Revolution*, he embodies consistently over time an individual in a high and awakened life state through his behaviour as a human being. For me this steady, grounded fusion with the higher reality is a more realistic and practical aspiration for ordinary people. We cannot all have extreme peak awakening experiences but we can, through regular chanting, ground ourselves in that transcendent state and use that experience to pervade our actions in daily life.

The downsides of peak experiences

The balanced and pragmatic approach to transcendent experience found in the SGI, is all the more important if one examines the downsides and pitfalls to awakening experiences especially in their extreme form. Scientific research on awakening experiences has often centred on similar high intensity states induced by drugs. For a scientist, this is the most predictable and trackable method to analyse, as the state can be induced chemically in the laboratory. Early studies in the 1960s centred on LSD before the risks and downsides of this drug were fully ascertained. More recently, research has looked at a similar hallucinogenic drug called psilocybin which, it is claimed, in a supportive and controlled environment can result in positive mystical experiences. Hallucinogenic drugs may well induce awakening experiences in controlled circumstances, but to me the process seems fraught with risk. For every person who has a positive connecting experience, there is the possibility of another having a 'bad trip'. Human response to drugs and medicine varies greatly depending on an individual's metabolism and psychological make up. Chemically playing with a person's mind seems extremely dangerous even if only a minority have a negative reaction to the drug. I have met too many acid 'casualties' over the years to consider this could be a healthy and mass produced means to awakening.

Another area of peak experiences that must be treated warily are those that arise from the third of Taylor's key categories – psychological turmoil. One of the most lauded of the new age writers, Eckhart Tolle came to his awakening through having essentially a nervous breakdown. Tolle's depression got to a point when he kept repeating "I cannot live with myself any longer." From this point however, he experienced a kind of surrender of himself and his suffering, which resulted in a profound transcendent experience. What concerns me about lauding Tolle's experience is, that for many people at that point of mental collapse, enlightenment does not beckon and sadly suicide or hospitalization are a more likely outcome. To glorify Tolle's and others' extreme awakenings resulting from severe psychological turmoil, is to set them as aspirational, and yet the risks of such a route are extremely high. Tolle may advocate a different path, in which being present in the now is the route to enlightenment, but his own example is of a far darker and potentially more dangerous experience.

Tolle and many other new age writers see enlightenment and awakening as a process of dissolving the ego or rejecting the self. Although the ego or lesser self can be the cause of much suffering and unwise action in the world, its total rejection can also cause equally great psychological and social problems. Teachings and books which see the ego as the enemy, reinforce a view of enlightenment propounded by some other traditional Eastern philosophies and branches of Buddhism, that Buddhahood can only be achieved by fully rejecting the self. A healthy ego or sense of self in fact allows us to develop respect for oneself and others, resilience, the capacity to develop meaningful relationships and a sense of meaning. Trauma in childhood has been found to damage our ego, our sense of self-worth and to result in a range of social and psychological difficulties.

Is mindfulness meditation the answer?

Researchers Dr Miguel Farias and Catherine Wikholm have examined this issue in their book, *The Buddha Pill*. They describe the limitations to some of the research on mindfulness and also some of the adverse effects of meditation practice centred on dissolving the ego. One experience they describe is of a woman who, having been on many meditation retreats, found her sense of self dramatically changing. Despite thinking that this was part of the ego dissolving process, she couldn't help feeling anxious and frightened. The retreat teacher encouraged her to keep meditating, yet by the next day she was seeing a psychiatrist and spent the next 15 years being treated for psychotic depression, of which part of the time she was hospitalized.[38] Farias and Wikholm go on to outline further examples and a body of research, on the potential negative effects of meditation including depression, anxiety, panic and disorientation. This is not to say that all meditation is risky or results in adverse effects, but it is worth being wary, particularly in the example above, where a focus on the dissolution of the ego is involved.

In contrast, SGI philosophy seeks to fuse with the greater self and to put the ego in proper perspective but not to destroy it. As Ikeda stated in a speech to the University of California on April 1st 1974,

"To live for the greater self does not mean abandoning the lesser self, for the lesser self is able to act only because of the existence of the greater self. The effect of that relationship is to motivate the desires and attachments common to all human beings to stimulate the advancement of society."

There can also be a presumption that awakening experiences by themselves, confer a change in behaviour for the better. Wikholm and Farias examine the role of Zen Buddhism in Japan, its involvement in supporting the Japanese imperialist war effort and its lack of interest in morality or social ethics. The renowned Zen authority D.T. Suzuki wrote:

"Zen is....extremely flexible in adapting itself to almost any philosophy and moral doctrine as long as its intuitive teaching is not interfered with. It may be found wedded to anarchism or facism, communism or democracy, atheism or idealism."[39]

Brian Victoria researched Zen's involvement in World War Two in which the Japanese militarist authorities used Zen philosophy, meditation techniques and the explicit support of Zen Buddhist leaders to advance the war machine. Violence and killings were even regarded as synonymous with Zen

Buddhist compassion.[40] These examples starkly contrast with the actions of the first two presidents of the Soka Gakkai, Makiguchi and Toda who stood up against the militarist authorities in World War Two. This example is important to highlight the need for a grounding philosophy behind any spiritual practice to fully realise human potential.

The current explosion of mindfulness meditation practice has been driven by extensive scientific research on its health benefits and by the appeal of its secularisation separated from any philosophy, religion or moral code. Many have found beneficial effects from this practice, but in examining the hundreds of studies of the effects on participants, Farias and Wikholm found that barely any research had involved an active control group to ensure scientific rigour.[41]

There has also been a backlash from established meditation groups, that what is being produced is 'McMindfulness' which may afford relaxation but does not offer deep personal change. In focusing merely on non-judgmental awareness in the now, mindfulness can allow individuals to passively accept their circumstances and without an ethical backbone, participants' choices will not necessarily be wiser.

It has also been noted by Farias and Wikholm, that large multi-national corporations have embraced mindfulness in the workplace because a happier and more relaxed employee is more productive. The end goal is not self-improvement, but the interests of the company to maximise profits.[42] More worryingly, the US Marine Corps have also used mindfulness to increase the military effectiveness of their troops.[43] A far cry from Buddhist pacifism and with echoes of Zen's role in World War Two.

NAM-MYOHO-RENGE-KYO

My experience of meditation

My own experience of awakenings and meditation echo some of the research I have outlined above. After ten years of practising Nichiren Buddhism and receiving many conspicuous and inconspicuous benefits, I came to a major obstacle with my health. I began suffering severe insomnia which in turn led to anxiety. This was initially triggered by a personal conflict with someone, but was derived from my underlying tendencies. In desperation I began practising mindfulness meditation for its mental health benefits and to help me sleep. I initially found it helped relax me and so, although I never stopped chanting or going to SGI discussion meetings, they took somewhat of a back seat to a more lengthy meditative practice. Along with meditating for around an hour a day, I read associated literature, which although secular, was prescribing a philosophy associated with the mindfulness of living in the moment, of non-judgmentalism, the rejection of the ego and moral relativism.

After a month or two the insomnia returned, but I continued with the meditation in the hope of a breakthrough. I aspired to a 'new me' - a wiser and more enlightened version of my former self. However, I had a shocking argument with the teacher I was working with that year, which on reflection, was due to my increased passivity as a result of the meditation and to the fact that I was not 'pulling my weight' anymore in planning lessons with her.

At the end of the year, I moved to another job as a senior teacher in another school which was even more challenging. My anxiety and insomnia increased and I desperately tried to use the meditation to diminish them, in the main unsuccessfully. I wondered if I would get to a point of ego dissolution, but instead I suffered more and became more selfish and dysfunctional with my family. Psychological turmoil did not provide awakening or peace. The idea of a long retreat away from the challenges of the world appealed to me greatly and I went spiritually shopping around various retreat and religious centres. Just at that point, when I was about to book a holiday to India on my own, away from my family, I finally sought medical treatment for my insomnia. Within weeks of getting the right treatment, my insomnia and anxiety were gone and I had what I describe as a 'lightbulb moment'. Mindfulness had not given me the health benefits I sought and I decided to fully reconnect with my Buddhist practice with the SGI, where I truly had received benefit and an approach that engaged me with society. This is merely my personal experience. I acknowledge that many people derive benefit from mindfulness and, occasionally, I will use the breathing and techniques at extreme moments of stress. But I have never looked back after that moment of reengagement with the act of chanting with the SGI.

A middle way

The chanting of Nam-myoho-renge-kyo is a grounded practice which provides an ongoing awakening experience. This, as Richard Causton describes, is neither, "a supernatural quality which enables you to perform superhuman or magical feats... (nor) a transcendental state, divorced from the everyday reality of this world."[44] The daimoku is a middle way which avoids the extremes of awakening experiences (desiring as I did an epiphany or hallelujah moment), and instead is refreshing, vital and connected to the greater self, but also connected and concerned for the potential of others as well as our own.

Overall, research on quantum physics, psi phenomena, near death experiences and awakenings is challenging the standard materialist reductionist view of science and the world. In turn, it is pointing to the likelihood of a universal mind or consciousness which could equate with a Mystic Law. Daisaku Ikeda's dialogue with the astronomer Chandra Wickramasinghe from the mid-1990s, outlines a similar viewpoint especially in the second chapter entitled 'Science and Religion'. Although much of the evidence I have discussed was not available at that time, Wickramasinghe challenges the reductionist position that the brain is the seat of all consciousness. Ikeda refers to Bohm, Maslow and Jung in the fields of science and psychology to outline levels of consciousness that transcend the individual. Ikeda states, "the limitations to the reductionist approach become all the more apparent when one moves from the realm of physics into that of biology,"[45] whereas Wickramasinghe takes the subject into neurology and the existence of consciousness as a separate entity. These ongoing discoveries are exciting and offer a new grounding to how chanting works.

PART 3 - THE SCIENCE OF CHANTING

Ikeda's dialogues with numerous eminent scientists, including chemist Linus Pauling, physicist Joseph Rotblat and cosmonaut Alexander Serebrov, have set SGI on an open minded path to engage with science. For the scientifically minded, hard evidence proven in the laboratory may be a prerequisite for giving any practice or method credibility and trustworthiness. As touched on earlier, the pervasive influence of mindfulness is the result of scientific research combined with a secularisation of the product on offer, the downside arguably being a commodification of the practice disembodied from a moral code and its philosophical roots. So has there been any similar research on chanting in general and specifically Nam-myoho-renge-kyo, and can it provide further insight and support for this particular model of practice?

Can we trust all of the research?

Before examining some of the scientific investigations into chanting, it is important to highlight some of the problematic issues of studies in this field. As noted earlier, Farias and Wikholm have re-evaluated the research on mindfulness, examining over 4000 articles and found the vast majority of studies were of poor quality, lacking a proper control group. They concluded there was no robust scientific evidence that mindfulness had any substantial effect on our minds and behaviours.[46] Control groups are an essential part of any fair test in order for scientists to examine conditions in the absence of the factor they are testing. Control groups are easy to establish when testing a new drug. A placebo drug is provided to the participants. But with meditation research, to create a control group by requiring the participants to do an alternative activity such as resting or exercising, will likely lead to the group knowing that they have been placed in the placebo group. This means the expectations of the participants get mixed up with the results. In addition, these expectations are rarely evaluated before meditation research. There is also the risk of high hopes on the part of the scientists to find a positive outcome, discounting neutral results and 'sexing up' any minor differences, something Farias and Wikholm have also evidenced.[47] In addition, it is important to avoid a 'sampling bias'. For example, examining only those who have experience of meditation may not reflect the make-up of the population as a whole in terms of ethnicity, social class and mental health profile.

All of these difficulties are encapsulated in the greatest body of research on a form of mantra meditation, Transcendental Meditation (TM for short). TM rose to prominence in the 1960s and 1970s with the initial public support of the Beatles. Its founder, the Maharishi Mahesh Yogi encouraged scientific studies in the 1970s and 1980s to support its main technique which involves the silent internal meditative technique of chanting a given mantra in one's head. The TM research claimed a wide range of health benefits related to stress, anxiety, depression, burnout and even wider societal impacts in grand experiments involving TM's effect on crime rates across a whole city.

However, a systematic review by Lynch et al of the Royal

College of Physicians in Ireland of 2171 records, of which 78% of the studies utilised the TM programme, found 90% of the studies were of poor quality hindering the extent to which one could be confident of the accuracy of their findings.[48]

What scientific evidence is there on the benefits of chanting?

Compared to the deluge of research on mindfulness that has been produced in the past decade, research on chanting in general is at a nascent stage and much of what has been investigated slips into the pitfalls outlined above. The most rigorous piece of research on Buddhist chanting so far was carried out by the University of Hong Kong in 2019, albeit on a different form of chanting. Brain waves are one of the most tangible factors that can be analysed for the effects of religious or therapeutic interventions. They are generated by electrical pulses working in unison via a vast network of neurons interacting with one another. Brain waves are categorised into five main bandwidths. The slowest of these are delta waves which occur, but not exclusively so, during deep sleep. The fastest are gamma waves prevalent in conscious perception. Alpha brain waves have been found to increase in experiments on mindfulness meditation, but also manifest in all forms of wakeful relaxation when our eyes are closed. Brain waves are monitored using an EEG (Electroencephalogram) which can measure electrical activity in the brain through the placing of electrodes across the scalp.

It is important to avoid unverified generalisations about the purposes of different brain waves. Scientists are not all in agreement in this field and furthermore, a number of 'new age' writers have manipulated the science to ascribe various qualities to each bandwidth which do not stand up to close examination based on the research.

The University of Hong Kong study used two active control groups, one who repeated the religious chant silently and the other who chanted the Chinese translation of "Santa Claus old man" to control for the potential effect of chanting just any phrase that comes to mind. The group who were chanting a Buddhist mantra aloud showed a greater increase in delta brain waves in comparison to the two control groups.[49] The researchers state that accumulating evidence suggests delta waves may be related to reduction of self-oriented thoughts and the temporary awareness of our senses. Due to the fact delta waves are prevalent in sleep they also likely have a restorative function for the brain and organs. Gemma Perry of Macquarie University, Australia has found a positive effect on mood and social cognition from vocal chanting but her study only used silent chanting as a control comparison.[50]

The chanting of Nam-myoho-renge-kyo has not received, as far as I am aware, any similar EEG studies. Two authors jointly have put themselves under EEG analysis during the chanting of the daimoku. The first experienced an increase in delta and theta waves during testing and the second, an increase in alpha and theta waves which crossed over during the recitation.[51] This alpha-theta crossover is associated with a hypnogogic state between waking and sleeping and is advocated in neurofeedback therapy to process trauma and addiction. With no control groups and such limited numbers of participants involved, however, nothing conclusive can be proved from these results. Certainly, it is only a matter of time before a fuller neuroimaging study of the chanting of the daimoku is performed at university level.

Would more scientific studies really prove how chanting works?

But even if a rigorous and comprehensive study was conducted in gauging the brain wave patterns of chanting Nam-myoho-renge-kyo, would this really be required to validate the practice? Chanting and practising SGI Buddhism are about far more than achieving altered states in the brain. It is about achieving our determinations, about our relationships with others and about deep personal change which manifests in daily life. We tend to latch on to the most tangible scientific evidence based on a testable hypothesis method which has its roots and clearest expositions in chemistry and physics. When dealing with a chemical reaction or an electrical event in the brain, experiments can achieve a clear cut answer. Yet there are many aspects of life: psychology, social science and behavioural science which are equally important but less unequivocal in their outcomes. For example, these latter sciences will often ask participants in studies to complete a survey about their views and feelings but these may garner subjective results based on the individual's mood that day, their expectations and experience of being in a scientific study and even if they had time to have a good breakfast beforehand. Sometimes results from such research can be approached in the media with the same scientific absolutes as the results from a test tube or a petri dish. Scientists can be viewed as the high priests of our contemporary society but the scientific method means new evidence can disprove old findings and conclusions can be overturned.

It is in these life sciences that the full benefit of Buddhist practice can be examined but we must be wary of making absolute judgements on their findings. As is so beautifully illustrated in Nichiren Buddhism, our lives are made up of a complex web of internal and external causes. In attributing a cause to any particular result there will be a myriad of other causes that also led to that outcome. In addition, there is the concept in Buddhism of latent and manifest effects. A cause we make now, may not manifest immediately just as an acorn planted today will not grow into a beautiful oak tree tomorrow. How could a study of the effects of chanting account for such delayed results as a latent effect?

The geographer, Jared Diamond compares proximate causes, the surface triggers for events and actions with ultimate causes, the deep causal origins of an event. He uses the example of a marriage counselling session where the husband attributes the break-up of their marriage to the wife slapping him in the face, whereas the wife attributes it to the husband having affairs. Digging deeper, the husband may attribute the affairs to his wife's coldness and his wife may attribute her coldness to the husband's lack of attention to her.[52] This could go on *ad infinitum* but above all, for Nichiren Buddhists the ultimate cause is the chanting of Nam-myoho-renge-kyo and therefore the manifestation of our truest, purest self, our Buddha nature.

As Nichiren states, "It is impossible to fathom one's karma." (WND 1, p303) If we could split our life in two, such as in the classic Christmas movie 'It's a Wonderful Life', and examine how our life transpired with chanting and without chanting, then we could truly evaluate the effects. As that is never going to happen, we must satisfy ourselves with examining our own responses to the difficulties of life after practising Buddhism and the overall trajectory our life takes. This is the actual proof we can all test in the laboratory of our own lives. As is made clear by Nichiren and Ikeda, struggles and problems will not vanish once an individual takes up Buddhism nor will life be easy. Buddhism's power is manifest in how one deals with the inevitable challenges when they occur.

It's all about vibrations, man!

A final recent scientific theory is worth noting at this point in relation to brain waves and physical phenomena more generally. Tam Hunt and Jonathan Schooler of the University of California, Santa Barbara have recently proposed a 'resonance theory of consciousness'[53]. Hunt and Schooler posit that resonance, another word for synchronized vibrations, is at the heart of physical reality. All things in the universe are constantly vibrating. Every object in the room you are sitting in is vibrating at various frequencies, and on an ultimate level, all matter is a vibration of underlying fields. In addition to this view, Hunt and Schooler highlight that many things in proximity to each other start to 'sync up', to vibrate together at the same frequency, from fireflies flashing their lights in sync to the complex neurons firing in the human brain.

Hunt states, "Resonance is a truly universal phenomenon and at the heart of what can sometimes seem like mysterious tendencies toward self-organisation."[54] Could this universal tendency in phenomena to vibrate and sync in the future explain further the logic and power of chanting Nam-myoho-renge-kyo?

Pascal Fries, a German neurophysiologist has explained how this synchronisation process in gamma, theta and beta waves produces human consciousness. On a material level, it is the working together of these electrical waves that produces various types of human conscious experience. This does not resolve the difficulty in defining the ultimate source of consciousness, but Hunt and Schooler go further based on a panpsychist approach to consciousness outside the brain. Their view is that all entities are to some extent conscious, that consciousness is an inherent part of the universe and that through simpler elements combining into more complex elements through vibrational harmony (an example being the neurons that make up the brain), ever more advanced manifestations of consciousness occur.[55]

The universe's 'fine-tuning problem'

The likelihood of the universe existing of itself, with all the laws of physics in perfect balance, is incredibly slim. J.M. Walsh describes seventeen independent cosmological factors that must be at or near their observed values and the chances of all these functioning as they do to be a vanishingly small probability[56]. The issue of the cosmological factors is known as the 'fine tuning problem.' The universe is fine-tuned for life to a statistically impossible degree. Scientists have developed mathematical theories of limitless multiple universes to allow for the chance of the universe and our planet to exist under such laws and the even remoter outcome of the emergence of life. The multiple universe theory can only remain a theory however, because it is impossible to find or enter other universes.

How the universe brought forth life and mind, we do not know, but the idea of a universe dynamically driven towards life and mind- a compassionate law- is an alternative theory gaining increasing acknowledgement from scientists and philosophers. It is a theory not as yet fully proven, but the multiple universe theory supported by many others can never be proven other than in mathematical models. Secular materialists see the idea of universal consciousness, an underlying dynamic law that produces life, as a dangerous threat and a return to a pre-Darwinian reliance on God. But giving "space for the possibility that life and mind were in some way woven into the natural order from the beginning,"[57] as Adrian Nelson puts it, does not require us to return to the religious dogma and superstition of the past.

The concept of a Mystic Law with some compassionate intent makes the dynamic development of life and the universe plausible, and finds a place for mind and consciousness whereas a purely mechanistic explanation does not. It also connects us with our environment and becomes a basis of value in the world, rather than casting us as isolated biological robots with no ultimate worth.

Daisaku Ikeda has stated, "In the universe itself, there is a unifying compassion. The universe itself is originally compassion."[58] and, "The compassion of the universe is a function of the Buddha.... When we pray, speak out and take action for the happiness of a friend, the eternal life of the universe manifests through our thoughts, words and deeds."[59] Based on the evidence I have outlined earlier in this chapter, I believe it is fair to remain open to the existence of this compassionate intent and, as Ikeda outlines, through compassionate actions we attune with this underlying law. For Nichiren Buddhists, the quintessence of this compassionate law is revealed in Nam-myoho-renge-kyo.

Transcending differences

But if this Mystic Law, all pervading consciousness or mind, is a universal aspect of existence infused everywhere and an aspect of all of us, can Nam-myoho-renge-kyo be an exclusive means to connect with this universal element or are there other means? SGI sees Nichiren as having fully fused with the ultimate law of life and he recognized that this law could be fully expressed in the current age as Nam-myoho-renge-kyo.

But equally, Ikeda's engagement outside SGI in dialogues with those of other religions expresses a sympathy with a universal message found in all religions and a desire to transcend differences. Ikeda, in elaborating on Toda's views, hypothesises that if Mohammed, Jesus and Nichiren had been able to meet, they would have quickly been able to reach agreement on the way forward, difference only having arisen among their later followers.[60]

Steve Taylor describes how the Lakota native American tribe called the spirit force they believed in as *Wakan-tanka*, which more accurately can be translated as 'The Great Mystery', a divine force, not a sacred being, much like the concept of the Mystic Law.[61] J.M. Walsh refers to other SGI publications in which the authors acknowledge that all major religions seek the same reality, and that the SGI does not claim exclusive truth.[62]

My perspective on this question was coloured by my spiritual crisis which I referred to earlier in the chapter. Whilst I was meditating heavily and chanting minimally, I went on what can only be described as a spiritual shopping tour, participating in a variety of retreats, seminars and services from Hindu, Christian and other forms of Buddhism. Although I enjoyed each one and saw a spiritual connection manifest each time, none came close to the warmth, support and engagement I had found in SGI meetings. My conclusion therefore was, that there are many ways to access the universal ultimate reality but that Nam-myoho-renge-kyo is a particularly refined and accessible method, combined with a practical and reasonable philosophy which can result in major positive impact on the individual and society.

Can anyone benefit from chanting?

So can anyone who chants benefit, whether or not they are connected to a specific organisation such as SGI? My answer to this would be yes but with a caveat, most illustrated by a quote from Nichiren's writing:

"'How great is the difference between the blessings received when a sage chants the daimoku and the blessings received when we chant it?' To reply one is in no way superior to the other... The gold that a fool possesses is no different from the gold that a wise man possesses. However, there is a difference if one chants the daimoku while acting against the intent of the sutra." (WND 1, p756)

The chapter on the Lotus Sutra looks at this in more depth, but that 'intent' can be summarised as the philosophy of the dignity of life. Therefore, chanting in isolation may be beneficial, but a wise organisation, aligned with the intent of the sutra, is really key to ensure one is manifesting that intent to maximise the power of chanting. Chanting isolated from others limits growth and one's positive impact on others. It can also more easily come from a distorted perspective. Further chapters will look at this in more detail with regard to SGI, kosen rufu and the mentor/disciple relationship.

I have attempted to provide in this chapter some further perspectives on the chanting of Nam-myoho-renge-kyo, some of which are indicated by science. And yet it is important to acknowledge the difference in perspective that religion affords. It deals with consciousness in a way that science may never be able to, because *we are* the conscious observers and the observer observing one's own consciousness is part of what scientists describe as the 'hard problem' regarding consciousness. Instead religion and, more specifically in this case, SGI Buddhism, come from a different angle most eloquently summed up by Arnold Toynbee in his dialogue with Daisaku Ikeda, *Choose Life*:

"Scientists limit their objectives to observing phenomena, seeking to explain them rationally and trying to test their conclusions. In contrast to science, religion offers human beings a chart of the mysterious world in which we awoke to consciousness and in which we pass our lives. Although this chart is conjectural we cannot do without it. It is a necessity of life."[63]

CHAPTER FOUR

THE GOHONZON

ENTERING THE TREASURE TOWER

"I am entrusting you with a Gohonzon for the protection of your young child. The Gohonzon is the essence of the Lotus Sutra and the eye of all the scriptures. It is like the sun and moon in the heavens, a great ruler on earth, the heart in a human being, the wish granting jewel among treasures, and the pillar of a house."

On Upholding Faith in the Gohonzon (WND 1, p624)

A mirror, a banner, a road map for life, a scroll, an insignia, a reflection of enlightened cosmic reality. However you describe the Gohonzon, it is without doubt the most widely distributed devotional mandala in the history of humankind. Millions around the world chant to the Gohonzon (which literally translated means supreme object of devotion) every day in their homes. As one of the three key elements to the practice of Nichiren Buddhism which Nichiren described as the Three Great Secret Laws (secret in that they had never before been revealed), the Gohonzon is an essential part of SGI Buddhist practice.

What is the Gohonzon?

The Gohonzon is a graphic reflection of enlightenment, inscribed in Chinese and Sanskrit calligraphic characters, an embodiment of ultimate reality. Down the centre, bigger and bolder than the rest, is written Nam-myoho-renge-kyo Nichiren – the essential teaching fused with the human being who has revealed his Buddhahood, Nichiren himself. Surrounding this central inscription are many smaller ones which represent all aspects of life both positive and negative, and notably including the Ten Worlds or life states that we referred to in chapter 1. All the forces of the universe which affect us; the sun, the moon and the stars are also all included. These representations are all depicted in the form of figures from Buddhist iconography, which in turn allows the Gohonzon on another level to be a depiction of the crucial event in the narrative of the Lotus Sutra – the gathering around the treasure tower known as the 'Ceremony in the Air'. The central inscription of Nam-myoho-renge-kyo is the treasure tower surrounded by the Buddhas – Shakyamuni, Many Treasures and the leaders of the Bodhisattvas of the Earth. The mandala is inscribed in a fashion to involve those who face it in actually taking part in the ceremony in the air. The two Buddhas face us whilst the surrounding characters are flipped so as if they are facing towards the treasure tower like us, in three dimensions. It is as if we are participating in this timeless event whilst chanting to the Gohonzon. SGI President Daisaku Ikeda writes:

THE GOHONZON

"The moment of relation provides a sublime seat where you join palms together to become one with the true entity of all phenomena. It contains the overflowing power to embrace, integrate and motivate all existences."[1]

An object of devotion or worship is somewhat alien to Western tradition particularly those countries influenced by Protestant Christianity's rejection of the worship of images (though the Gohonzon's abstract form is far removed from an idol). However, Richard Causton in *The Buddha in Daily Life* elucidates the point that we all have a fundamental object of devotion which we value above all else, regardless of religion. This could be a partner, a career, possessions or even pets. In developing the Gohonzon, Nichiren offered a transcendent focus for our natural tendency to centre on something.

My experience of receiving the Gohonzon

I kept a diary during my first years of practising Buddhism and wrote the following when I received my Gohonzon:

"Receiving the Gohonzon was a flowering for me. In our chapter (Buddhist group), three people were receiving Gohonzon, the scroll which represents one's life on May 6th. Deciding to receive it is a momentous step; it fully equips you to connect with your Buddhahood (though you can do it without a Gohonzon) and it is a statement of intent to follow this Buddhism no matter what... As I went forward (to receive the Gohonzon) I felt an incredible sense of elation, greater than I had ever experienced before. As the leader handed me my scroll, I said to him, 'I will never give up.' 'Good boy', he replied enthusiastically. I had made the vow ultimately to myself but had promised it to the General Director of SGI-UK. I would keep such a vow.

After it was all over, I shed a few tears as did many people; they were tears of the purest kind, not dipped in excessive emotionalism of any sort. They were simply tears of happiness."

Can there be a special Gohonzon?

The Gohonzon, which SGI members enshrine in their homes, is a version of Nichiren's mandala inscribed in the 18th century by Nichikan, the 26th Abbot of Taiseki-ji temple (Nichiren Shoshu as it is referred to now did not exist as an official entity under that name until 1912). This Gohonzon in turn is based on the layout of what has been known in Nichiren Shoshu tradition as the Dai-Gohonzon, which correlates with the basic template of Nichiren's own fully developed Gohonzons from his later years. Dai means 'great' or 'big' as in Daishonin, 'Great Sage', an honorific title for Nichiren. Nichiren Shoshu's take on this particular Gohonzon, the Dai-Gohonzon, has resulted in a fundamental difference with SGI philosophy which we can explore to valuably draw out the universal significance of Nichiren's mandala format.

For the Nichiren Shoshu priesthood and followers, the Dai-Gohonzon in their possession enshrined at their head temple is a supreme Gohonzon, greater than the rest, the reason for Nichiren's appearance and the master to all other subordinate Gohonzons. An analogy that was once frequently used was that the Dai-Gohonzon was like an electric generator powering the outlets, which are the Gohonzons enshrined in people's homes. And like a flow of electricity, flipping a switch could allow the

THE GOHONZON

outlets to go dead. The flipper in this case being the high priest who, according to Nichiren Shoshu, has alone received the heritage of the law – all a convenient basis for asserting priestly authority if he could at will stop Gohonzons from working.

The concept sounds outlandish and ludicrous, yet SGI accepted the status of the Dai-Gohonzon until 2014 when a doctrinal revision quietly dropped these particular claims and henceforth the Dai-Gohonzon was regarded as one of many equal Gohonzons. It began to be referred to in SGI as 'the Gohonzon of the second year of the Koan era.' This move is wholly to be approved of, and in this chapter we will look at how this issue can be an opportunity to deepen our understanding of the universal relevance of Buddhist practice. Furthermore, SGI's revision of its stance has been a prime point to rebuke SGI by Nichiren Shoshu. By investigating the Gohonzon more thoroughly, not only can SGI practice be empowered further but the basis of Nichiren Shoshu's authority and philosophy dissolves. For ease of speech rather than any acknowledgement of its power, I will refer to it as the Dai-Gohonzon rather than SGI's rather wordy new title for it. Long before the split of 1991, Daisaku Ikeda wrote:

"All religions have objects of worship which are usually expressions of some supernatural or external power governing life and human destiny. People have a subservient attitude in prayer when asking for salvation, forgiveness and compassion or, in some cases, try by subservience to satisfy those powers and avoid their wrath. Such attitudes have contributed to creating the special position of the clergy as intermediaries between man and his object of worship."[2]

THE EVOLVING BUDDHA

Origins of the Gohonzon

Before looking more deeply into the issues and lessons from the controversy surrounding the Dai-Gohonzon, let us look at the Gohonzon in broader terms. The Gohonzon is a Buddhist mandala, and a mandala is an object that serves as a focal point for devotion, ritual or meditation. The first proto-mandalas originated in the Stone Age some 25,000 to 30,000 years ago and were simple circles drawn on the walls of caves. Mandala means circle in Sanskrit, and the first Buddhist mandalas were circles marked on the ground. They most likely entered the tradition through direct borrowing from Hinduism which has utilised them in worship since ancient times.

In Vajrayana (Tantric) Buddhism, the mandala represents the universe through proscribed circular and rectangular areas. Two key mandalas which Nichiren refers to and undoubtedly came into contact with during his years of study, were the Womb World and Diamond World mandalas centring on the Buddha Mahavairocana in their middle. Although the Gohonzon is unique in many ways, it does contain elements that bear relationship to previous mandalas. For example, Nichiren used the ancient Indian Siddham script to inscribe the Wisdom Kings, Aizen and Fudo or Craving-Filled and Immovable who represent earthly desires are enlightenment, and the sufferings of birth and death are Nirvana, respectively. Craving Filled appears on the Diamond World Mandala and Immovable on the Womb World Mandala. In addition, part of the Hindu pantheon, Brahma and Indra are also included on the Gohonzon, Gods who had been adopted in early Buddhism from the Hindu scriptures.

THE GOHONZON

In 1254, one year after Nichiren declared the practice of chanting Nam-myoho-renge-kyo and many years before he developed the Gohonzon, Nichiren produced two beautiful drawings of Craving Filled and Immovable in pictorial form flanked by Sanskrit and Japanese inscriptions. The two drawings are still preserved to this day and although no explanation for them is found in Nichiren's writings, it has been inferred from their inscriptions that Nichiren drew them after a visionary experience. Certainly the prominence of these two esoteric deities on the Gohonzon can be linked to these early depictions by the Daishonin.

How did Nichiren create a Gohonzon?

Nearly 140 original Gohonzons inscribed by Nichiren himself still exist to this day, preserved in temples of a variety of Nichiren denominations over the centuries. Historians estimate that between 1271 and 1282, Nichiren inscribed between 300 to 800 Gohonzons for his disciples. The simplicity and accessibility of the Gohonzon, since only paper, ink and brushes were needed to produce them, made it a form of mandala accessible to all. Long lasting mulberry paper would have been fabricated by Nichiren's disciples and sheets pasted together to create the scroll inscription. Black sumi ink was used but also blue ink and in general long, soft tipped brushes. Once the materials were prepared, most likely with followers silently gathered around him, at his dwelling on Mount Minobu, Nichiren would begin to inscribe the Gohonzon without hesitation, starting with the central inscription of Nam-myoho-renge-kyo.[3] Some original Gohonzons even have clear indications of Nichiren's fingerprints perhaps left by mistake when slipping, as the Daishonin could not lean on his left arm or hand due to injuries sustained in the Komastsubara attack of 1264.

The Gohonzon inscription would vary to a certain extent depending on the recipient and the circumstances of the time. For example, Nichiren would add a quote from the 'Medicine King' chapter of the Lotus Sutra for a sick person or during times of epidemics. Craving-Filled and Immovable would be inscribed thick and large at times of persecution of the community of believers. In both Shijo Kingo's and his wife Nichigen-Nyo's Gohonzon, like pillars protecting the mandala, these two Sanskrit characters are enormous in proportions, taking up almost all the length of the Gohonzon. Nichiren's letters to Shijo Kingo and Lady Nichigen-Nyo attest to the troubles they encountered from their lord and through family illness.

Nichiren varied the size of Gohonzon from small personal *omamori* Gohonzon, which may have been rolled and tied to a person's body, to enormous scrolls using numerous sheets of paper for a community of believers. The largest recorded mandala ever produced by Nichiren comprised 28 sheets of paper and was bestowed in November 1278 to Mitsunaga and his group. Various lengthy passages from the Lotus Sutra are included in this mandala, the space affording their inclusion.[4] On a rare occasion, Nichiren would make mistakes on the Gohonzon, missing the 'ten' from Bonten or doubling the loops on the Sanskrit Aizen.

One notable feature of Nichiren's Gohonzon are the '*komyo*', sweeping brush stroke lines coming from the ends of the central inscription of Nam-myoho-renge-kyo. These unusual and dynamic strokes have been interpreted in a variety of ways. Traditionally they have been seen to represent the widespread propagation of the daimoku but they could also be seen as a physical representation of the voice chanting Nam-myoho-renge-kyo and reverberating out into the universe transforming the ten life states.

How did the Gohonzon evolve?

Nichiren's Gohonzon was not immediately created at the outset of his mission to propagate the daimoku of the Lotus Sutra. In fact it evolved over time to the fully formed Gohonzons we are familiar with near to the end of his life. One way experts can assess whether a Nichiren Gohonzon is a later forgery is his *kao* seal, his cursive signature at the bottom of the Gohonzon. It was very difficult for others to copy and it also changed stylistically over Nichiren's lifetime, allowing us to determine the time of the inscription as well.

The first historically surviving and recorded Gohonzon was inscribed on 9th October 1271, in Echigo village, Sagami as Nichiren awaited to be transported across the sea to Sado Island for his final exile. It is known as the 'Toothpick Gohonzon' as it was simply inscribed with a twig or implement similar to a toothpick on good quality paper. Nichiren most probably produced it for a follower who came to bid him farewell and there is a sense that the initial necessity of inscribing Gohonzon derived from Nichiren's dislocation from his followers.[5]

THE EVOLVING BUDDHA

This first Gohonzon is very simple with Nam-myoho-renge-kyo down the middle flanked by Craving-Filled and Immovable, with Nichiren's kao seal and his name. Whilst on Sado, Nichiren began to inscribe the Gohonzon for his disciples. Many that survive from this period are of the 'abbreviated' simple style similar to the 'Toothpick Gohonzon', but other figures are gradually added starting with Shakyamuni Buddha and Many Treasures Buddha. Bestowing these simple but profound scrolls on his followers, Nichiren was not just providing an object of devotion to complete the believers' practice. Nichiren refers to the mandala as 'a banner of propagation' and sending the Gohonzon back over the sea from Sado was a call for action for his disciples on the mainland. Banners had huge significance in the medieval world as heraldic symbols for feudal armies and war lords. Nichiren's banner was not a call to arms on the battlefield but a call to his disciples to stand up to the persecution heaped upon them by the authorities for spreading 'the correct teaching for the peace of the land' in Kamakura and elsewhere.

The first full 'formal style' Gohonzon was produced when Nichiren arrived to take up residence on Mount Minobu. Even at this stage, Nichiren experimented with various depicted figures before reaching a full and essential composite structure. For example, he included the Buddha Mahavairocana and some other esoteric imagery before discontinuing their use. In the Koan era from February 1278 until his passing in 1282, the distinctive composite structure of the Gohonzon had been established reaching its peak in the years 1279-1281.

The 'comprehensive' version of the Gohonzon stated by Ken Mandara of the Nichiren Mandala Study Workshop has eleven key features:

i) Nam-myoho-renge-kyo

ii) The Buddhas Shakyamuni and Many Treasures

iii) The four leaders of the Bodhisattvas of the Earth

iv) The voice hearers Manjushri, Shariputra etc

v) Kishimojin and her 10 demon daughters

vi) The sages who propagated Buddhism (T'ien T'ai, Dengyo etc)

vii) Japanese deities (Hachiman)

viii) The esoteric deities Craving-Filled and Immovable

ix) The four Heavenly Deva Kings

x) Nichiren's name and kao signature

xi) The laudatory inscription 'This great mandala was never before revealed...'[6]

The Nichikan Gohonzon chanted to by SGI members includes all these features with the exception of the voice hearers. Instead the Four Bodhisattvas are attributed to representing the life state/worlds of Learning and Realisation in addition to the state of Bodhisattva. In fact in only 65 of the existing 130 plus Gohonzon are the voice hearers included. The author, Yukio Matsudo, suggests a simplification of the requirements of the comprehensive Gohonzon to i),ii),iii),ix) and the ten worlds or life states represented by various of the above characters.[7]

Nichiren's signature also merges with the central inscription of Nam-myoho-renge-kyo in later Gohonzons. This is considered to reflect the oneness of the person and the law, Nichiren as an ordinary person revealing his Buddhahood. Of the scriptural passages that Nichiren placed in varying forms on his mandalas, the 'curse and blessing' passages found on the SGI

Gohonzon are the most common quotes that Nichiren used, demonstrating the law of causality.

Gohonzon inscribed by Nichiren's disciples

Many of Nichiren's direct disciples authored their own Gohonzon inspired by their master. Their varying efforts reflected the extent of their own understanding of the import and meaning of the great mandala. Nissho omitted the lower worlds whilst Nichiro, who stayed in Kamakura and was not present at Minobu in the period when Nichiren inscribed the comprehensive Gohonzon of his later years, produced rather dull and lifeless renditions with none of the sweeping energy of his master's komyo lines or Siddham depictions. It may not be a coincidence that it was Nichiro's school who first took to worshipping statues rather than Gohonzon.

The independent Nichiren Mandala Study Workshop recognises that Nikko most understood his master's intent in the Gohonzon and created the fullest exploration of the medium.[8] Nikko also reconferred at least twenty of Nichiren's original mandalas. Nikko, being considered the founder of the Fuji school has had an enormous influence on the philosophy of Nichiren Shoshu and the Soka Gakkai.

The current Gohonzon which SGI members chant to in their homes is a mandala inscribed by Nichikan, 26th Abbot of Taiseki-ji temple in the 1720s. Nichikan is seen as a great restorer of the Fuji school who reinterpreted and reformulated the branch's doctrine. It is noteworthy that the current SGI Gohonzon is not the first Nichikan matrix to be reproduced for members. In the 1940s, a Nichikan Gohonzon was one of the first mandalas distributed to Soka Gakkai members in the foundational years of the movement. Nichiren Shoshu priests and followers have criticised the Nichikan Gohonzon as invalid because SGI removed the inscription to the original recipient, a priest named Honsho-bo Ajari Nissho. However, as noted above with Nikko, the founder of their own school, cancellation and reconferral has been a common practice in the past, especially at Taiseki-ji and even on original Nichiren mandalas, a point confirmed by the Nichiren Mandala Study Workshop.[9] Nichiren Shoshu have also claimed the Nichikan Gohonzon has been significantly altered, yet researchers from the Fuji Religious Studies Workshop who could observe the original Nichikan Gohonzon are of the opinion that no significant alterations were made and certainly not with the intent to forge the original matrix.[10]

Another important Gohonzon for SGI members is the Gohonzon bestowed on the Soka Gakkai as a whole group by Mitzutani Nissho on 19th May 1951, which is now housed in the Hall of the Great Vow in the Soka Gakkai Headquarters precinct of Shinanomachi, Tokyo. The content of this Gohonzon differs slightly from the Nichikan Gohonzon, as it includes the voice hearers and more of the sages of the past, for example Nagarjuna.

Chanting to statues

Although the Gohonzon's central importance is unquestioned in SGI practice, in other branches of Nichiren Buddhism, notably Nichiren Shu (as opposed to Nichiren Shoshu), an assortment of statues are at the forefront of altars, whilst the

THE EVOLVING BUDDHA

Gohonzon or even just an inscription of Nam-myoho-renge-kyo, are relegated to the background. Certainly, Nichiren's writings indicate he did keep a statue of Shakyamuni his whole life, and it is also recorded in the list of Nichiren's possessions by Nikko. The Daishonin did have a flexible attitude to his disciples fashioning statues. For example, he wrote to Shijo Kingo's wife Nichigen-Nyo:

"I have inscribed the Gohonzon for your protection...Lady Nichigen-nyo, who fashioned the wooden statues, three inches in height, of Shakyamuni Buddha, the lord of teachings in the three-fold world." (WND 2, p811)

While tolerant of a variety of forms of worship, research has shown that it does not follow on that Nichiren's central intent was for his object of worship to be a statue. His references to statues diminish in his later writings as he fully formulates the Gohonzon. Matsudo has clarified through textual analysis, that Nichiren's references in his writing to the worship of Shakyamuni of the Essential Teaching, refers not to a statue or person, but to the Mystic Law, Nam-myoho-renge-kyo, inscribed down the centre of the Gohonzon.[11] In September 1278 in 'Questions and Answers on the Object of Devotion', Nichiren writes, "They should make the daimoku of the Lotus Sutra the object of devotion," and quotes T'ien T'ai to fully elucidate his point, "One need not adorn it with any statues of the Buddha." (WND 2, p787)

Even on a practical level, the simplicity and accessibility of a scroll mandala has made the Gohonzon the pre-eminent devotional object in Nichiren Buddhism, whilst time, money and greater resources are required in the purchasing and fashioning of statues. The Gohonzon was a revolutionary and egalitarian means for revealing one's higher potential, and on every Gohonzon he inscribed with slight variants, the statement, "Since more than 2220 years after the Buddha's demise, this great mandala has never before existed."

Most surprising for an SGI member entering a Nichiren Shu temple, would be the large statue of Nichiren himself positioned centrally at the front of the altar arrangement. A development from later generations, it smacks of founder worship and wholly distracts from the Gohonzon positioned far behind. It is the abstract nature of the Gohonzon which is one of its key strengths in reflecting back our own potential, our own enlightened self, rather than the image of another person.

Some Nichiren denominations regard an eye opening ceremony, a specialised ritual by a priest or religious authority, as necessary to endow the Gohonzon with its power or soul. Nichiren Shoshu cite the importance of this ceremony, to claim their Gohonzons, having undergone such a process by their High Priest, are thus the only valid working Gohonzons. In fact, Nichiren refers to eye opening ceremonies only in the case of statues and mostly in his writings prior to his Sado exile. There is no evidence he ever performed such a ceremony or left instruction to do so. Such a practice falsely creates a barrier between the practitioner and his own enlightenment through a ceremony only deliverable by a select authority. In this sense, it is a manipulation of power by a priestly class rather than anything central to Nichiren Buddhism.

THE EVOLVING BUDDHA

The controversy surrounding the Dai-Gohonzon

Perhaps the greatest manipulation by a priestly authority is the case of the Dai-Gohonzon itself. Carved on a lacquered black camphor wood plank, the Dai-Gohonzon is enshrined in the Hoando hall of Taiseki-ji replacing the Sho-Hondo hall which was built in the early 1970s from millions of sincere offerings by Soka Gakkai members. The Sho-Hondo was considered a masterpiece of modernism but its association with SGI was too much for the priesthood and, on the pretext of structural deficiencies, this architecturally significant building was destroyed in 1999.

According to Nichiren Shoshu doctrine, the Dai-Gohonzon was inscribed by Nichiren on 12th October, 1279 and later transferred into wood by one of his disciples, Nippo. Adherents believe the Dai-Gohonzon is supreme to other Gohonzons in that it was inscribed for the entire world as the fulfilment of his purpose. This was inspired by Nichiren receiving reports of how his disciples in Atsuhara had remained steadfast in their faith despite the persecutions they received, ultimately resulting in the beheading of three farmer believers. To substantiate this claim, they quote from a passage in Nichiren's 'On Persecutions Befalling the Sage' (WND 1, p996) which reads, 'The Buddha fulfilled the purpose of his advent in little over forty years... For me it took twenty seven years and the great persecutions I faced during this period are well known to you all.' The one word 'it' is inferred to mean the inscription of the Dai-Gohonzon.

Whilst affiliated with Nichiren Shoshu, SGI adhered to this position. 'Tozan' pilgrimages to the Dai-Gohonzon were an integral part of SGI members' practice until the split with the priesthood. Even after the separation of the two organisations in 1991, philosophy on the Dai-Gohonzon did not radically change, though pilgrimage for SGI members was not permissible by the priestly authorities. The silent prayers in gongyo (sutra recitation) continued to refer to the Dai-Gohonzon whilst other differences in the priestly and lay approaches were laid bare more fully.

A change of view

Finally, on 8th November 2014, Minoru Harada, President of the Soka Gakkai announced, "We will not consider the Gohonzon of the second year of Koan (1279) to be the object of worship for us to uphold." Henceforth in SGI doctrine, all Gohonzons would have equal worth and equal power in that they were the means to activate the individual's power and were not an external source of benefit. The change took place with minimal fanfare and emphasis in publications around the world. Sometime later, the references to the Dai-Gohonzon in the prayer books were replaced with the Gohonzon.

This soft landing approach was necessary for members who had a nostalgic attachment to the Dai-Gohonzon. Some would inevitably be upset by the change. Others, attached to a rigid set of rules or dogma, could likewise be disturbed by such a fundamental change to the certainties they had held dear. Naturally, Nichiren Shoshu trumpeted this move as a distortion and rejection of their perceived true law. Using quotes from Daisaku Ikeda prior to 2014 to show the contrast with previously held views, they hoped to prey on those believers who could not accept or understand the development.

Conversely it could be asked what took SGI so long to free itself from the association with this object? J.M. Walsh interprets the SGI's former acceptance of the object's claimed superior status as nothing more than a necessary collaborative spirit whilst both organisations were affiliated.[12] As a lay movement of Nichiren Shoshu, SGI was obliged to go along with its doctrine. Once liberated from priestly authority in the 1990s, movement towards this change could begin, especially once the priesthood began brandishing the Dai-Gohonzon as a weapon to hold over SGI members. This needed to be gradual however, because it challenged deeply held beliefs cultivated over decades, which for some would be less easily changed than for others.

This subtle approach, which acknowledged the sensitivity of the subject, was right and proper in the circumstances. The Dai-Gohonzon was henceforth referred to as the Gohonzon of the second year of Koan (1279). And yet, this approach in hoping to assuage long standing members' concerns, left SGI vulnerable to counter attack by Nichiren Shoshu. The Dai-Gohonzon's authenticity or provenance as a Nichiren original mandala has not been officially questioned by SGI. It just became one of many Gohonzon inscribed by Nichiren. The priesthood continued to argue over the Dai-Gohonzon's relevance, superiority and power to draw converts.

THE GOHONZON

How does the evidence stack up?

However, the evidence derived from independent research is compelling. The Dai-Gohonzon is not merely one of many Gohonzons Nichiren created, but a later pious forgery. An examination of the Dai-Gohonzon puts the whole basis of Nichiren Shoshu in doubt. For without this supreme object of worship which they use to justify their superiority, their claims for exclusive truth vanish.

Although Nichiren Shoshu zealously keep the Dai-Gohonzon away from analysis, and photography is strictly forbidden, this was not always the case. Photographs from the first half of the 20th century exist, and Kaiso Inada, a scholar-priest who was an acquaintance of the 59th Abbot of Taiseki-ji, Nichiko Hori, was able to examine both the Dai-Gohonzon and the Nichiren mandala said to have been used as a matrix for the plank itself. Inada who had an extensive knowledge of Nichiren's Gohonzons having travelled across Japan, was of the opinion the Dai-Gohonzon was fabricated using different sheets traced from at least two different mandalas.

The ten worlds depicted figures and Nichiren's *kao* signature are considered to be in Nichiren's handwriting but from two different Gohzonzons. The dedication caption to a specific individual called Yashiro Kunishige and the laudatory inscription "for more than 2220 years after the Buddha's passing..." are believed to be in the handwriting of someone else. The central inscription of Nam-myoho-renge-kyo is most likely to have been traced from another original matrix that Nichiren bestowed on a priest disciple named Shosuke-bo Nichizen. This would date the central part of the Dai-

Gohonzon to the 9th May 1280, 8 months later than claimed.

From existing photographic evidence, when the Nichizen Gohonzon is compared to the Dai-Gohonzon, every character is the same and in the same position, except the date and the conferral inscription. As discussed earlier, to find two Gohonzons inscribed by Nichiren which were identical in every character was extremely rare, if not completely anomalous. In a direct pictorial comparison of the Dai-Gohonzon and the Nichizen Gohonzon, the central inscriptions are perfectly identical.

Nichiren Shoshu refute this claim but as they strictly limit access to the Dai-Gohonzon to the faithful only and ban any further photographs of Gohonzon, it is difficult for them to prove their case. In addition, the calligraphy and proportions of Nichiren's mandalas in 1279 were all very different to the Dai-Gohonzon, with a shorter central inscription and spiked and elongated tips to the writing.[13] The argument that these differences are due to the special nature of the Dai-Gohonzon are hard to sustain when the differences relate not to substance but Nichiren's calligraphic style at the time.

Signs of a later creation

The Dai-Gohonzon is dedicated to an individual of a Hokkeko (Lotus) confraternity, known as Yashiro Kunishige. Nichiren Shoshu explain this very particular dedication by claiming Kunishige represents 'everyman' in the mandala which is dedicated to the whole world. Kunishige is also described as someone involved directly in the Atsuhara persecution. However, proof of his existence is all but non-existent, with

Nichiro Hori, the learned 59th Abbot of Taiseki-ji, stating, "I do not know the basis for the matter of Yashiro Kunishige."[14] Furthermore, the Hokkeko confraternities referred to did not exist at the time of Nichiren and only appeared later in the Muromachi era (from 1336 to 1573). Likewise, carved mandalas on wood were a later invention not referred to in Nichiren's time. Nichiren's disciple, Nippo is said to have carved the Dai-Gohonzon under Nichiren's supervision from his original paper version. Yet given that Nikko as Nichiren's secretary carefully documented every single activity that took place, there is a surprising lack of any record of this activity. Nor does the Dai-Gohonzon bear any similarities to Nippo's calligraphy or include his signature which he put on all the Gohonzon he inscribed.

In fact, the earliest verifiable reference to the Dai-Gohonzon is almost three hundred years later, in 1561, by Taiyu Ajari Nichiga, an abbot of a temple near to Taiseki-ji. Any earlier references are considered apocryphal and are not found in the original author's handwriting, such as Nikko's will which was questioned in its authenticity even by Nikko's own disciple Nichidai, as well as modern scholars.

Another issue of concern is that the Dai-Gohonzon seems to have been processed with a planer, a tool that did not come into existence until 140 years after the Daishonin's time. According to research by Hiroshi Kawasaki, from the 17th to the 19th century, the Dai-Gohonzon was recorded in records with varying sizes and differing inscriptions. For example the curse and blessing inscriptions are not present on the current Dai-Gohonzon but are on earlier transcriptions of it. Kawasaki believes that there may have been several reproductions made after fires destroyed previous copies and that the current Dai-Gohonzon was produced around 1865 after a great fire at the time. Between 1569 and 1945 there were 9 major fires at Taiseki-ji temple.[15]

Questions also surround the feasibility of Nichiren receiving news in time of the Atsuhara persecution executions to inscribe the Dai-Gohonzon on the purported date. Even more importantly, there are absolutely no references in any of Nichiren's writings regarding the Dai-Gohonzon. If this really was the reason for his purpose in this world, surely a direct reference to the Dai-Gohonzon would have appeared in his writings from October 1279 onwards. In the previously cited passage from 'On Persecutions Befalling the Sage', " For me it took 27 years…" there is nothing which clarifies what Nichiren is actually talking about and no direct mention of a special mandala. A number of other letters from October 1279 exist specifically giving advice to Nikko and others regarding the ongoing escalation of events in Atsuhara. Again, a mention of this all powerful object linked to the trials of these believers is gapingly absent.

The only verifiable Nichiren Gohonzon which he refers to as a Dai-honzon is the Mannen kyugo Dai-honzon (usually he referred to Dai-mandalas) inscribed in the 12th month of 1274.[16] This Gohonzon was recorded as originally bestowed on Nikko and transferred to Nichimoku, his successor, and oblique references to a Dai-Gohonzon in one of Nikko's unverified transfer documents to Nichimoku may well refer to this Gohonzon instead. The Mannen Kyugo Dai-honzon is no longer in the possession of Nichiren Shoshu temples and has never been claimed to have special powers.

THE GOHONZON

Implications of this new understanding

So what are the implications of the overwhelming evidence questioning the validity of the Dai-Gohonzon? To challenge one's beliefs is difficult and it has been shown scientifically that people are unlikely to change a belief on an issue if there is a conscious or unconscious benefit to them in holding such a conviction, even if a body of evidence contrary to their belief is arrayed before them. For the faithful of Nichiren Shoshu, this may well be the case with its central focus on the Dai-Gohonzon. For those who have taken solace in the idea of an all-powerful Gohonzon, who have experienced spiritual emotions in front of it, there is too much vested in its power for any of the evidence to shift a viewpoint, however reasoned the argument is.

Yet for those of us without attachment, the case I have outlined in this chapter gives the opportunity to go deeper into what the function of the Gohonzon is, to come to a broader, more inclusive perception of its meaning: A universalist approach to the Gohonzon.

The Gohonzon is within

Central to this understanding is the timeless statement from Nichiren which is an axiom of faith for many SGI members, "Never seek this Gohonzon outside yourself." (WND 1, p 822) Far from revering one exceptional Gohonzon to bring us benefits, chanting to the Gohonzon is a process.

"When we revere Myoho-renge-kyo inherent in our own life as the object of devotion, the Buddha nature within us is summoned forth and manifested by our chanting of Nam-myoho-renge-kyo." (WND 1, p887)

Our life, the Buddha nature, Nam-myoho-renge-kyo and the Gohonzon are all one and the same. There is no special Gohonzon, just as there is no special life in the universe. All life is precious, all life is sacred, all is universal. The difference in outcome in our chanting before a Gohonzon does not come from the Gohonzon itself. It comes from ourselves.

An experience of this point came to me early in my Buddhist practice. At the time I was introduced to Buddhism, my main ambition was to achieve fame and fortune with my rock band *Sun Machine,* in which I was the lead singer. I had even previously reduced my day job to three days a week to concentrate on writing new music and promoting the group. Despite having a professional manager and some critical acclaim including approval from Chris Martin of *Coldplay*, a highly sought after record deal eluded us.

After starting to chant, things seemed to shift. We were booked to play at a festival in Cardiff organised by a major national radio station and achieved a showcase performance in front of the executives from a global record company. But I wasn't happy. Even this actual proof did not inspire hope in me or provide satisfaction. Soon after receiving my Gohonzon, I was chanting earnestly in front of it when it seemed to be telling me, 'Quit the band.' Of course the Gohonzon was not telling me anything. This was my inner voice, my inner wisdom revealing itself in the connected space created by chanting to the Gohonzon. I decided to take action based on this realisation to the initial shock of my manager and bandmates.

THE GOHONZON

The band folded and we never 'made it big' but I realised that my deepest intention had never been to become famous in the music industry. What I really wanted to do all along was to create wonderful music. In an example of the synchronicity of events, in the week I made my announcement, my keyboard player had just bought enough equipment to build a home recording studio. We re-formed as a duo and recorded five albums together, fulfilling my true determination.

We never became famous but, on reflection, I have created exactly the life I would want to have for my deeper happiness along with a family, rewarding career and a happy home. The itinerant gigging lifestyle and relentless spotlight of a successful front man, I am certain, would have ultimately not made me happy and, knowing my tendencies, would likely have been detrimental to my well-being and mental health.

The power comes from us

Shin Yatomi points out that Nichiren's enlightened life is revered in the Gohonzon but so are our lives. We can fall into the trap of admiring the Gohonzon's beneficial power whilst not giving the same respect to our own lives. This power is not something mysterious beyond our reach or available to a chosen clergy. The power comes from us.[17] The efficacy of the Gohonzon derives from the inner faith of the individual – faith in themselves, faith in the potential of life.

This was Nichiren's message in inscribing the Gohonzon as an embodiment in visual form of *ichinen sanzen*, three thousand realms in a single moment of life. With the ten worlds arranged around the central totem of Nam-myoho-renge-kyo, this is the visual fulfilment of every person's potential to respond, to change, to win in a given life moment. Criticism that the Nichikan or Hall of the Great Vow Gohonzon derive from the Dai Gohonzon's template, a Gohonzon now in doubt, does not stand up to examination. First, there are a number of differences in iconographic content between the three mandalas, such as the curse and blessing phrases and the inclusion or absence of Manjushri and Shariputra. But more importantly all three mandalas, irrelevant of their provenance, are directly inspired and derivative of the comprehensive Gohonzons completed by Nichiren in the final years of his life. In that sense, they can all work as a summation of the principle of *ichinen sanzen* to reveal our Buddhahood from within.

The development of SGI's view on the Gohonzon and Dai-Gohonzon, far from being a betrayal of profound principles, is another crucial marker in the development of Buddhism, another evolution to grow nearer to the ultimate reality based on greater knowledge and wisdom. The universality of the practice of Nichiren Buddhism comes to the fore when anyone who chants to any Gohonzon can reveal their greatest self in the moment. The simplicity, beauty, power and wonder of the Gohonzon is brought centre stage with this new understanding: a simplicity that comes from a humble man with ink and brushes, the sounds of the mountains around him, drawing our enlightened selves on a patchwork of paper.

CHAPTER FIVE

THE SOKA GAKKAI AND SGI

THE VALUE CREATORS

"I am entrusting you with a Gohonzon for the protection of your young child. The Gohonzon is the essence of the Lotus Sutra and the eye of all the scriptures. It is like the sun and moon in the heavens, a great ruler on earth, the heart in a human being, the wish granting jewel among treasures, and the pillar of a house."

On Upholding Faith in the Gohonzon (WND 1, p624)

PART 1 - WHY DO I NEED AN ORGANISATION?

I am writing this chapter in April 2020 at the seeming peak of the first wave of the Coronavirus pandemic sweeping the globe. Over half of the world's population is in some form of lockdown or severely restricted in their personal movement. What this crisis augers for the future, I cannot say, but for the first time since 1945 the gathering of Soka Gakkai members in Japan and Soka Gakkai International (SGI) members across the world has ceased. No physical discussion meetings (*Zadankai*), the beating heart of the SGI movement, are taking place and visiting and supporting members in their homes is not even allowed for fear of transmission of the virus, COVID-19.

And yet, the SGI movement continues. Joint chanting sessions at set times are co-ordinated across continents, SGI members reach out to support those in their local communities and online meetings proliferate using video conferencing. When this is all over amidst the sorrow, the loss, the isolation and the pain, connections will have been made; value will be created. This is the conviction of the SGI.

This chapter is about the Soka Gakkai or in its international context SGI, described as the world's largest lay Buddhist movement. I have benefited enormously from being part of the SGI community in my practice. The encouragement, support and purpose it has given me has been indispensable in effectively using Buddhism to move my life forward and to overcome obstacles and difficulties. For a start, I feel enormous hope in the midst of the greatest worldwide disruption since the end of the Second World War, a conviction that poison can be turned into medicine and victory can spring from defeat, borne from the experiences and learning I have derived from the SGI movement.

We will look in this chapter at why we need an organisation to practice Buddhism and how the Soka Gakkai and SGI have undergone their own evolutionary process based on the times and people's expectations and values.

A profound experience of connection

The value of connection within SGI was most powerfully evoked in an experience that took place during my most recent visit to Japan. Staying with friends in Saga City in Japan's southerly island of Kyushu, we were invited to the local SGI centre on a humid working day in late July. The Kansai Soka High School Koto Orchestra were in the area to compete in the national schools' competition and had arranged a warm-up gig at fortuitously our nearest local centre. News of the event had only been passed around the day before, but a gathering largely of the retired, mothers and children assembled at the centre that afternoon.

The koto is a Japanese stringed instrument with 13 strings strung over a horizontal piece of carved wood and is the national musical instrument of Japan. I sat down in the front row, a little jaded from the previous night's hospitality, not having felt I could say no to my friend's father's largesse as he proffered me, an occasional drinker, a range of beers and sake. I had no expectation of the performance as 27 High School students in crisp white shirts, the girls in dark green Scottish tartan skirts, the boys in dark trousers, took their places in front of their kotos.

As the first notes were plucked, my heart seemed to expand endlessly. The purity, precision and depth to their playing tapped something essential in me and I was overwhelmed with a wave of emotion which seemed to pulse out from the centre of my heart. It lasted only 20 minutes but was one of the most profound experiences of my life. When the last notes faded, a few of the students quietly wept. I deeply felt Daisaku Ikeda's heart and care in these young people and his appreciation of the profound value of culture for humanity. It was kosen rufu (world peace) manifest, but the individual actions and support that had brought these pure hearted young people to perform so magnificently encapsulated why I put faith in SGI and how incredible this movement is. The team went on to place in the top 4 of 56 finalist schools as did the Tokyo Soka High School. Life is about connection and I truly felt it that day.

The first Western account of the Soka Gakkai

Probably the earliest personal account of the Soka Gakkai from a Western perspective comes from Noah S. Brannen, an American Baptist Missionary and academic who had been living in Japan since 1950 and saw at first hand the incredible growth of the Soka Gakkai movement after the Second World War. Although he published his book on the Gakkai in 1968, it records his experiences from the late 1950s onwards. A mix of astonishment, reprobation, awe, misunderstanding and respect colour Brannen's conflicted opinions of the movement. He opens with an encounter with a cobbler in one of Japan's outlying islands.

"His face was beaming. Seldom have I seen a face so expressive of the joy of living. It was not long before I discovered the source of his exuberance; it was his religious faith which had become a hidden spring welling up within him until it was ready to burst through at any provocation... An hour and a half later I left the shop with shoes well laced and tied, and a never-to-be-forgotten impression of the sincerity of a simple island cobbler and his faith."[1]

In June 1960, Brannen travels to Taiseki-ji and gate crashes a pilgrimage to what was then considered the Dai-Gohonzon. Awed by the spectacle, he finds himself bowing in reverence at Second Soka Gakkai President Josei Toda's tomb and questioning the absolutism of his own beliefs.

"Is Christianity after all just this: the faith of my own people?... Why, O why didn't more Japanese Christians die for Christ in prison during the war, as Makiguchi died for his faith? Would that have been too much to ask of them? Here is something we Christians in Japan today must face every day of our lives."[2]

Origins

The Soka Gakkai traces its founding to November the 18th 1930 and the publishing of a book on value-creating education by founding President, Tsunesaburo Makiguchi, the publisher listed as the Soka Kyoiku Gakkai. In essence at this point, the organisation was just two men: Makiguchi and his disciple and fellow educator, Josei Toda who funded the publication of the book. Although training courses were organised with members by the mid-1930s, the formalisation of the Soka Kyoiku Gakkai (Value-Creating Education Society) did not fully take place until January 27th 1937 when a meeting of some 60 members was arranged in a restaurant in Azabu in Tokyo. Makiguchi's death in prison for standing up against the militarist authorities would be a powerful totem and example for the oppressed post-war Japanese reeling from defeat, but it was Josei Toda, who had joined Makiguchi in prison, who would reformulate the retitled Soka Gakkai (Value Creating Society) and drive the phenomenal expansion that so awed Noah S. Brannen. At Toda's first lecture on the Lotus Sutra after leaving prison, there was an attendance of three people. By his death in April 1958, he had achieved his dream of more than 750,000 member households practising Nichiren Buddhism with the Soka Gakkai. As Clark Strand, a contemporary pan-Buddhist commentator, describes:

"We see in the Soka Gakkai, as conceived by Toda, a dynamic and practical philosophy that, for the first time in human history, privileges life over religion, rather than religion over life."[3]

An international stage

However, it was Daisaku Ikeda, the third president of the Soka Gakkai who built on this momentum to expand the movement not only in Japan but to internationalise it to promote peace, culture and education across the world, founding the SGI in 1975.

In 1955, the first foreigner group was established made up mainly of American servicemen stationed in Japan. By June 1960, there were 710 members overseas including 460 in North America, 2 in India, and 1 each in Italy, West Germany and France. By SGI's own account on its website in 2020, there were over 2 million members in 191 countries and territories outside Japan including 352,000 in North America, 256,000 in Central and South America, 130,000 in Europe and 1.42

million in the rest of Asia and Oceania. The most notable recent expansion of SGI has been the dynamic and rapid growth of the movement in India from a membership of 4,000 in 1997 to 150,000 in 2016 and some 240,000 by early 2020.

Secularisation and isolation

The ongoing development of SGI comes at a time of increasing secularisation in many developed countries and a rejection of organised religion particularly in the West. According to the British social attitudes survey of 2018, the proportion of those who say they are "very or extremely non-religious" has more than doubled from 14% to 33% in the past 20 years. Trust in scientific institutions is increasing (82% for University Scientists), whilst only 11% trust churches or religious organisations.[4] American research paints a similar picture with confidence in churches and organised religions down from 68% in 1975 to a new low of 36% in 2019 with fewer Americans also identifying with an official religion.[5] This does parallel a decline in trust in many secular organisations including government and the media. Since the 1950s, the question "Do you think people can be trusted?" has been a commonplace survey question across Europe. In the U.K. in the 1950s, 60% answered yes to this question whilst by 2019 this had halved to 30% of those polled.

As trust in society has declined, social isolation has increased. In the U.S, 20% of people consider loneliness, "a major source of unhappiness in their lives." and one third of Americans over 45 years old state they are lonely.[6] In 2010, a study examined what was driving the increase in mental illness among high school and college students. The research found a correlation between the likelihood of suffering poor mental health and an increase in social detachment. A sense of belonging and connection really does matter. Positive psychologist Sonja Lyubomirsky puts a sense of connectedness or engagement as the most important factor in a well-balanced and happy life stating, "The centrality of social connections to our health and well-being cannot be overstressed."[7]

The importance of connection

The quality of these connections also matter. Jane E. Dutton of the University of Michigan's research shows that high quality interactions at work, which can be as simple as a positive remark by a manager or noticing the efforts of others, can result in employees feeling more engaged, more resilient and also helps teams work more cohesively.[8] At the heart of high quality interactions is compassion, the positive and empathetic regard for the other person. With its locally based system of districts, the SGI is well placed to develop connections centred on discussion meetings in members' homes, personal support derived from home visits and a philosophy which holds respect for the individual as central. Furthermore, chanting in and of itself is connecting and outwardly directed, lending itself to communal practice.

Robin Dunbar, the acclaimed evolutionary psychologist from Oxford University, identifies three cultural adaptations which he proposes were developed in early humans to strengthen bonds of friendship and co-operation and put our ancestors at an advantage for survival. They were laughter, chanting or singing and the advent of language enabling communication and the bonding of groups of people.[9] There is a substantial body of research on the power of positive and supportive networks. For example in 2009, Nicholas Christakis of Harvard Medical School found that "...someone's chances of being happy increase the better connected to happy people."[10] But this sense of happiness or well-being is of itself powerfully derived not from individual pleasure but from altruism, the care of others. The father of positive psychology, Martin Seligman, has stated, "kindness produces the single most reliable momentary increase in well-being of any exercise we have tested."[11] Happiness is the by-product but compassion is the focus.

Based on research by Robert Sampson from Harvard, it has been shown that the strength of social connections and the levels of compassion and concern for others are crucial in determining how communities work effectively and how they deal with momentous challenges.[12]

A response to a crisis

One example of what has been termed the 'neighbourhood effect' in action and how SGI as a community stood up to a major crisis, is the communal response to the Great East Japan Earthquake and Tsunami of March 11th 2011. My wife comes from Sendai, in the Tohoku region which was particularly badly hit by the Tsunami. I have had the opportunity to visit a number of times the area where that human tragedy unfolded. Nearly 16,000 people lost their lives and thousands more lost everything else: their homes, their livelihoods and their loved ones. A year after the disaster, standing on a road bridge overlooking the outlines of where homes and businesses once had been was a deeply moving experience. The force of the wave that destroyed everything in its path was clear. Only the foundations remained and a few larger buildings, a school and the shell of a factory, colourful carp shaped banners fluttering beside it - symbols of hope in the devastation.

Even more emotive, however was attending a local discussion meeting further north where the tsunami had not hit, but displaced members were taking up temporary residences. One elderly couple related how they had been at home when one of their grandchildren's toys inexplicably began making a noise. Going upstairs to turn it off, the wife of the couple saw the great surge of the tsunami bearing down towards the house. Calling her husband upstairs, they survived but would have certainly died if they had remained on the ground floor. Now that they were uprooted and had lost nearly everything, it was the Gakkai and their faith that was sustaining them.

Beyond individual stories of hope, the collective response of SGI as a movement was second only to governmental support for the relief effort after the disaster. 42 Soka Gakkai centres offered approximately 5000 people temporary shelter and sustenance; 641,700 items such as clothing, foodstuffs and equipment were delivered through the Soka Gakkai's network. 540 million yen were donated to relief funds in the name of the Soka Gakkai and $2.23 million were donated from SGI overseas organisations. Around 17,000 volunteers in addition to Soka Gakkai staff supported operational and logistic operations. Local members offered their homes to accommodate the displaced and to provide relay points. As an integral part of the local community, Soka Gakkai volunteers were at times able to provide relief efforts in advance of Japan's Self-Defense Force such as in Kesennuma. Local community members could also offer emotional support and ensure the continuing safety of local residents, sharing information with a wider network.

I visited the exhibition on the 2011 disaster at the new Tohoku Culture Centre in 2019. Rebuilt after the earthquake, it is now the grandest of Japan's Soka Gakkai facilities outside of Tokyo. The scale of the tragedy and the heart rending stories of the loss of loved ones was humbling, but the exhibition also illustrated most vividly the power of the human spirit to triumph with hope over despair in the direst of circumstances, something that was clearly more difficult without the network of support the people had received. In a wider perspective, a wall of the exhibition displayed the countless messages of encouragement still being sent to this day by SGI members around the world, the most beautiful of which was a huge banner of an orange hued rising phoenix, illustrated with numerous messages of support from the youth division of Los Angeles. Being part of something matters. Being part of something can make a difference.

Meaning as the source of happiness

Since the turn of the millennium, there has been an explosion in books related to well-being and happiness. However, author on psychology, Emily Esfahani-Smith posits that this relentless focus on personal happiness has not resulted in any demonstrable improvement in the well-being of humanity as recorded in scientific observations. Instead, Esfahani-Smith suggests that in order to improve well-being, the focus should not be on happiness, a subjective term on which writers and thinkers have found it difficult to concur, but rather on meaning in people's lives and that the research points to meaning being the greatest determinant of good mental health and overall well-being.[13]

In 2010, a study by the Universities of Ottowa and Rochester on college students asked the group to either pursue activities related to personal happiness such as shopping, sleeping in and comfort eating or partake in activities associated with meaning such as studying, helping another person or thinking of one's values. The immediate effect was that those choosing personal happiness related activities did feel better but the mood boost did not last and it was those who had made meaning the priority who felt better three months later, feeling 'enriched' and inspired with fewer reported negative moods.[14]

Declining mental health and happiness levels in the West have gone hand in hand with a lowering of meaning in life as a priority for people. In the late 1960s, the top priority for American college freshmen was "developing a meaningful philosophy" (86%). By the 2000s, this had dropped to 40% and the top priority was instead "being very well off financially". Research on happiness, meaning and suicide levels from the University of Virginia and Gallup which studied 140,000 people across 132 countries, found that wealthier countries did tend to score well on respondents reporting they were happy but had dramatically higher suicide rates than poorer countries. When the researchers re-analysed the data, they found a strong correlation between the lack of a sense of meaning in a country's population and their suicide rate. Countries with the lowest rates of meaning such as Japan, had the highest suicide rates.[15]

Developed societies across the world have, in tandem with an individualist and acquisitive mindset tied to free market capitalism, prioritised pleasure over meaning, what Aristotle described as 'hedonia', hedonism described as 'feeling good' as opposed to 'eudaimonia' meaning 'being and doing good'. One of the clearest summations of this mindset in my own country of England, are the comical signs sold in every gift shop in the country, a huge number of which seem to focus on wine as the answer to life. 'You can't buy happiness, but you can buy wine, and that's kind of the same thing!' is one popular example. This is of course all good fun and there is nothing wrong with a bit of pleasure, but the issue comes when meaning is relegated and pleasure becomes the centre of people's lives as shown in the research.

"Happiness without meaning," Roy Baumeister and his team from Florida University wrote, "characterizes a relatively shallow self-absorbed or even selfish life, in which things go well, needs and desires are easily satisfied and difficult or taxing entanglements are avoided."[16] The origins of this mindset may be an inherent part of human nature going beyond Jeremy Bentham's utilitarianism which described pain and pleasure as the defining human emotions or Aristotle's definitions cited earlier. From a Buddhist perspective this focus relates to the life state of Rapture or Heaven in the Ten Worlds which constantly function in all human beings. And yet this state finds credence and magnification in the dominant materialist view of our times. In positing that matter is all there is, as discussed in chapter 3, Steve Taylor of Leeds Beckett University proposes that the materialist viewpoint easily leads to a worldview that is bleak and barren in which having a 'good time' and taking what we can from the world without concern for the consequences, through consumerism and hedonism, seems to be the best option in life.[17] The science is now proving that such an approach lasts longer than the hangover the next morning in terms of its detriment to our well-being, and that the true route to happiness lies in finding a meaningful life philosophy.

What values you choose matter

Although meaning in life provides long lasting benefit, it is important to note that what kind of meaning one imbues one's life with, matters a great deal. In our pluralist and democratic societies where freedom of thought and expression are enshrined in law, it is quite easy to regard all cultures of meaning or philosophies as equally valid. It is important to respect and listen to others' perspectives, but cultures of meaning can be destructive as well as productive. No one can deny that Islamic State had a strong culture of meaning. Its participants in terrorist suicide attacks most likely derived a great sense of well-being, purpose and camaraderie from the meaning they ascribed to their acts and yet, in rejecting the dignity and equality of all human life, they have ascribed to a distortion of the Islamic faith which is pure evil.

In citing this extreme case we can see the logic in Nichiren's uncompromising stance against the government authorities and other schools of Buddhism of his day. Nichiren evaluated the relative depth of major philosophies and religion at the time through his system of the fivefold comparison and the three proofs, which determine how different teachings explain the causality of life ultimately behind happiness and unhappiness. The three proofs of the validity of a teaching being documentary proof, theoretical proof and actual proof, the last of the three being the driving force behind the personal experiences of SGI members around the world. This is supplemented by the study movement related to the first two proofs, which provides substantiation to personal experience.

Nichiren has been described as a firebrand and confrontational by some historians, but the value of standing up for the most value creating philosophy and the justification of his criticism of belief systems he saw as destructive and contributing to the social malaise was brought home to me in my most recent trip to Japan.

A 'special' temple in Japan

Family friends had driven us to see a Tendai temple in Tochigi prefecture in central Japan. As the tradition in which Nichiren had first trained in, I was particularly interested to have a look. Driving towards the temple I was immediately struck by the opulence of the temple roofs emblazoned with gold leaf and unlike many of the local temples I had come across. As we entered, a ceremony was taking place. A father and daughter knelt before an altar which contained a large fire. Three Tendai priests were performing a ritual to rid the couple of bad luck for the year. A sign at the entrance (sadly Seicho-ji had a similar sign) outlined the birth years that were particularly unlucky that year. A minimum fee for a basic exorcism of this kind was charged at 5000 yen ($40-50 US dollars). No wonder the priests could afford to bedeck their roofs with gold. This temple was particularly noted for this lucrative ceremony but such operations are a normal part of Japanese Buddhist temple life. The passivity and superstition on the part of the participants in such an arrangement and the sheer contrast to the fundamental tenets of Buddhism, brought home to me why Nichiren and the three presidents had made their stand for a culture of meaning that focused on personal responsibility, equality and empowerment.

What is kosen rufu?

In Nichiren Buddhism the concept of ultimate aspiration and meaning is the ideal of kosen rufu. The literal meaning of kosen is to widely declare and rufu - to let flow in all directions. More than merely the propagation of a religious teaching, it has developed in its conceptualisation for SGI members over the years. In the early post-war years, it was more simply conceived by many members as a fixed time in the future when the majority of the world would practise Nichiren Buddhism.

However, in line with the broadening and liberalising of the movement, Daisaku Ikeda describes it in far more fluid and all-encompassing terms. He states that kosen rufu is unending, not something that will end at some time and has no set form. Often defined as world peace, it more accurately summarises the active efforts of SGI members on an ongoing basis to awaken all people to their inherent and unlimited value and potential. Sharing the practice of Nichiren Buddhism is still seen as the most noble and effective way to create a shift in the depths of people's lives and therefore bring forth a happier and more humane society.

Furthermore, it now also means making the philosophy of respect for the dignity of life the foundation of society and that this can be achieved by aligning with like-minded individuals of all faiths and none, as Ikeda has done in dialogues with world leaders, thinkers and intellectuals. In this sense, kosen rufu is not bound exclusively to the SGI or even Buddhism but becomes a broad alliance to bring about peace, happiness and prosperity to humanity in the ongoing realities of conflict, division and hatred. The ideal of kosen rufu provides SGI members with the power of meaning in every activity they undertake.

THE EVOLVING BUDDHA

PART 2 - OUR COLLECTIVE CONDITIONING

As we have seen, research points to the physical, social and emotional benefits of being part of a group: in having high quality interactions; a sense of belonging and a greater meaning in life, all traits which religion is perfectly placed to offer and the SGI as an open, non-exclusivist and socially engaged model, a good place to start. And yet, we have also noted societal trends towards greater isolation, distrust of organisations in general and particularly suspicion of religion per se. Where does this come from and can it be challenged?

How are we conditioned?

We are conditioned life forms. The conditioning process is a part of every human society. It includes the values of a society, what a society believes about itself and others, acceptable behavioural codes and what we should aspire to achieve to create a 'good life'. For pretty much everyone, this conditioning, starting in childhood and continuing throughout our lives, is something we are barely aware is happening. Conditioning is not inherently a bad thing and in fact is a prerequisite for a functioning human society in terms of expected behaviours and communication. However, the subconscious beliefs that derive from our everyday conditioning can lead us to assumptions that we are always right and that others see things the same as ourselves, without full reflections on the merits of our viewpoint. Matthew

Lieberman, a psychologist at the University of California showed through brain imaging, how people's beliefs categorise human beings in general and racial groups unconsciously as good or bad and that because the responses were irrespective of the participants' own race, this was most likely learned from prevailing cultural conditioning. The neuroscientist Kathleen Taylor of Oxford University considers beliefs and ideas the most important 'currency' for modern humans now that our physical needs are met.[18]

Beliefs arising from our conditioning significantly affect our decision-making process. And yet, in a society that rejects the co-ordinated conscious framework of belief which religion offers, belief becomes more subconscious, less explicit and, I would suggest, more easily manipulated by external drivers. Manipulation of belief happens all the time. Fake news and online conspiracy theories have magnified this process in susceptible individuals but the media and our social groups can have this influence on our collective beliefs. For example, Taylor has noted that in the wake of the 9/11 terror attacks and the invasion of Iraq, more than half of Americans believed Iraqis were involved in the 9/11 attacks despite no explicit evidence in this regard or this being directly suggested by politicians.

It is only when we gain awareness that we have internalized ideas from family, community and society that we can then make our own choices in terms of our beliefs. Yet also, fear of change can be an important factor in holding on to an ingrained belief system and rejecting personal change or engagement with a new set of beliefs or outlook. Researchers Farias and Wikholm describe this well documented tendency thus: "even if you're unhappy, you know where you are. The prospect of change brings uncertainty-what will happen? Who will I become? For many people, the unknown is unsettling: much more so than a familiar feeling of unhappiness. Perversely, there may be a sense of comfort within long-term, enduring discomfort."[19]

Even for those who are motivated to take action for personal change, our conditioning can lead us to taking easier and hassle free options which chime with society's prevailing conditions. I would suggest this is why many (though not all) would feel more comfortable paying for a yoga class with limited interaction with the other participants than to join their first discussion meeting, filled with the opportunity for new interactions and costing nothing. The yoga class subscribes to the market driven model of paying for a service. Although there are practitioners and organisations promoting yoga very much rooted in spirituality and a set of principles, the average class in the West does not require participants to reflect on their beliefs and values. For the majority, it is there for relaxation and stress release which is all well and good in and of itself. On the other hand, a discussion meeting involves no monetary exchange but far greater interaction and connection. The rewards are far greater too, as we have seen from the research, but this can be challenging for those conditioned in an increasingly isolated society.

Suspicion of religion – New Atheism

The decline in engagement in religion, the rise in distrust in general terms and the rejection of organisation can all be seen in the context of a collective shift in the beliefs of the West.

Shifts may seem like an organic process but they are driven by events and ideas promulgated by the media, leading thinkers and political leaders.

Suspicion of religion may have also grown due to media coverage of controversies within established Christian denominations and contradictions to traditional teachings highlighted by scientific advancement. One particular view of organised religion as being a particularly nefarious and manipulative set of beliefs is promulgated by the 'New Atheists', led by 'the four horsemen' of New Atheism, Hitchens, Harris, Dennett and Dawkins. Most influential of these is Richard Dawkins whose world bestseller from 2006, *The God Delusion* has undoubtedly contributed to the growing atheism in Western society.

As a Nichiren Buddhist, one can read *The God Delusion* and find much of it relevant, inspiring and in agreement with Nichiren's admonition that Buddhism is reason. Dawkins, at the outset, clarifies that his focus is on a supernatural God or Gods most familiar in the Old Testament, not an impersonal law-like God such as perceived by Einstein. In fact, he explicitly states, "I shall not be concerned at all with other religions such as Buddhism or Confucianism. Indeed, there is something to be said for treating these not as religions at all but as ethical systems or philosophies of life."[20] Dawkins' invective is directed at the claims and narrative of traditional Christianity in the main part.

Certainly, you can often find in SGI-UK meetings members who prefer not to call SGI Buddhism a religion at all and much prefer the term philosophy. I am comfortable with using the term religion in relation to SGI as it confers a system of organisation, faith and community which does not necessarily require the worship of a deity and covers the many facets of SGI practice far more than the term philosophy, though I respect those who prefer otherwise.

One area on which I find myself in agreement with Dawkins, is on the labelling of children as being of a particular religion and the segregation of schools based on religion. "Small children are too young to decide their views on the origins of the cosmos, of life, and of morals,"[21] he writes.

I do, in contrast to Dawkins, find it perfectly reasonable for parents to share their spiritual and moral convictions with their children. In fact, as we have seen, this process will take place whether it is conscious or not. However, once a child has become an adult who can weigh up the evidence and make the choice for themselves, then it is up to them to choose to practise any particular religion or not. SGI-UK has a well-developed programme of activities for young people which aim to provide connection, community and inspiration, but it is not possible to become a member of SGI-UK before the age of 16 and there are no childhood ceremonies, such as baptism, to initiate the unknowing child into the faith. SGI is very much in accord with Dawkins' perspective on establishing the free choice of the adult in terms of faith even for those brought up in a religion.

Dawkins explains the wonders of life on earth effectively through the evolutionary process of natural selection without the need for creation myths or miracles, but he does acknowledge there is no similar satisfactory explanation for the wonders of the universe and the perfect balance of the laws and building blocks of physics. This is the Achilles heel in the materialist scientific belief system which we examined in more detail in chapter 3.

On this next point, I wish to beg to differ with Dawkins. For him, human conditioning is victim to a 'maliciously designed program', the self-replicating false beliefs of religion, 'memes' which spread like mind viruses from generation to generation. This perspective, clumsily, in my view, lumps all religious belief as inherently negative. Dawkins claims that our moral progress in the past century is a natural development of the moral zeitgeist outside of religious belief but fails to recognise the spiritual convictions of some of the key leaders of the 20th century who had a profound influence on political and social structures as well as providing moral leadership: Gandhi and Martin Luther King being the two most obvious examples of this.

The New Atheists espouse a somewhat fundamentalist position whilst attacking (and in many cases quite rightly so) fundamentalism in religion. Dawkins claims he would abandon his position overnight if the evidence appeared to disprove it, as all good scientists should. In contrast, Steve Taylor and Rupert Sheldrake both argue that the materialist and, in tandem, atheist perspective is based on assumptions, not proven facts on the nature of consciousness, matter, brains etc. It is a meme and a belief system like any other.

The New Atheist position goes further than just attacking extreme and fundamentalist religion, it sees more balanced and reasonable religion as leaving the gate ajar for fundamentalist religion to enter and cause havoc. This creates suspicion surrounding all religious practice and I believe is a contributor to society's current fear and rejection of all organised religion.

THE EVOLVING BUDDHA

I challenge this argument. It is like stating that all people should reject watching football because there is a committed group of hooligans in many countries' fan base. What really is the problem, are the claws of hatred, division and anger within the human heart. Atheists are often prone to cite the wars that have been fought in the name of religion, but Stalin and Pol Pot, both avowed atheists, killed more people than any religious war in the 20th century. (I avoid mentioning Hitler as he seemed to flip between Catholicism and Atheism in his speeches.)

We all have belief systems

Again we return to Nichiren. Belief systems are with us whether we like it or not, whether we are conscious of them or not, whether they are religious or not, but surely the defining value of a belief system should not be whether or not it is religious but whether it can successfully promote respect, harmony and a peaceful world. Is it not better to consciously choose a belief system on a logical and rational basis that creates value, well-being and peace rather than be unconsciously swept along by the social zeitgeist?

Dawkins offers science as a source of meaning to replace religion, but I would suggest that this is insufficient when it comes to values, morality and decision making as evidenced by the distortion of morality in science's creation of nuclear weapons. Furthermore, science's limited understanding of consciousness and mind leaves a gaping hole in what it can currently offer humanity in terms of wisdom. This is not to reject science and its value to us all but not to elevate it to replace religion wholesale.

Faith, a word that is an anathema to atheists, need not be blind faith, unquestioning faith. In the case of SGI, it can be based on empirical evidence and the three proofs, as Nichiren outlined. This book aims to contribute to that process. Blind faith, on the other hand, asserts itself not only in manipulative religions but in every human being who takes their belief system and societal values as a given. Consciously choosing a belief system and/or a religion actually empowers the individual to make a positive selective change for themselves, those around them and the world as a whole.

What is a cult?

Another prevalent factor in society's conditioned response to involvement in religious organisations is the concept of cults. The idea of a cult and fear of cults is part of our collective conditioning in the West but derives from the relatively recent anti-cult movement of the 1970s and 1980s. Although references to cults will appear from time to time in the media, considered academic research across the world has questioned the very concept of a cult. I will therefore use the term 'new religious movement' (NRM) when not specifically referencing the idea of a cult.

The anti-cult movement was begun in the 1970s by parents of young people of the hippy generation who had joined new religious movements such as the Hare Krishnas and the Moonies (Unification Church). Researchers suggest the majority of parents were tolerant of their children's life choices but a small percentage found the rejection of an expected career path and the devotion of time, energy and finances required in being part of one of these groups as intolerable. The anti-cult movement was bolstered with literature from previous decades by Christian writers who were threatened by new religions and had coined the term 'cult'.

In November 1978, a U.S. congressman and his entourage along with 900 followers of a socialist-Christian church commune named the People's Temple died in combined acts of murder and suicide. The unequivocal horror of the Jonestown massacre, as it became known, made 1979 a bumper year for media attacks on all religious movements, unfairly lumped together in the term 'cults' and the anti-cult movement was emboldened across the world. Professor James Beckford of the University of Warwick considers the media portrayal of all religion to be sensationalist and their treatment of new religious movements particularly unfair.[22] Professor Eileen Barker of the London School of Economics has stated:

"New Religious Movements come in a vast variety of forms. They are successful or they fail for a multitude of reasons. Facile generalisations are bound to be wrong... through their studies of NRMs, social scientists have found that many of the statements in the popular media are blatantly untrue about the majority of the movements, and others refer to only a tiny proportion of their number."[23]

Carefully considered and checked academic scholarship provides a critical balance against, "the generalisations and stereotypical images which all too often pass for 'in-depth journalism,"[24] as Professor Beckford describes the media's portrayal of so-called cults.

However, it is this emotive media creation of the fear of cults which has embedded in the collective conscience and even inspired some European governments to issue reports against a wide range of religions. For example the French government issued a report in 1996 against 172 minority religions as dangerous 'sectes' while ignoring the work of French scholars of new religions and the negative reaction of the academic community to the report as an unreasonable attack on a wide spectrum of religions with very differing structures, beliefs and outlooks. In Germany the anti-cult campaign consisted mainly of officials of the established Christian churches in the country.

Ironically, the anti-cult movement behaved in not dissimilar ways to the cults they depicted. Bryan Wilson of Oxford University stated, "Their (anti cult movements) general attributes are single-minded fanaticism, the supreme conviction of their own righteousness, a determination to 'save' individuals from their delusions, and indeed, thereby 'save the world'."[25] George Chryssides from the University of Wolverhampton considers that the anti-cult movement also provided an outlet for prevalent racism in Britain towards Eastern ideas and culture in general.[26] Wilson notes that, "it takes a long time for a dissenting religious body to win any degree of disinterested approval from the general public,"[27] the Quakers and Salvation Army being two examples who have done so after many decades, even centuries.

Brainwashing

At the heart of the idea of cults is the concept of 'brainwashing' in which psychologically vulnerable individuals are enticed into cults through subtle and overpowering psychological techniques and which result in the recruit losing his/her ability to think or choose another way. The idea of 'brainwashing' derives from the thought control practices used by the Chinese against American prisoners during the Korean War and was being widely used as a term in the anti-cult movement by 1975. The idea has been consistently reinforced in the media as an emotive hook to stories about supposed cults and become part of popular vocabulary and perception. And yet, academics universally and resoundingly reject the idea of brainwashing in relation to religious movements. Lilliston and Shepherd of Oakland University, Michigan state that 'brainwashing' is "refuted by both the data on the development of religious organisations and the inadequacy of the proffered psychological explanation: there is no research evidence to support the notion of 'brainwashing' as offered by critics."[28]

In fact, the collapse of a court case in the US involving evidence by Margaret Singer, a key advocate of the 'brainwashing' hypothesis, discredited her theories and contributed to the collapse of the anti-cult network in America. Perversely, many anti-cult groups also supported the 'de-programming' of people involved in new religious movements against their will, using some of the techniques which they themselves associated with 'brainwashing'.

In contrast to the unsubstantiated charge of 'brainwashing', academic studies of new religious movements have found a general conclusion that good mental health is typical among adult members.[29] In addition, the suggestion that new religious movements display a large number of common characteristics has been debunked by a number of academic writers. As we will see later in this chapter, the health benefits of religious experience can depend on the theological thrust of the religion.

Finally, even if a small minority of religious movements do manifest some traits of a cult, it is deeply unfair to tar all religious movements with this brush. Bryan Wilson of Oxford University concluded that SGI does not show the "secrecy, authoritarianism, inflexibility and entrenched resistance to change,"[30] which popular opinion identifies with a cult.

An experience of heart-to-heart bonds across the world

From a naturally suspicious and typically British mindset, I was soon confident in my early days of practice, that there was no hidden agenda behind the warmth, friendship and hope filled convictions of the first SGI members I encountered. This openness and pure heartedness was encapsulated in an experience I had only a matter of months after I began to practise Nichiren Buddhism.

My mother and I had decided to take a walking holiday in Nepal in the spring of 2001 in celebration of her retirement. I phoned the SGI-UK national centre at Taplow Court to see if I could connect with some members in Kathmandu. As luck would have it, the receptionist volunteering that day had lived in Nepal in the preceding years and gave me the phone number not only of a member but of the General Director of Nepal-SGI, Keshab Shrestra!

On arriving in Nepal's capital, I called Keshab and was welcomed with warmth to the extent that he invited me and my mother for a Chinese meal to celebrate Nepali New Year with the top leaders of Nepal-SGI. This was before I had even become an SGI member and received Gohonzon. I remember being collected in an already packed small Fiat car and driven just 100 yards to the next tenement where the restaurant was. The next day, we were invited to the main SGI centre in Kathmandu for their New Year's Day celebration meeting, in which they asked me to play a song on the guitar. They were somewhat surprised that I didn't know any of the rousing traditional SGI songs that they also conducted as group singalongs that day.

The warmth and unfettered regard for us by people from the other side of the world truly touched our hearts and when I met Mrs Shrestra at Taplow Court last year, I was overwhelmed with gratitude for the welcome they gave that fledgling Buddhist 20 years before. My mother, inspired by my own personal transformation and trusting in the SGI members she had met in the UK and abroad, began chanting a few months afterwards. During that meal in Kathmandu, I was sat next to Keshab, a great man who sadly died a few years later. I wrote in my diary of that time, "At one point he turned to me and gave guidance which had a profound impact on me. He told me that Buddhism is about helping others, that it is the key to our own fulfilment and the well-being of the whole planet. Although I had read this before, it was only now that it truly lodged in my heart."

Research on the benefits of religion

In contrast to the societal conditioning that could turn us against religion, research is increasingly pointing to the benefits of being involved in a religious group. Researchers at the Mayo Clinic concluded, "Most studies have shown that religious involvement and spirituality are associated with better health outcomes, including greater longevity, coping skills and health-related quality of life (even during terminal illness) and less anxiety, depression and suicide. Several studies have shown that addressing the spiritual needs of the patient may enhance recovery from illness."[31] The religious report more happiness than the non-religious, have been found to have lower blood pressure and in a 1999 study attending religious services more than once a week was linked to an additional seven years of life compared to those who never go.[32] The *Handbook of Religion and Health* in 2012 reviewed thousands of data-based studies since the year 2000 and came to the conclusion that religious and spiritual practices conferred a wide range of physical and mental health benefits.[33]

In a 2010 study Dr Andrew Newberg, a neuroscientist at Thomas Jefferson University, Philadelphia found that meditative prayer (such as prayer that repeats a particular phrase as is the case in chanting daimoku) activates areas of the brain involved in regulating emotional responses.[34] Even religion apart from a contemplative element may change brain circuits according to Michael Inzlicht PhD of the University of Toronto. He analysed a particular brainwave that spikes when people make mistakes and found those with greater religious zeal had a dampened brain spike and calmer response when making mistakes.[35]

However inconsistent and differing religions are in practices and rituals, on the whole they promote the conviction that our existence is purposeful and our lives worthwhile. Research indicates that the meaning this confers in people's lives creates optimism in the religious. Wide-ranging investigations in the field of positive psychology have shown optimists are healthier and of course happier. The social support mechanisms of religions can also account for some of the health benefits seen in religious participation.

It should, however, be fairly noted that research into well-being has found intensely religious people have the highest levels of life satisfaction but that strong atheists have quite high levels of life satisfaction, higher than the nominally religious.[36] Having strong meaning in one's life seems to be the determining factor here. However, further research has shown that well-being very much depends on the religious belief system one subscribes to. Newberg has pointed out that if a religion advocates hate for non-believers, these negative pattern beliefs and emotions show up in brain patterning.[37] For those filled with guilt, fear or severe religious conflicts, religious beliefs can have a negative impact on health and well-being. In a study by Pargament et al (2001) religious patients experienced a 19-28% greater mortality rate due to the belief that God was either punishing or abandoning them.

Can a secular alternative work?

From an atheist perspective, all this evidence may be true but it doesn't make religion truthful. I hope in the rest of the book I have outlined the clear rationale behind Nichiren Buddhist belief, but mainstream society may more often than not try to acquire the social and sense of meaning benefits conferred by religion through non-religious means. So could the benefits of religion be equally derived from secular alternatives?

Alain de Botton, one of the UK's most noted contemporary

philosophers, has attempted to do just that in his book *Religion for Atheists*. He points out that, "we invented religions to serve two central needs which continue to this day and which secular society has not been able to solve with any particular skill,"[38] namely living together and overcoming pain and suffering. He notes that, "religions merit our attentions for their sheer conceptual ambition: for changing the world in a way that few secular institutions ever have."[39] Having sympathetically cited successful religious examples, what follows are de Botton's attempts at secular alternatives to all of the pillars of religious organisation: community, education, art and values/perspective. Undoubtedly creative and at times humorous, de Botton's suggestions appear wholly unrealistic in terms of actually being implemented in real life. For example, he proposes building temples to reflection and perspective, psychotherapeutic travel agencies which would align mental disorders with parts of the planet best able to alleviate them and advertising hoardings preaching accepted moral values. Finally, he cites Auguste Comte, a 19th century philanthropist who in a parallel to de Botton, attempted to start a non-religious secular religion and failed miserably. As indeed Richard Dawkins himself has pointed out, "organizing atheists has been compared to herding cats."[40]

De Botton's ideas seem so fanciful because secular society and atheism in particular lend themselves naturally to individualism. No conclusive, credible alternative to religion has been offered that could be practically implemented. Far more likely to succeed is not an extraction of the religious model grafted on to rational secular ideals, but a rational religion based on reason and evidence. SGI Buddhism is just such a religion.

Count Richard Coudenhove-Kalergi, founding father of European unification stated in 1970 in Daisaku Ikeda's first dialogue with a leading thinker outside Japan, "Only a new religious movement can prevent the drift (toward a Third World War) and save humankind. The Soka Gakkai is thus a tremendous source of hope."[41] *The New Human Revolution* series of novels powerfully illustrates how this source of hope transformed the direst of situations of individual practitioners. Could a secular alternative have broken through the despair felt by Noriyoshi Yamaue (NHR pen name), a second generation victim of the atomic bomb dropped on Hiroshima, his family decimated and his own health destroyed? Reading Ikeda's guidance ignited the flame of hope in him and with the encouragement of the youth division members and a strong daily practice, he dedicated his life to making sure later generations never had to experience war, eventually becoming the Chair of the Hiroshima Youth Division Anti-War Publications Committee.[42]

A family experience

My own family were in the main part deeply unreligious, my paternal grandfather being a case in point. His father, my great grandfather, had been a Methodist preacher but like many academic people of his generation in the 1920s and 30s, he rejected Christianity, becoming a Professor of Economics. The grandpa, I knew was a troubled man, however. By the time he was in his 70s and 80s, he would spend most of the morning in the bathroom due to a deep seated terror of germs, illness and death, resulting in a prolonged bathroom routine which would last at least a couple of hours. Around 11.30am he would appear with a cheery "Morning all!" I am sure modern psychotherapy would have helped him with what was Obsessive Compulsive Disorder, but I also feel in ritualising the bathroom routines, he was in some way filling the gap that was left after the loss of religion. Death was his greatest enemy, imbued with a materialist mindset of this being the only existence and yet, when I visited him in hospital near to the moment of death, all those worries and fears that had tormented him in life seemed to have vanished like clouds departing from the sky. Drifting in and out of consciousness, there was a deep serenity and calm to him, transcending what could be termed in Buddhism, the lesser self.

There are many aspects of our modern society that can support people to lead fulfilled lives; psychotherapy including Cognitive Behavioural Therapy, social services, charitable organisations, community groups and clubs; the list is endless but the comprehensive depth and breadth of religion to make a positive change, in my opinion, is still unrivalled.

PART 3 - WHY CHOOSE SGI?

It is the right in any free society for the individual to choose whether they want to be part of an organisation or even a religion at all. For some, the idea will hold no appeal and that must be respected. I hope that the research I have outlined at least indicates the sound and substantial scientifically proven benefits to participation in a religious group.

But if one were to choose to be part of a religion, why particularly choose SGI Buddhism? What makes it stand out from other organisations? Without negating the effects of other faiths, I will suggest that SGI offers a highly evolved organisation on a grass roots level which has proved adaptive to the challenges of the modern age and been able to change to suit different cultural contexts around the world.

What is different about SGI?

Alfred North Whitehead wrote, "(Religious) principles may be eternal, but the expression of those principles requires continual development."[43] SGI has created a new paradigm of religion. In focusing on people, on actual proof and most importantly on life, the formality and convention of religious practice has dropped away in the SGI. Clark Strand, former Zen Buddhist monk and spiritual writer, places great hope in SGI's radical reconfiguring of religion. With "no dress code, no priests or monks and no identifiable architectural style," what, asks Strand, is left when the appearance of religion falls away? He finds the answer in the core life values of SGI, basic human concerns that transcend religion.[44] In his three hour dialogue with Minoru Harada, current President of the Soka Gakkai, Strand is astonished that not one Buddhist term was used, his message of peace and goodwill transcending cultural affectations.

The spirit of the SGI movement is distinctly modern, but takes its cue from Nichiren himself in his flexible revisionist approach. "When it comes to studying the teachings of Buddhism, one must first learn to understand the time," he wrote (WND 1, p538). In a democratic age, a religion focused on and for the people needs to have as its focus the difficulties and challenges that come up in daily life and provide a network of moral support to sustain people to overcome obstacles and enact real personal change. Jane Hurst of Gallaudet University describes SGI as a pragmatic religion aimed at making things better in the here and now based on its values.[45]

The importance of discussion meetings

Central to SGI are the locally based district discussion meetings, gatherings of local members and their friends which take place in a member's house. Unlike a religious service or a philosophical lecture, the dynamic is interactive and the floor is open for anyone to share, inspire or offer and receive support. A good discussion meeting holds a space where people can be authentic and return home rejuvenated and refreshed. During some of the most difficult times, discussion meetings have been there for me to share my challenges and receive support and guidance. In one year as a class teacher, I had a particularly challenging and difficult class with a pupil seemingly pulling the strings of many of his classmates and subtly trying to undermine the learning. It was the opportunity to even shed a tear in my local discussion meeting and receive inspiration and support that kept me going. In turn, I go to discussion meetings with the aim to inspire and bring hope to those who need it.

The discussion meeting format goes back to the leadership of Tsunesaburo Makiguchi in wartime Japan, who appreciated the capacity of open dialogue to empower all the participants. As Clark Strand describes it,

"The monthly discussion meeting is 'Where the rubber meets the road,' Buddhism is put to the test, and the truth of its teachings are manifested by members through personal stories of overcoming obstacles to happiness."[46]

Strand also describes the discussion meeting model as 'a post-tribal delivery system', the reason why SGI can, through the natural lines of human relationships in a locality, grow and spread exponentially with no need for facilities, resources or buildings. The autonomous nature of these meetings is also empowering. The local district or group sets the theme, moderation is shared by the participants each month and other than chanting for a successful and rewarding meeting, no one knows quite how it will unfold!

An egalitarian and accessible structure

This focus on the grassroots as the centre of the SGI movement is also special. It is egalitarian and co-operative as opposed to didactic and instructive. I could not describe myself as a classic rebel. I kept my head down at school and made it to Cambridge University, but I have felt keenly the sense of oppression when forced to conform and submit to organisational structures where an individual has little real say. I hated being a prefect at school; by the end of my time at University I had cut myself off from my college and was doing 'my own thing'. At work, I found certain kinds of bosses intolerable to work under. Within SGI, however, I have always felt free not only to express myself but also to be myself in terms of my response to the teachings and my spiritual journey. This book is in and of itself an expression of that sense of freedom.

The Buddhist scholar, David Chappell commented, "This universal affirmation of the value of every human being is found in Buddhism, Christianity and Islam, but the way Soka Gakkai applied this principle to all strata of society without demanding a change in lifestyle was exceptional and represents a distinctive feature."[47]

With no robes, no change of names, no rejection of worldly goals, no requirement to live communally, SGI integrates with normal mainstream society, making membership possible not only without compromising one's normal daily life, but through its personal empowerment, providing a lever to be even more successful and integrated in society.

The accessibility of SGI is also down to the lack of expense in practising its teachings. Unlike many contemporary self-development courses or even other forms of Buddhism centred on residential retreats, the core of SGI practice is free. For example, in SGI-UK there is no cost to receiving the Gohonzon, no charge to attend local meetings and any contributions to the upkeep of centres in what is known as the 'kosen rufu fund' are entirely voluntary. This model of participation, free of cost, is very important in ensuring the diversity of SGI. Whether you live in a gated mansion or a council flat, whether a successful business person or an unemployed student, you can access SGI equally and benefit from the practice equally. This has also led to the racial diversity of the movement, SGI-USA as a case in point, being by far the most racially diverse Buddhist movement in America with a large proportion of African American and Hispanic members. Hurst also notes that as early as 1968, there were a high proportion of LGBT participants in some SGI-USA districts.[48]

SGI's teaching of enlightenment in the here and now also has a practicality to it which opens it to all willing to try the practice. There are no hidden complicated teachings gradually revealed to the practitioner in stages, no esoteric or otherworldly philosophy to grapple with. Whilst there is plenty to study, to deepen one's understanding, the simple practice of chanting Nam-myoho-renge-kyo is ultimately a great leveller. Someone who has chanted for a week and someone who has chanted for thirty years can still attain the same life state in the moment.

A system of support

The anti-authoritarianism which sent Toda and Makiguchi to prison for their beliefs colours the organisational structure of the SGI in unique ways. The organisation is a highly structured system of support. Jim Cowan a social scientist and pioneer member of SGI-UK describes it metaphorically, "Just as atoms are in molecules which are in cells which are in an organism, so local groups form together to create a larger group, which combine with other larger groups,"[49] and so on until a large group covers an entire country. In each of these groups are leaders who take responsibility for their respectively sized group, but are conceived not in a role of authority but, as Daisaku Ikeda has emphasized, to serve and support those leaders and members in the next groups smaller to themselves. This in turn creates what is often described as an inverse pyramid of support rather than of authority, with the 'top' leaders at the bottom and the local groups spread out at the top and at the forefront of the movement.

Jim Cowan writes in his recent book, *The Britain Potential*, about the make-up of organisations based on Wilber's consciousnesses. These colour code an organisation based on strengths and weaknesses. For example, at one extreme, a red organisation has strong egocentric leadership and is ruthless when it responds to threats and opportunities internally and externally (the Mafia being one example). Market based organisations are quite often orange which, although led by reason and responsive to change, are materialistic and disconnected from the inner life of their employees/members. Cowan classifies SGI as a teal organisation with self-organising autonomous teams and humanistic leadership. He describes a rare kind of unity fostered in SGI, "a unity built on the uniqueness of what each individual brings of themselves, combined with a profound spiritual unity of sharing the same profound purpose in life," that purpose ultimately being the deep happiness of ourselves and all others. "SGI members experience one another's hearts and the organisation itself is transparently ablaze with heartfelt interactions, friendship and trust." Cowan proposes that this is a completely different way of "doing organised religion."[50]

THE EVOLVING BUDDHA

Challenging corruption and authoritarianism

SGI is made up of diverse human beings, diverse in outlook, diverse in where they are in their own personal development and spiritual journey. So it is testament to the openness and transparency of the organisation that the inherent tendency in humanity towards corruption, authoritarianism and self-interest is warned against in Ikeda's writings and openly challenged.

For example, in Volume 10 of *The Human Revolution* which records the Osaka campaign of 1956, a turning point in the Soka Gakkai's expansion in Japan, the imperious and authoritarian behaviours of some senior leaders visiting from Tokyo are written about in detail, one leader foisting unreasonable targets and labelling those who did not agree with him as 'drop outs'. Instead of glossing over these difficult realities, Ikeda uses them as a case study in how not to behave as a leader. In *The New Human Revolution* Volume 19, Shin'ichi (Ikeda's pen name) admonishes the central leader in the United States about behaving in a dictatorial and authoritarian manner:

"Becoming authoritarian and bureaucratic is a sign of ineffectiveness. If a leader lacks credibility and humanistic qualities others respect, he inevitably starts abusing his position and authority in an effort to make others follow him. But arrogantly issuing orders only alienates others... Never forget to be grateful and appreciative of everyone's efforts. Its one's humanity and character that attracts others."[51]

I find this confrontation with authoritarianism refreshing. Some may find the idea of organisations problematic precisely because of this human tendency but for anything to spread and have an impact on humanity, organisation and cooperation is necessary. Instead, it is SGI's wariness of corruption that signals its willingness to challenge such tendencies when they arrive. Shin Yatomi, the late study chief of SGI-USA, summarizes this succinctly when he points out that whilst organisations and leaders consist of human beings, corruption will inevitably appear at some point. Acknowledging this reality is key for a religion to then develop an 'antidote', the wisdom to see wrongdoing and authoritarianism as it truly is and the courage to challenge it.[52]

My experience of facing authoritarianism

My own experience of an imperious leader almost upended my practice. Whilst I was in the youth division of SGI-UK, my local Men's Chapter Leader was very castigating about how I encouraged members to participate in activities. I was very upset by this and had a dialogue with him which, from my perspective, did not resolve our disagreement. How could a Buddhist behave like this? I asked myself. Does this practice work if people can act like this within the organisation? This was the obstacle in my thinking and also my delusion. He was coming from a different place and perspective and had no more intention of triggering seething anger in me and doubt in my practice as I had in him. He saw himself as being helpful in strictly correcting me. During this time, I caught a senior leader after a talk for very brief guidance. He simply said to me, "This is your anger, not his," in other words, I had to take responsibility.

I kept chanting for him and the issue, despite my resentment, directing my chanting for his happiness and well-being. The situation affected me so greatly that it led me to allow my practice to take a back-seat in my life, though I continued to chant a bit and attend discussion meetings. The resolution was not overnight and took much chanting and reflecting but I eventually came to realise that the anger I felt was down to my own ego's attachment to my status as an SGI leader, not merely his authoritative tone. He too was on his own journey and over the next couple of years softened in his style as a leader, doing his own 'human revolution', inner transformation with his Buddhist practice.

Before he moved out of the local area, our relationship had completely transformed and he greatly supported me in a difficult situation that arose. When he moved away, I felt genuine sadness at his loss and gratitude that what seemed to be a completely intractable conflict had been transformed with the power of the chanting. The experience gave me great confidence that any relationship can be transformed with this practice.

A philosophy of flexibility and adaptation

SGI offers a radical reconfiguring of the religious framework but equally important is the fact that this structure is not set in stone. One of the potential weaknesses of the old religious model is its resistance to change and improvement. All religious organisations inevitably change over time, but those with a mandate supposedly set by an all-supreme deity or those which have an authoritative priestly or monastic body in a position of privilege and power, may find moving with the times difficult. Such organisations are likely to come up against what may be perceived as 'the way things should always be' according to scripture. This can result in a potentially traumatic conflict between conservative and more liberalising elements.

SGI suffers less from this difficulty because it is underpinned by a philosophy of flexibility. This derives from two contrasting precepts in Buddhist theology: *Zuien shinyo no chi* (wisdom to adapt truth to varying circumstances) and *Fuhen shinyo ri* (the rationality of immutable truth). The immutable truth in Nam-myoho-renge-kyo must stay the same but how this is shared and conveyed can have a myriad of different manifestations. As a result, SGI can interpret and apply Nichiren Buddhism according to the times, unfettered by orthodoxy.

This process of adaptation and evolving is seen clearly in the case of SGI-USA. Beginning in 1960 with President Ikeda's first visit to the States, the organisation started with a small number of mainly Japanese female members, wives of American servicemen who had returned from the Far East. Meetings were held exclusively in Japanese until 1963. By 1970 however, the American movement had expanded rapidly across a cross section of the American public, particularly the baby-boomer generation. SGI-USA had transformed itself from a distinctly Japanese organisation to one that was overtly American not only in its membership, but in consciously celebrating American values and festivals such as Independence Day. David Machacek of the University of California describes this process as 'isomorphism', where organisations take on key features shared with other organisations in that culture.[53] SGI would consciously describe this process with the Buddhist term *Zuiho-Bini* – acting according to local custom as long as the fundamental principles of Buddhism are not violated.

In the 1970s, concert groups and marching bands celebrated America's bicentenary and, in later years, outward facing institutions such as the Boston Research Center for Peace (later the Ikeda Center for Peace, Learning and Dialogue) and Soka University of America, involved SGI-USA in established frameworks of public life. As a result, SGI-USA, by complying with the widely accepted rules of behaviour of American social life, has not been attacked by the American media to the same extent as other new religious movements. This, Macachek points out, has also been the case with family and friends of those practicing who, at first potentially concerned, come to realise nothing untoward or outside normal social expectations takes place when someone becomes a member of SGI.[54]

The growth of the movement in India in very recent years can also be in part accounted for by a cultural adaptation. In a deeply religious society, Bharat Soka Gakkai members in India are told that they can still celebrate Hindu festivals and have Hindu shrines left in their homes whilst still practising Nichiren Buddhism in the spirit of *Zuiho-Bini*. BSG members and beginners are told they are practising a teaching rather than exclusively a new religion and so they can continue to maintain Hindu rituals. An exclusivist stance, as was taken in 1950s Japan, is seen as a relic of the past and just would not have worked in India. This does not mean Indian members are any less focussed or passionate about their Buddhist practice, in fact, the contrary is the case, and this has been the determining factor in their growth. The scholar, Richard Hughes Seager, summed up this point when he wrote, "Buddhism of all sorts is found almost everywhere today, but few groups equal the Gakkai in either its programmatic effort to adapt to new situations and its genius for organisation."[55]

Spiritual independence

SGI's already existing evolving and adaptive mindset was given jet propulsion by its split with the Nichiren Shoshu priesthood. Rather than seeing this event as a sad and unfortunate occurrence, academics are generally in agreement that it was an inevitable part of the process of development. As the academic Jane Hurst wrote, "The pragmatic, goal orientated, this-worldly focus of the Soka Gakkai lay believers conflicts with the priestly, mystical, other-worldly focus of the Nichiren Shoshu priesthood. In light of this, it is remarkable that the co-operation between 1951 and 1991 lasted as long as it did."[56] Nichiren Shoshu members may still express bitterness and resentment towards SGI but for SGI members, the split was a liberation from the shackles of dogma, out-dated ritual and superstition.

Instead, SGI was truly free to express itself as a progressive, liberalised and flexible movement. The SGI Charter of 1995 encapsulated this sense of freedom by formally decentralizing control from Japan in Article 6, "SGI shall respect the independence and autonomy of its constituent organizations in accordance with the conditions prevailing in each country." Gongyo, the recitation of passages of the Lotus Sutra, was shortened from a liturgy that could take 30 minutes to one that could be achieved in 3, leaving time to focus on the core practice of chanting daimoku. Interfaith dialogue and respect for other religions became paramount with symposiums and events engaging with other faiths and other denominations of Buddhism.

At the turn of the century, only three other Buddhist groups had representation at the United Nations and sponsored local United Nations associations. SGI offers a model of 'Engaged Buddhism' where personal practice leads to solid social reforms, an example being SGI's involvement as a founder member of ICAN, the Nobel Peace prize winning campaign to abolish nuclear weapons. The United Nations Treaty on the Prohibition of Nuclear Weapons initiated by ICAN achieved its 50th ratification by a nation state and has therefore come into force. Although the major nuclear powers still stand against this move, it has the potential to undermine the worldwide acceptance of these devastating weapons and contribute to their abolition.

If there is value in Buddhist practice, it should lessen the suffering within society. Seager summarises this impulse well when he writes, "there is a strong pragmatic streak in Gakkai spirituality that does not shrink from the fact that the movement needs dedicated members, a strong motive, solid doctrine and practice, focused leadership, social awareness, money and political will to transform the world."[57]

A dynamic and highly organised movement

But let us not forget where the impetus for all of this comes from, the well spring derived from tapping the energy and potential within every individual through practising Nichiren Buddhism. Daniel Montgomery, a commentator of the movement in the 1980s, wrote that what stood out regarding SGI members, was not that they were more religious or even happier, as this may be true of any faith, "What is special about them is that they become more energetic; a new vitality permeates their activities. They chant vigorously, sing vigorously, walk vigorously (or even run instead of walk) and work vigorously. They expect to be successful at whatever they do, and generally they are."[58]

Montgomery also records the impressions of a manager of Akron Civic Center after his venue played host to the American association's general meeting in 1973,

"After a while I said, 'This thing is going to be the most fantastically organized thing I ever saw,' because everybody was taking care of all those little details to the last inch."

And when the show began, "we were glad we were in the dark because we were standing there with tears coming out of our eyes, and we weren't even members of the group!"[59]

This dynamism is something that was not just a bi-product of early enthusiasm, it continues to pulse vibrantly through SGI to this day. One recent experience of my own was in March 2018, when SGI-UK's youth division galvanised the movement to hold three events across the country with 6000 young people attending, to convey a sense of optimism and provide hope to a seemingly listless and downcast generation. Leading up to the event, ticket sales were sluggish but a sudden surge of activity and effort meant the events were many times over-subscribed. I took my elder daughter and her friend to the event. Outside the Hammersmith Apollo was a sea of people. The temperature was bitterly cold and a light flurry of sleet fell at times but once inside, the atmosphere was electrifying. We sat rapt as highly professionally staged dance, music and performance pieces were combined with film and heartfelt experiences. Just like at the Koto concert in Saga, my heart was touched deeply. This was something very special, far more than an ordinary performance and something very profound for the United Kingdom.

To change is to survive and thrive

Community is an integral part of what makes us human, an essential element of how we function that can be tracked back to our hunter gatherer past 70,000 years ago and beyond. But for communities and organisations (the structured framework for communities) to sustain, they must evolve, must adapt to thrive, must change to survive. This being the case, SGI's future looks bright if it continues to reconfigure in an age where social and technological changes across the globe are occurring at a pace unseen in human history.

Soka Gakkai and SGI have always been reform movements. With Makiguchi at first it was reform of education, with Toda it was to reform Japanese society and for Ikeda the world was SGI's stage. We will look at the development of Ikeda's vision and philosophy for world peace in more detail in the next chapter. But that desire for reform has allowed SGI to reform itself too and this must continue.

Clark Strand has high hopes for SGI when he writes, "a post-tribal, life-centred religious movement like the SGI – with its global mission to promote universal human values like peace, education and culture – is right on time."[60] At its core, SGI is about one thing, the one thing that Keshab Shrestra taught me in a Chinese restaurant in Kathmandu, that Buddhism is not about ascending the mountain to some perfect enlightenment but is about caring for others – deep, profound care based on the respect for the dignity of the person in front of us. Only through community and organisation can this take place in its fullest sense and through such altruistic actions we find liberation.

Daisaku Ikeda writes, "The organisation of faith is not something that holds you back or restricts you. Rather it is a springboard that enables you to develop yourself to the utmost and to lead the most dynamic existence. It is the most precious place for carrying out our Buddhist practice."[61]

Far from being a restriction, SGI provides true freedom, through social connectedness and social responsibility in an age where social cohesion and shared common consciousness have been lost.

CHAPTER SIX

DAISAKU IKEDA

THE BOND OF MENTOR AND DISCIPLE

"A blue fly, if it clings to the tail of a thorough-bred horse, can travel ten thousand miles, and the green ivy that twines around the tall pine can grow to a thousand feet."

On Establishing the Correct Teaching for the Peace of the Land (WND 1, p17)

PART 1 - WHY HAVE A MENTOR?

The night before I ran the London Marathon, I barely slept a wink. Maybe it was to be expected. I was running on behalf of my school, raising money to build a new hall, and the parent body had been incredibly generous in sponsoring me in the endeavour. A lot of people were anticipating me completing it, but at 5am that morning I felt alone and very, very tired. Sitting like a washed out zombie at my local station, waiting for the train to London,

THE EVOLVING BUDDHA

I was in a complete daze and had not even had the wherewithal to eat breakfast. Protection came in the form of a fellow runner on the platform who offered me the porridge and banana that he was eating.

I started the race very slowly and in a great deal of pain, but as I got into my stride, in each quarter of the race, I got faster and faster. In the end the last 4 miles were my fastest and I finished within 5 hours. I wept with relief when I made it through the finish line.

On receiving my medal, I decided I was not going to keep it. I would send it half way across the world to Japan as a gift to Daisaku Ikeda, founding President of Soka Gakkai International (SGI). A few months later, I received a message of gratitude from him and a large book of his colour photographs of nature.

So what made a 28 year old Englishman send a treasured lifetime achievement to an elderly Japanese man whom he had never met? By that point in my Buddhist practice, having chanted for three or so years, I was developing my understanding of the mentor-disciple relationship and my connection with 'Sensei', which literally means teacher in Japanese. The concept of a mentor is somewhat alien to the Western mindset and in addition, for SGI members, the living mentor is one man, Daisaku Ikeda.

In this chapter, we will look at the logic and development of the mentor-disciple concept, to find why it is so important in Buddhism and what value it brings to the practitioner. We will also place a spotlight on Ikeda's life, achievements and philosophy, and unpick why he has been persecuted in his tireless efforts for peace. By again considering the academic research outside of SGI, we can bring a new perspective to the individual most central to the international growth of Nichiren Buddhism, and see how his thought too has evolved and crystallised over time.

Who is Daisaku Ikeda?

Ikeda is a Tokyoite, born in 1928 and raised in the Omori district of Japan's capital. Ikeda's father's nickname was 'Old Diehard', a tribute to his obstinacy, but for most of Ikeda's childhood his father was bedridden with rheumatism, leaving his mother and her children to maintain the family business harvesting seaweed which saw a decline through the 1920s and 30s. As a boy, Ikeda's sister-in-law asked him what he wanted to do when he was older. He replied, 'I will do something that will astonish the entire Japanese nation.' In his interview with Professor Richard Hughes Seager of Hamilton College, Ikeda bashfully passes this statement off as a typical thing an 'Edokko', a colloquial term for one raised in Tokyo, might say.[1] And yet, as his sister-in-law later pointed out, he really did what he said he would.

The rise of militarism and the catastrophic involvement of Japan in the Second World War defined Ikeda. All four of his elder brothers were sent off to fight in Asia to further Japan's Imperial expansionist agenda, and his elder brother Kiichi never returned from Burma, killed seven months before the war's end in 1945. Ikeda's sense of mission to eradicate war, to forge a truly peaceful world stems from the deep suffering inflicted on his mother and family at this time. In addition, afflicted with tuberculosis, Ikeda knew his life could be cut short at any moment.

THE EVOLVING BUDDHA

It was in this war ravaged state, questioning the purpose of life, that the young Daisaku was invited in the summer of 1947 to what he thought was a life-philosophy talk on the thought of the French philosopher, Bergson. In fact, it was his first Soka Gakkai meeting and his first encounter with the man who became his mentor, Josei Toda. Awed by Toda's response to his questions, Toda's conviction and the fact he had stood up against the militarists, Ikeda felt he had found a man he could truly put his faith in. He became a member of the Soka Gakkai on 24th August of that year.

Ikeda became President of the Soka Gakkai in 1960, furthering the dynamic expansion of the movement under Toda. His achievements are well recorded. Ikeda stepped out of Japan to expand Nichiren Buddhism overseas and in turn internationalized the teachings centring on peace, culture and education. He engaged in dialogues with a wide range of intellectuals, artists, politicians and scientists to find common ground towards peace. He established a range of institutions including a school and university system and various cultural organisations. Above all, he developed a profound philosophy of Buddhist Humanism which transcended the confines of a particular school or even a specific religion. A 1999 survey of the Japanese public put him in the top twenty authors in the country. Twenty years earlier, another major poll placed him as the sixth most respected individual in Japan with the only living person in the five ahead of him being the then Emperor, Hirohito.[2]

A story of his life

The narrative of Ikeda's life and those of many pioneer members who walked along with him, is mapped out in his novels *The Human Revolution* and *The New Human Revolution*. His purpose in writing the series is tied to his own relationship with his mentor:

"I have taken writing *The New Human Revolution* as my life's work. In it, I am determined to continue to record, to the limits of my ability, the diamond-like genuine path of mentor and disciple, and depict the grand portrait of glory created by the precious children of the Buddha as they have advanced... Truth and falsehood, good and evil, winners and losers- all will be vigorously depicted. I cannot help thinking that President Toda is steadfastly watching me."[3]

The fact that the work is novelised and that the author acknowledges characters may have been combined for ease of narrative has been criticized by detractors as producing revisionist history. However, as Clark Strand the pan-Buddhist author points out, the story-like retelling of the Soka Gakkai movement is foundational in creating a 'gospel' for SGI, a coherent narrative for the movement, of mentor and disciple and which epitomises in its essence the spirit of Buddhist Humanism, to inspire future generations.[4]

As Ikeda has often pointed out, "you are the scriptwriter of your own life". Recent research has supported this approach. The American author, Emily Esfahani-Smith states, "We are constantly taking pieces of information and adding a layer of meaning to them; we couldn't function otherwise. Stories help us make sense of the world and our place in it, and understand why things happen the way they do."[5] George Harrison once said that everyone had a different idea of what it was like being a Beatle, and that applied even to the Beatles themselves, even if they were experiencing the same moment. In this light, one understands that all history, all journalism comes from a particular perspective and *The Human Revolution* and *New Human Revolution* series creates a specific narrative aimed at offering a perspective which inspires readers to take action (modelled in a similar vein), in the same spirit.

Dan McAdams of Northwestern University advocates that we all have a 'narrative identity', described by another author as "about who we are deep down – where we come from, how we got this way, and what it all means."[6] This is our own personal myth and it is based on our interpretation of events that have happened to us, which can naturally differ from how others viewed the same events. It is this 'interpretative' quality that has allowed psychologists to encourage the reframing of tragic or traumatising events from 'contamination' stories to 'redemptive' narratives.[7] Meaning and value can be gleaned from suffering and hardship, something which very much resonates with the Buddhist concept of turning poison into medicine. In a study from 2012, Adam Grant and Jane Dutton found that when university call-centre fundraisers were asked to write a journal recounting the times they contributed to others at work, they made 30% more calls than those who had been asked to write narratives about being passive recipients of generosity.[8]

Our personal narratives can affect our psychology and our actual behaviours so *The New Human Revolution* is not merely a positive angle on the SGI movement. It provides a coherent narrative of the mentors and disciples of Soka, and in doing so provides a benchmark, a model on how to behave to fully reveal one's best self, one's Buddha nature. It should finally be noted that, as was pointed out in a previous chapter, this does not mean that the narrative avoids tackling the problems, difficulties and mistakes that took place on the journey. These are equally brought up including the more controversial events which will be considered later in this chapter.

A Youthful Diary

As a roadmap for Buddhist practice, *The New Human Revolution* is pre-eminent. However, to get a more immediate and visceral account of the young Daisaku Ikeda, his *A Youthful Diary* allows the reader to feel the emotions and heart of this young man. What comes across are his sincerity, his values, his sufferings and his frailties. The honesty of the entries is refreshing. Here is someone to look up to who is not perfect, who has felt weakness, illness and fear, like all of us.

Two years into practising on June 13th 1949, Ikeda writes, "Had a headache since morning. Have to take better care of myself. My mind changes from one moment to the next. I know what my goals are but I waver all the same. Pathetic. One moment I'm in high spirits, bursting with youthful intensity, and the next moment I'm as petrified as though I were standing on the edge of a cliff." But he rouses himself in the same entry admonishing himself, "Youth, stand up! Advance! Otherwise there will be no human revolution. Plunge into the whirlpool of reality and fight. Fear nothing. Remember your great mission."[9]

Over ten years later, in April 1960, a few days before assuming the presidency of the Soka Gakkai, Ikeda is still emotionally torn regarding whether or not to accept it. On 9th April he writes, "Ah is there no one else who can take leadership in place of my tired, worn-out self? Have no one to talk to. My wife quietly watches over me in agony." But by 15th April, he has overcome his fears and resolves to accept the role, "I was raised by President Toda as his direct disciple. He trained me continually and repeatedly. How could I fear any battle? The time for me to repay my debt of gratitude to him has come."[10]

I find the honesty and humanity of Ikeda in *A Youthful Diary* empowering. Here is a mentor who goes through suffering, who is tough on himself, but who also holds high ideals and follows through on them. Just as he could place his trust in Toda, I can place my trust in him.

Our preconceptions of mentor and disciple

But why bother to have a mentor and what exactly does having a mentor mean? These are questions prevalent in the Western mindset in which the concept is not culturally embedded. In fact, the idea of mentor and disciple can seem frightening – even threatening – to a Westerner. The term 'mentor' is generally only used on a professional basis in the West, such as supporting trainees in a job and the word disciple is associated in European and American minds with the twelve disciples of Jesus who gave up everything to follow him. Combine these cultural pendants with suspicion of Eastern gurus who have manipulated and extorted followers, plus the strident individualism of modern first world societies, and you have a recipe for misunderstanding for SGI's emphasis on the mentor-disciple relationship.

Lawrence Carter, Dean of Martin Luther King Jr. International Chapel, Morehouse College (King's Alma Mater), describes a trend towards spiritual individualism, "where one can choose an idea from this tradition, a ritual from that one, to fashion a wholly individual, even idiosyncratic, spiritual worldview."[11] While our spiritual journey is personal and requires looking within ourselves, Carter argues that something is lost when we are not practising with a community of believers, something we examined in the last chapter. Furthermore, he questions how individual such a journey really is. We are always taking inspiration from those who have walked a path before us.

What is the mentor-disciple relationship?

Across all forms of Buddhism, the mentor-disciple relationship has been an essential element from the foundational days of Shakyamuni Buddha. Clark Strand asserts that this reflects the Buddhist understanding of the interdependence of all life. Individualism is a delusion which risks us falling into isolation, when in fact, "we stand or fall based on the quality of our relationship to others and to the world. No one of us exists alone."[12] It is wholly inaccurate to treat SGI's development of the mentor-disciple relationship as a completely new innovation. It is in fact an essential part of all Eastern spiritual traditions in varying forms. Nichiren's letters are permeated with the spirit of the mentor-disciple relationship, none more so than when he states, "My wish is that all my disciples make a great vow." (WND 1, p1003) Nichiren had made his own vow at the risk of his own life to uphold the philosophy of the Lotus Sutra. He now wanted his disciples to do the same and share this lofty task.

Mentor-disciple is a relationship of trust, of learning and spiritual inspiration. As is often stated in SGI, it is the disciple who chooses the mentor and it is the mentor who desires the disciple to exceed him in his personal growth and achievements. Outside perspectives often misunderstand the respect Ikeda is held in as veneration. However, the respect and value one holds for the mentor in SGI is not to put him on a pedestal, but at its heart, to catalyse individual empowerment for the disciple. When Strand interviewed pioneer members who had been directly mentored by Ikeda, none of them praised him merely for his personal qualities but associated his inspiration and encouragement with their own life transformation.

The mentor-disciple relationship is essential for the relaying and endurance of great teachings and philosophies. This is, in a sense, why the relationship in SGI is focused on Ikeda as the mentor, for multiple mentors across the world who may not live up to this standard could muddy the clarity and consistency of the essential philosophical underpinnings of Buddhist Humanism as developed by Ikeda. Socrates, Plato and Aristotle are a classical Western example of this tradition. This focus does not mean that there cannot be a culture of inspiration between SGI members as well, through the mutual support and guidance they receive on a local level. Furthermore, in following a teacher's life example, we do not lose our individuality but challenge our egoistic tendency to already know all the answers. This takes courage not submissiveness.

How has the mentor-disciple relationship evolved in SGI?

As with every concept we have looked at in this book, the mentor-disciple relationship has evolved as SGI has developed over the decades. For Ikeda, his own relationship with his 'Sensei', Josei Toda was forged from the outset of his practice, and that first meeting with Toda in the summer of 1947. In that moment, he chose to absolutely believe Toda's words and take him as his mentor. This could be contrasted with the Western approach which would be to pick and choose the statements or ideas we personally find appealing. But such an approach stultifies growth by limiting our choices to what we already know and perceive. Instead, by absolutely trusting him, Ikeda regards his ten years of mentorship by Toda as the source of everything he has achieved and become. The very first entry in *A Youthful Diary* from 31st May, 1949 includes the line, "Must advance toward the dawn, never wavering in my conviction, following my lifelong – no, my eternal mentor."[13]

Many later passages show how keenly Ikeda felt to aim to fulfil his mentor's expectations, calling out to him, "Mr Toda, no matter what, I will fight till the last moment. Please wait a little longer. Please don't misjudge me – you'll see."[14] In 1954 he writes, "A lifelong mentor makes me profoundly happy. No honour in the world compares to that of having a lifelong mentor."[15]

In post-war Japan, the culture of mentorship was a universal creed embedded in society from masters and mistresses in tea ceremonies and calligraphy to martial arts and flower arranging. Toda became the Soka Gakkai members' 'Sensei' (teacher) and on his passing Ikeda became the new mentor over time. In writing *The Human Revolution* in the mid-1960s, Ikeda developed the concept of mentor and disciple and the oneness of mentor and disciple,

"Oneness meant a perfect unity or fusion... For Shin'ichi (Ikeda's name in the novel), everything started from his oneness with Toda - the oneness in the depths of their minds."

Ikeda was therefore elucidating the difference between mentorship when one merely follows instructions and learns from someone and the spiritual bond of mentor and disciple which involves deeply connecting with the heart of the mentor and following his actions in this spirit.

Outside Japan, the mentor-disciple relationship was sometimes less explicit in the foundational decades of SGI, at least for local members. It was clearly expounded during the expansive growth phase of the American organisation in the early 1970s[16] but was less prevalent in the British movement, perhaps because the UK organisation did not start to grow to any great extent until the 1980s. This lack of emphasis on Ikeda as mentor may have been in part because it was distinctly unfamiliar to Westerners. However, I believe it is more likely a result of the relationship with the Nichiren Shoshu priesthood in the late 1970s and 1980s. The priests did not want to afford Ikeda any special status in comparison to their High Priest, given the difficulties between the priests and lay organisation that led to Ikeda's resignation from the Soka Gakkai presidency in 1979. During this time however, Ikeda was President of SGI and an inspirational figure for overseas members. For example Gary McCarty's book, *Daisaku Ikeda – Ambassador of Peace* published by the American organisation in 1984 affords great respect to Ikeda's achievements and personal character. He is described as 'confidant and counsellor' to millions of SGI members but there is no reference to the mentor-disciple relationship anywhere in the book.[17]

The split with the Nichiren Shoshu priesthood afforded SGI the opportunity of bringing the mentor-disciple relationship back to the forefront. Beginning in the mid-1990s, and fully developed in the 2000s, Ikeda as the mentor has become an essential aspect of SGI Buddhism around the world. This is tied to the idea of successors and the transmission of the teaching to future generations. As Ikeda states in *The Wisdom of the Lotus Sutra* after discussing the oneness of mentor and disciple,

"In a broader sense, no important undertaking, no movement, nothing of truly great import can be completed in a single generation."[18]

For some older members, attached to the teachings as they were espoused in the 1980s, the change can be unwelcome. However, I would argue that, like all the developments we have noted in this book, this is a worthwhile evolution. The teachings, with a lack of emphasis on the mentor-disciple relationship at that time, were no more a 'traditional orthodoxy' than at any other point in the evolving continuum of Buddhism.

THE EVOLVING BUDDHA

Nichiren Buddhism on a different, darker path

In understanding and appreciating the mentor-disciple relationship, it may be useful to consider what SGI would be like without it. Clark Strand hypothesises that without Toda following his mentor into prison, a revived Soka Kyoiku Gakkai would have continued to be a limited educational reform movement after the war, if any of Makiguchi's other followers had tried to reignite it.[19] It is in life-to-life relationships that Nichiren Buddhism has spread, not in mere ideas.

Furthermore, SGI's particular brand of Nichiren Buddhism-humanistic, universalist, tolerant and cross cultural is not an automatic given. This has come about through the inspiration and leadership of the three founding presidents. When people are suspicious of the respect afforded Makiguchi, Toda and Ikeda, the connection between their actions and teachings and the warm, dynamic and compassionate discussion meetings that participants are involved in, is rarely understood.

To illustrate this, it is useful to highlight that it is not inevitable if you follow Nichiren Buddhism, that you would end up with an inclusive peace-orientated model such as SGI. This is thanks to Ikeda.

The case of Chigaku Tanaka (1861-1939) shows how Nichiren Buddhism led by the wrong man can go down a far darker path. In creating an interpretation called, 'Nichirenism', Tanaka manipulated Nichiren Buddhist philosophy to support nationalistic ideas and the militarist expansion that dominated Japan in the 1930s. He set up a society and lectured around the country, associating the spread of the Lotus Sutra with the unification of the world under Japanese rule and reverence for the Emperor. This is in stark contrast to Makiguchi's rejection of militarism at around the same time.

Tanaka's ideas not only supported the motives of the Japanese Imperial war machine, at times they inspired some of the decisive moments in the conflict. A notable example is that of Kanji Ishiwara, an operations officer in the Japanese force stationed in the early 1930s in Manchuria, China, who was a follower of Tanaka, believing in a warped militarist version of Nichirenism. Ishiwara instigated the 'Manchuria Incident' on Sep 18th-19th 1931, when the Chinese garrison was attacked. Although not authorised by his superiors, the action played into sentiment at home towards a more aggressive policy in China. Ishiwara was made a hero, and the government became committed to a military takeover of Manchuria which would lead to the tragic Japanese invasion of much of East Asia in World War Two.[20] The extreme difference in interpretation of Nichiren's mandate by the pre-war Nichirenists, elucidates the importance of following a good teacher and a wise teaching but also makes clear how easy it is to fall into arbitrary and conflicting reinterpretations without clear guidance.

Eastern and Western perceptions

In considering the mentor and disciple relationship, Clark Strand describes a dialogue he had with a New York University professor who was a leading researcher on the neuroscience of meditation. They compared notes on the difference in interviewing American and Asian Buddhists about their Buddhist practice. "The difference was this. A person raised in

America would speak frankly and openly about their individual experience with Buddhism and the spiritual benefits they felt they had gained from it. Ask someone raised in Asia, and they would speak about their teacher – the spiritual mentor who had taught them the practice – and the benefits of their *relationship* with that person. If they had experienced significant gains or improvements in their life, these would be explained in the context of that relationship, as if the relationship itself had been what made these things happen."[21]

Despite this stark cultural difference, Westerners have come to understand the mentor and disciple relationship within SGI and to choose Ikeda as their mentor. Orlando Bloom, the Hollywood actor is a practising SGI Buddhist who has chosen Ikeda as his 'Sensei'. In his filmed recount of his encounter with Ikeda, Bloom describes the warmth, positive regard and even strictness of his dialogue with Ikeda. He describes Ikeda's authenticity and how he found a true connection with his heart and spirit which encouraged Bloom to embrace his own authenticity.[22] What is even more notable is that renowned figures outside SGI and from diverse religious traditions have not only appreciated the mentor-disciple tradition but have even chosen Ikeda as a mentor in their lives.

Lawrence Carter, Dean at Morehouse College and protector of the legacy of Martin Luther King Jr. has even written a book about his relationship with Ikeda, *A Baptist Preacher's Buddhist Teacher*. Carter elucidates his path of discipleship with Martin Luther King, Jesus and Ikeda.

"Being a disciple is not the same as joining a club. It is not as simple as declaring allegiance or choosing a side. It is a purposeful decision to try to understand the greater vision held by a mentor and to try to actualize that vision in our own life. The decision to be a disciple is fundamentally a choice about the values, virtues, and the vision of victory we have for ourselves and the world, and how to avoid vices."[23]

On the other side of the world, N. Radhakrishnan, Chairman of the Indian Council for Gandhian studies, New Dehli, has extolled the efficacy of the mentor-disciple relationship writing his own book, *Ikeda Sensei – The Triumph of Mentor and Disciple*. Radhakrishnan acknowledges the challenge the concept faces from Western thinking as contrary to rational, critical scientific enquiry. But he counters that the mentor-disciple relationship is far from exotic or irrational and that all great individuals have a mentor, citing the example of Gandhi and how he affected change in his disciples including the founding father of modern India, Jawaharlal Nehru.

"What sustains the mentor-disciple relationship is the devotion and understanding – devotion to the ideals the mentor represents and admiration on the part of the mentor of the essential qualities of the disciple,"[24] states Radhakrishnan.

He further clarifies the practical logic in having a mentor:

"The human mind, which Gandhi described as a 'restless bird' needs spiritual nourishment and proper anchoring. The inner turmoil needs proper management so that the boat does not turn over or capsize. It is here the role of an experienced boatsman in the form of a mentor or one who has mastered the forces which govern the mind, body and spirit comes in."[25]

THE EVOLVING BUDDHA

My experience of developing the mentor-disciple relationship

For most SGI members if not all, their relationship with Daisaku Ikeda as their mentor is a developing journey rather than an immediate and absolute outcome of beginning to practice SGI Buddhism. As we have seen, there is considerable conditioning in the West that must be challenged and reflected upon before engaging with having a mentor in Buddhism.

And so it was with my own experience. In my first couple of years of practice, I would often tell people I found Founding Soka Gakkai President Tsunesaburo Makiguchi the most appealing of the three presidents, the scholarly primary head teacher who looked like a kindly grandfather. It took some time of studying Ikeda's writings but, more importantly, hearing others' experiences of their relationship with 'Sensei', for me to begin to approach taking Ikeda as my mentor.

I had the good fortune of being part of the SGI-UK youth division for ten years and in that time had the opportunity to receive training as a 'Dedicated Soka', a group for young men who would give support with the organisation of major Buddhist activities. We would also study together and have talks given by youth leaders. One highlight was a course in a hostel high up in the mountains of the Lake District in Northern England, where we profoundly shared, bonded and sang songs around the campfire. I remember one lecture at such an event by our then Soka Chief, later Youth Division Leader, which particularly moved my heart when he relayed his connection with Sensei which brought him to tears. I finally resolved to make Ikeda my mentor and told the Young Men's Division leader that this was my vow.

Although I have never met Ikeda, this vow of mentor and disciple has been an essential part of the expansion of my life in the intervening decades. I always try to end my daimoku in the morning with connecting to Ikeda's heart and to act as he would in the challenges to come that day. In particularly, in nerve wracking situations, such as speaking in front of a large hall of people, imagining Ikeda standing next to me, sooths my fears.

Having a mentor has, for example, been instrumental in how I responded to the many challenges thrown at me at work during the COVID-19 crisis from difficult parents and stressed staff to major logistical issues in reorganising my school to be 'COVID safe'. I reached for Ikeda's guidance and chanted to take action as his disciple rather than from a place of ego and fear. The actual proof came in successfully and safely returning all pupils to school by the end of the summer term when many schools in the UK remained shut, bringing staff and parents on board through dialogue and support.

A relationship of choice and freedom

Above all, the mentor-disciple relationship should be understood as based on choice and freedom. The scholar, Richard Hughes Seager interviewed Einosuke Akiya, the then President of the Soka Gakkai in the early 2000s regarding the mentor-disciple relationship, who told him:

"It's really the disciple's choice and decision to follow the mentor's vision. In response, it is the mentor's wish to raise and foster the disciple so that he can become a greater person than the mentor himself. His wish is to pull him up to where he is or even surpass him. It is the right spirit of the disciple to earnestly absorb as much as possible from the mentor."[26]

In 1967, Ikeda explained the non-hierarchical and participatory aspect of this approach by stating,

"Soka Gakkai has no leader who is absolute and supreme. Both the members and myself are comrades, moving forward toward the common objective of kosen rufu. This is the reason why I receive the members' support and cooperation – to build the solidarity that gives the Soka Gakkai the power to develop."[27]

The bond of mentor and disciple is a heart-to-heart connection, a spiritual transmission at its basis. However, it is also a means of sharing an integrated philosophical position which ensures the unity of a religion and its furtherance in the world without the risk of fragmentation, discord and the creation of a variety of arbitrary views. As we have considered with the case of Nichirenism in the 1920s and 1930s, any philosophy can take a turn towards darkness and hatred. Holding fast to SGI's interpretation of Nichiren Buddhism as evinced by Ikeda protects the community of believers from this risk.

PART 2 - IKEDA'S PHILOSOPHY

But what is so special about Ikeda's philosophy to justify following it above other positions? Before examining the key elements, it is important to point out that Ikeda's contribution to SGI philosophy is part of a continuum with Makiguchi and Toda both also providing new insights and perspectives on Nichiren Buddhism that Ikeda has built on. To a dogmatist, it is easy to attack this philosophical development as straying from the original and correct path. However, as we have seen in preceding chapters on the Lotus Sutra, Nichiren and the Gohonzon, there are no absolutes to the framework of practice since so much has evolved and changed. Even the philosophy that the followers and priesthood of Nichiren Shoshu adhere to has undergone an evolutionary process, first with Nichiren's disciple Nikko, then in the 18th century with the reformist High Priest, Nichikan who among other changes, raised the status and centrality of the Dai-Gohonzon, and finally, even with the influence of the Soka Gakkai who developed the form of gongyo under Toda that lay Shoshu practitioners still follow.

The dignity of life

Ikeda's great contribution has been in interpreting Nichiren Buddhism for modern times. Such an approach is synonymous with Nichiren himself who wrote, "When it comes to studying the teachings of Buddhism, one must first understand the time." (WND 1, p538)

To make a teaching relevant and accessible, in order for it to continue to help those who are suffering, it must be revisited through the language, understanding and values of contemporary society without compromising the heart of its message. This is what Ikeda has done so successfully and is the root of SGI's success from the 1970s onwards.

Rooted in his mentor's awakening that the Buddha is life itself, Ikeda has placed respect for the dignity of life as the central tenet of SGI's philosophy. Life is a universal value, open and flexible enough to find common ground with people across the world but also clear enough an anchor to root and affirm the philosophy. Do one's actions protect and nurture life in front and all around you or do they not? A simple, practical reflection that every individual can apply to their circumstances.

Inner transformation

Secondly, Ikeda has taken Toda's concept of human revolution and made it the central purpose of Nichiren Buddhist practice. As is oft quoted from his novel, *The Human Revolution*, Ikeda's vision of this process is summed up when he wrote,

"A great revolution in just a single individual will help achieve a change in the destiny of a nation, and, further, will enable a change in the destiny of all humankind."[28]

The process of human revolution aims, therefore, to reform social and institutional structures but does so through individual inner transformation. Personal change through practising Buddhism then enacts wider change; the changed individual makes different choices to the ones they would have made, therefore interacting with their environment in a way that creates significantly more value. For example, before I started practising Buddhism I had never stuck with a job for more than 2 years before becoming so bored or restless that I just had to quit it. When I started my first teaching job, 2 years after starting to chant, I determined to stick with it for 7 years. In the end I stayed at that particular school for 8 years. This was a clear example to me of my human revolution. The revolution was in fact internal change – greater patience, resilience and fortitude in a far more challenging job than I had ever been in before. The external 'effect' manifested as my not giving up in my workplace.

The inner change of human revolution also affords the practitioner the opportunity to reframe difficulties and seemingly negative events in line with the Buddhist concept of changing poison into medicine. This corresponds with much recent research on the effects of trauma. Most of us have heard of post-traumatic stress disorder or PTSD, but few know about 'post-traumatic growth', a term developed by Richard Tedeschi and Lawrence Calhoun of the University of North Carolina at Charlotte. The researchers found that trauma and adverse life experiences did not necessarily lead to stress and disorders. They could lead to a renewed sense of purpose, stronger relationships, inner strength, a greater appreciation for life and a deeper spiritual life.[29]

But what factors allow some to experience growth and inner revitalisation from negative life experiences whilst others are seemingly damaged and traumatised? Although neither are mutually exclusive, resilience researchers Steven Southwick of Yale School of Medicine and Dennis Charney of the Icahn School of Medicine at Mount Sinai found a series of key characteristics which led to a resilient response. These included: having a worthy goal or mission in life; receiving social support and having a transcendent or spiritual source of meaning.[30] In other words, key aspects of our Buddhist practice that we have examined: kosen rufu, the support of SGI meetings and the chanting of the daimoku are components which could develop resilience in the face of negativity. Scientists have shown that although genetics can contribute, resilience is not a fixed trait and we can change, reframe and revitalise our lives regardless of our circumstances thus, in Buddhist terms, carrying out our human revolution.

Buddhist Humanism

Thirdly, Ikeda has introduced the notion of Buddhist Humanism. In contrast to Western Humanism which puts humanity above nature, Buddhist Humanism centres on the human being as an interdependent part of the chain of life. Its pillars are peace, culture and education which can be adapted to different countries and cultures. Seager has stated, "Buddhist Humanism seeks to inspire, empower, and unite people around the globe by basing its appeal on the universal human experience."[31]

It is this universalism in Ikeda's thought based on 'our shared humanity' irrespective of religious affiliation and ethnic or cultural boundaries that has led to the emphasis on global citizenship in SGI and its engagement in interfaith dialogue. Olivier Urbain, former director of the Toda Peace Institute, defines Ikeda's philosophy for peace, encompassed in the term Buddhist Humanism, as containing three key elements: inner transformation, global citizenship and dialogue.[32]

Rabbi Abraham Cooper of the Simon Wiesenthal Center, a Jewish human rights organisation has collaborated with SGI in creating a Japanese version of the Holocaust exhibition at a time when the tabloid Japanese media was still promoting the views of Holocaust deniers. Cooper recalled to Seager that the first time he met Ikeda around the time of the Jewish festival of Hanukkah, "It dawned on me after about three minutes that Ikeda knew all about Hanukkah. I was explaining it but, yeah, he knew all about it. He seemed like a nice guy, very approachable. A really sharp guy, very open."[33]

The evolution of Ikeda's philosophy

The SGI movement today is established on this broad, inclusive and global path set by Ikeda. But it is important to note that, as with Nichiren, Ikeda's philosophy and understanding have been on their own evolutionary journey through a process of reflection and refinement. Ikeda often refers to how he is the man he is today thanks to the guidance of his mentor. Toda was an inspirational leader with the grandest of visions. However, he was also a man of his time. His powerful firebrand oration and absolutist approach empowered the suffering populace of Japan reeling from the war. In so doing, his form of shakubuku, the sharing of Nichiren Buddhist practice, rejected erroneous religions and encouraged the removal of previously sacred objects in the new practitioner's homes. The rapid expansion of the Soka Gakkai in the 1950s may have also resulted in some unintended consequences.

Kiyoaki Murata in *Japan's New Buddhism – An Objective Account of Soka Gakkai* notes, "In the heyday of the shakubuku drive, there were clearly many cases of extremism through genuine misunderstanding on the part of the overzealous members of the lower ranks of Soka Gakkai. But such excesses should not be identified with Toda himself nor with Soka Gakkai's policy on shakubuku, for Soka Gakkai leaders did stress the need for moderation and reasonableness."[34] For example, Toda told an audience not to remove a convert's Shinto tablet themselves from their home but the convert should choose to do so themselves with consent from their family.[35]

Ikeda assumed the presidency in 1960 still reflecting Toda's exclusivist approach and in his May 3rd inaugural address reiterated the aim of challenging erroneous religions. However, in a short space of time Ikeda began to travel a new path. James White of Stanford University, an early observer of the Soka Gakkai observed that, "since 1962 a tolerance and willingness to work with groups on non-religious matters has developed,"[36] and that around the same time the Gakkai daily newspaper, the Seikyo Shimbun moderated its language. In 1967, members could say, "If someone feels he is happy with the Nembutsu or Shingon sect, that's OK."[37] By early 1964, Ikeda was stressing a gentle and reasonable form of conversion based on showing a good example rather than confrontation of beliefs. In the editorial of the Seikyo Shimbun on 4th January, 1967, readers were encouraged by the following, "Let us carry out shakubuku without being bound by narrow viewpoints but always with a broad, flexible attitude."[38]

Around the same time, Ikeda rejected the concept of building a 'national hall of worship' with the support of the state. He reclarified that in Nichiren's time, this would have referred to an ordination platform for priests contributed by the monarch. In contrast, in the modern democratic era, a temple funded by the people (in this case Gakkai members) would be the aspiration. This led to the building of the Sho-Hondo or Grand Main Temple at Taiseki-ji in the early 1970s. By 1969, Ikeda's conciliatory and open approach was fully established where he could find the commonalities in Christianity and Buddhism and state: "Therefore we can respect each other, not being mutually hostile. We can study each other's doctrine and thus elevate ourselves."[39] However, events in 1970 would accelerate this process further.

A crisis becomes a turning point

With continued expansion and success came envy and suspicion. Hirotatsu Fujiwara, a conservative political commentator and professor described by author Henry Scott-Stokes as a "rebarbative hack", wrote a book, *I Denounce, Soka Gakkai* in which Seager describes the "deliberately incendiary quality of his arguments in which he skewed recent events and reiterated old charges,"[40] much of the book making oblique attacks on Ikeda.

Rather than repudiating or ignoring the charges, a group of Gakkai members foolishly approached Fujiwara to correct his inaccuracies and when this failed, requested he delayed publication. Fujiwara then used the event to attack the Soka Gakkai further for trying to disrupt free speech, resulting in the issue being debated heatedly in the Japanese parliament, the Diet.

Turning poison into medicine, Ikeda used the crisis as an opportunity to develop the Soka Gakkai's universalist and progressive approach even further. Seager describes his May 1970 speech at the 33rd Soka Gakkai General Meeting as a watershed moment, for his philosophy and the movement in general. Whilst affirming to take lessons from the incident and not make the same mistakes again (which included formally separating the Komeito political party from the Soka Gakkai), he called for further openness, democratisation and moderation in approach, including an absolute commitment to free speech and religious freedom.

He outlined three key principles as the bedrock of this new approach as Seager describes, "the heart of Nichiren's message to the modern world: absolute pacifism, the sanctity of human life, and respect for human dignity. 'These principles are universal to humankind, transcending the limits of religions, race, nationality or ideology.... They derive from the essential nature of human existence. Everything starts from this humanism,'"[41] Ikeda explained.

Emboldened by this outward looking, universalist approach, Ikeda set out to actively engage in cultural exchange through dialogue, starting with his meetings with British historian, Arnold Toynbee. Toynbee encouraged Ikeda to continue to meet other great thinkers, providing him with further connections such as Aurelio Peccei, first President of the Club of Rome. Through his many dialogues, Ikeda has had the opportunity to further hone his perspective and humanistic outlook.

The 1991 split with the priesthood liberated Ikeda further to express these views and to further democratize SGI. In the year prior to this, he had already urged SGI-USA on a visit to the States, to become a less rigid organisation, to reject authoritarian leadership and to become more democratic, participatory and open so there was no discrimination between members and non-members.[42] The SGI charter formalized in 1995 was the culmination of Ikeda's vision affirming a spirit of religious tolerance, respect for cultural diversity and the independence and autonomy of the constituent organisations in each country.

Ikeda's life example

"The purpose of the appearance of Shakyamuni Buddha, the lord of teachings, lies in his behaviour as a human being." (WND 1, p851-2)

However noble a philosophy Ikeda may espouse, it is his life example, his behaviour as a human being which must inspire his disciples to enact a human revolution in their own lives. For the members who worked alongside him in the pioneer days, it was his commitment, compassion and action which instilled in them, "a confidence that allowed us to change our lives. It was he who taught us the oneness of mentor and disciple,"[43] stated Tadashi Murata, a member from Kansai in those early days.

For Gary McCarty, the SGI-USA writer who worked alongside Ikeda in the 1970s and 1980s, he was never self-serving and always warmly embraced and thanked McCarty, even though he was one of innumerable people Ikeda would be dealing with every day. Ikeda's lack of affectation, great compassion and vision for peace resonate powerfully in McCarty's study of him.[44]

Ikeda is a source of inspiration for SGI members the world over and for those who have never met him through the drama that plays out on the pages of *The Human Revolution* and *The New Human Revolution*. Yet the testaments of those outside of SGI provide greater proof to the cynic of Ikeda's genuine personality and motive.

Lawrence Carter found him, "a profoundly authentic and humble person, spiritual genius that he obviously was."[45] On his dialogue with Ikeda, he said,

"What I sensed most from him was a tremendous sincerity, unpretentious, open and honest, with no ego at all. He seemed to be coming from a place of such profound non-violence, humility and concern for humanity that even after spending a relatively brief time with him, I felt heard, seen, known, and whole. I was at peace."[46]

Carter saw in Ikeda someone who wanted and could empower him to revitalise his own Christian practice and concludes, "of all the spiritual and philosophical leaders I have met…it is this Japanese lay Buddhist,… who has been the most impressive in terms of sincerity, learning, action, integrity, achievement and global vision. Daisaku Ikeda has captured my heart, my mind and my spirit in a way that I find difficult to describe – except to say that at last, after many years, I have found another mentor."[47]

The scholar Richard Hughes Seager found in his research, "As I grew to admire his disciples' consistency in expressing empowerment for self and others in ways both healthy and sane, I also came to trust Ikeda according to the principle which is both Buddhist and Christian – that by the fruit you shall know the tree."[48]

In his chapter 'The Ultimate Declaration', Clark Strand, the pan-Buddhist writer, explains to a new SGI member suspicious of why 'Ikeda's name is written large' within the organisation. It is because, like Toda and Makiguchi, he stood at the forefront for kosen rufu and has taken the ultimate risk, taking all his actions, "with his life force and his life blood." Strand asks her if she too will make that stand, "to add your name to that declaration? And if not, why not?"[49]

PART 3 - ON PERSECUTIONS

Despite the respect, praise and friendship of many leading figures from Gorbachev to Mandela (the latter having sought out a meeting with Ikeda, rather than the other way round), and, to date 396 honorary degrees from 380 different universities spanning all regions of the world, Ikeda has been attacked and pilloried in the media and online. Why is this? Gwee Yee Hean, a senior academic from Singapore explained the controversy to Seager, "When you become a great man... there will always be people who do not like you."[50]

Why has Ikeda been attacked?

But I consider there to be more than Ikeda's greatness as a cause for the attacks on him. By slandering Ikeda, those who wish to do the SGI harm have a human target to undermine the whole Buddhist movement. The human propensity to gossip is hardwired from humanity's ancient ancestry and so a human target is far more tangible than an organisation to cause consternation and concern. Furthermore, by attacking Ikeda, his detractors aim to sow doubt in the members' hearts and drive a wedge between mentor and disciples.

So behind the accusations against Ikeda is a desire to undermine the SGI movement. But what are the reasons that the Soka Gakkai and the SGI would attract persecution and calumny? The first reason is the unprecedented and enormous expansion of the Soka Gakkai in the 1950s and 1960s in Japan.

With literally thousands of people converting to a new faith in a local area, sometimes in a matter of weeks or months, long-established temples and their vested interests were losing their parishioners at an alarming rate. Fighting back at this new movement was a response to defend their tradition and sometimes in the case of priests, their livelihood.

At the same time, especially in the 1950s as noted by Murata earlier in the chapter, the growth was so rapid that new members at the grass roots could be sharing the practice in a forthright manner after a few days of chanting, not sanctioned by the leadership of the movement. This could cause misunderstanding and upset. Ikeda's presidency in the 1960s, as we have seen, reinforced a policy of moderation to ensure such incidents did not recur and it has been noted that reports in newspapers regarding overzealous propagation were largely confined to a short period between 1952 and 1956.[51]

The second reason for criticism of the Soka Gakkai was its decision to be involved in politics by founding a political party, the Komeito or Clean Government Party. This is not so unusual; for example, the Christian Democratic Union Party in Germany was founded in 1945 and has been the dominant political party in the country leading many governments since World War Two.

Komeito was established as a reformist movement to challenge the corruption of Japanese politics still led by families associated with the wartime militarist regime. SGI has consistently reiterated that it has no intentions to found political parties in any other country and has never done so. As referred to earlier, in 1970, along with other reforms, Komeito formally separated from the Soka Gakkai and has continued to function as a separate entity whilst continuing to enjoy voter support from Soka Gakkai members.

In fact, the Komeito has been in the ruling coalition in Japan for the past twenty years but prior to that, in the 1990s, it was part of a number of opposition parties who posed a substantial threat to the dominant Liberal Democratic Party. It is no coincidence that the most vociferous attacks on Ikeda came in the mid-1990s from established media and with the tacit support of the LDP, an example of which will follow.

Thirdly, the split with the Nichiren Shoshu priesthood in 1991 created a whole new contingent who became bitterly opposed to SGI's liberal, reformist agenda led by Ikeda. The priests in losing the support of the vast majority of lay members had cause to feel vengeful.

It is also important to note that scholars have absolved Ikeda from any of the accusations made against him. For example, Takesato Watanabe, a professor of Media Ethics at Doshisha University, Kyoto and Adam Gamble, an investigative reporter have concluded, "Indeed, despite his many detractors in Japan, it is well-nigh impossible to come up with any hard facts that justify an indictment of Ikeda's character."[52]

A perspective from the Lotus Sutra

Persecutions of Ikeda and SGI also resonate on a scriptural level for practitioners, with the three powerful enemies as outlined in the 13th chapter of the Lotus Sutra. These are the three groups of people who persecute the votaries of the Lotus Sutra in the dark age after Shakyamuni's passing. They are 1) lay people ignorant of Buddhism who denounce the votaries of the

Lotus Sutra, 2) arrogant and cunning priests who think they have attained what they have not attained and slander the votaries, 3) priests revered as saints and respected by the general public, who in fear of losing fame or profit, induce the secular authorities to persecute the votaries of the Lotus Sutra. It is likely that the Mahayanan creators of the Lotus Sutra suffered persecution in stepping beyond the monastic confines of traditional Buddhism at that time, and these categories reflected their real experiences.

For modern SGI members, just as they did for Nichiren, they provide a scriptural reframing of their feelings under external forces. Rather than fall into victim mode, SGI members can consider the abuse and injustices hurled upon Nichiren and the three founding presidents, and feel emboldened that this negativity is part of the process, in fact a vital part, toward revealing our Buddhahood.

I have found the concept empowering in my own life when I have experienced criticism of my teaching, challenging conversations with school parents or conflict with fellow members of staff. I remember one day after work in which I had felt berated on all sides – from an inspector who had observed my teaching that day; from a parent who came to see me regarding their child and from a senior member of staff. I chanted to embrace these challenges whilst still asserting my 'best self'. Lying in bed that night, instead of feeling washed out and exhausted, the most incredible tingling sensation went through my body and I felt refreshed and revived. I felt my chanting was manifesting Nichiren's spirit when he wrote,

"When I think I will surely eradicate these karmic impediments and in the future go to the pure land of Eagle

Peak, though various grave persecutions fall on me like rain and boil up like clouds, since they are for the sake of the Lotus Sutra, even these sufferings do not seem like sufferings at all." (WND 1, p191)

In the same spirit, Daisaku Ikeda has calmly faced horrendous persecutions from the Osaka incident when he was falsely accused of election fraud and vindicated in court, to base slander from Japan's tabloid press. My persecutions seemed trifling in comparison. It is these media attacks on which I will now focus on.

Early media invective

The story of the media response to the Soka Gakkai and Ikeda begins in the 1950s when the press disparagingly labelled the movement, 'a gathering of the sick and poor'. Toda in repost took this not as an insult, but as a badge of honour. For what is Buddhism worth if it is not aimed at relieving the suffering of ordinary people? Incidents of forceful shakubuku by overzealous new converts were recounted in the Japanese press, but James White wrote that, "One notable feature of these data is that nearly all the incidents occurred before 1957," in other words during the initial time of massive growth and momentum.[53] Richard Hughes Seager asked Einosuke Akiya about those times and the criticism that Toda had to rein in the passionate drive particularly of the young men of those times. Akiya explained,

"'Young people were often criticized for their heated discussions during shakubuku," he recalls, "But you have to understand that to introduce somebody to a new practice – if that person already has a belief system – you have to dialogue with them to change their view. It's like revolutionizing a person's worldview. We were not savvy communicators. All we felt was passion and conviction: 'I really want to talk about this. I want you to understand. I want you to start this practice.' You can imagine the reaction."[54]

This heady expansion gave ammunition to the movement's detractors in the press but it also resulted in the empowerment and wellbeing of millions of families and was the initial cause for SGI's later success across the world.

As we considered earlier, Ikeda's guidance has been of moderation, tolerance and respect and indeed contrary to the perception created by the Japanese media in the 1950s, this was also the case with the vast majority of members even from the early days. James White found in an analysis of 5 surveys of the 1960s that only 4% of Japanese members named strangers as those who converted them and a study published in 1962 indicated that Gakkai members overwhelmingly recognized, the "social necessity of co-operation with individuals and groups of other religious persuasions: it noted a "surprising" degree of tolerance and liberalism."[55]

An experience of sharing Buddhism

Shakubuku, the sharing of Nichiren Buddhist practice is a challenge in any era. One's own reservations, self-consciousness and negativity must be challenged to share something deeply personal that can change a person's life positively on a fundamental level. Some of my most joyous moments have been when I have mustered up the courage to share the practice.

THE EVOLVING BUDDHA

One occasion took place a few years back when I was returning from a residential school trip camping in the woods for a couple of days to learn about the Stone Age with a group of Third Grade pupils. Exhausted from lack of sleep, things took a turn for the worse when our coach broke down just outside Birmingham on one of the busiest parts of motorway in the UK known as 'Spaghetti Junction'. The motorway was closed for us at the peak of the Friday rush hour and we made the local press that evening due to the ensuing chaos. After transferring to two different replacement buses, I plonked my rattled self down next to the coach driver.

Tomasz came from Poland and had studied philosophy at Warsaw University. A lively conversation ensued, including a discussion on Buddhism. We exchanged numbers and a few weeks later I drove the 2 hours out of London to take him to his local discussion meeting. Eventually, Tomasz decided to take up chanting along with his fiancée and found immediate benefit. When Brexit arrived in the UK, Tomasz and his partner decided to move back to Poland but they continue to chant. Last year, I received a text from him. Tomasz had been made Deputy Mayor of his town and signed off with 'This chanting really works.' Nothing gives me greater joy than to empower somebody in this way.

Japanese media atrocities

For critics of SGI and Ikeda, spurious claims on the internet or in Japan's tabloid press are perfect ammunition. But is there no smoke without fire? You don't have to take my word for it or anyone else aligned with SGI. Independent academics have consistently demolished the inflammatory claims made against Ikeda. One book stands out in this regard written by the aforementioned noted media academics, Watanabe and Gamble entitled, *A Public Betrayed - An Inside Look at Japanese Media Atrocities and Their Warnings to the West*. It tackles the often salacious, unverified and unaccountable tabloid press in Japan, who have, the authors describe, committed 'media atrocities' including denying the holocaust and Japan's role in war crimes such as the Nanjing massacre. They devote a whole chapter to the 'smearing of a Buddhist leader', Daisaku Ikeda.

In Japan, it is the weekly news magazines, *shukanshis*, rather than the daily newspapers that are quick to report sensationalist material. In an industry where powerful news and publishing corporations dominate and libel suits are extremely rare, intense commercial competition has motivated some of the weekly *shukanshis* to stretch well beyond the bounds of truth. Alongside this, the weeklies advertise their most sensational and eye-popping stories in simple, pithy headlines in advertisements on most train services. A group of scholars conservatively estimated that beyond the readership of the magazines, 10-20 million people are exposed to the headlines per week on public transport.[56]

There is a saying in Japan, 'the nail that sticks out is hammered down'. In a highly conformist culture, difference is not celebrated but attacked. The Japanese even have a word for it, *ijime* which means 'different from us' and represents the group psychology which results in bullying in the classroom and rejection in the workplace. Jun Kamei, a long-term writer and editor for *Shuhan Shincho*, the notorious weekly magazine that victimized Ikeda in the 1990s, acknowledges the magazine would regularly instigate media *ijime*.[57] SGI and Ikeda being non-conformist, pacifist and different to mainstream Japan were prime targets. Combine this with lax and unchecked reporting in which there is even a journalist term coined, *netsuko* meaning 'the manufacturing of the news', and you have a recipe for libellous content and bald-faced lies.

The smearing of a Buddhist leader

The case against Ikeda centred on the reporting of one weekly, the aforementioned *Shuhan Shincho*, who over a sustained period of years in the 1990s took particular delight in publishing spurious material about Ikeda and SGI. When SGI and Ikeda took the matter to court, they were vindicated in a strongly worded verdict which emphasized the false nature of the charges against Ikeda. Watanabe and Gamble note that this is underscored by the fact that less than twenty such verdicts were upheld in such cases between 1965 and 2001 in Japan.

The case in brief focused on the accusations of two former Soka Gakkai members Mr and Mrs Nobuhira. In 1992, the Soka Gakkai received complaints that the couple had duped and coerced local members to lend them large amounts of money which was not repaid. The Nobuhiras were removed from their leadership positions after refusing to step down and were taken to court with eight different lawsuits which ordered them to repay to the lenders what amounted to equivalent to $687,400 US dollars. They formally left the Soka Gakkai in December 1993. The couple also tried to sue Ikeda regarding a cemetery plot they had purchased, the courts dismissing it as baseless, as Ikeda had no involvement.

As Gamble and Watanabe point out, this pattern of dubious and immoral behaviour should have "raised a string of bright red flags for any journalists considering writing about the couple's charges against Ikeda."[58] Instead in February 1996 the *Shuhan Shincho* leapt on a false memoir which detailed allegations made against Ikeda by Nobuko Nobuhira, heavily promoting slanderous and bogus headlines. The Nobuhiras for their part, filed only a civil suit not criminal charges against Ikeda, even though they claimed to be victims of grave criminal behaviour. Rather than seeking to have Ikeda jailed, they sought financial compensation and publicity through the press. Gamble and Watanabe point out,

"Given the complete absence of supporting evidence, as well as the numerous inconsistencies of the claims, there is no doubt that (criminal) prosecutors would have dismissed the Nobuhira's claims outright."[59]

For example the later court hearing found many inconsistencies in her statements and concluded that the "reasons given for (her) confused memory are also very irrational without any convincing points, and lack credibility."[60] Mrs Nobuhira claimed an assault took place in 1983 in a building which did not even exist at that time. The final court case in its summation described the legal action "that severely lacks relevance with respect to the intentions and purposes of the civil litigation system, and is contrary to conduct in good faith and trust. Consequently, the complaint can be considered unlawful, because it abuses the right of legal action."[61]

In the meantime, *Shuhan Shincho* had everything to gain from publishing the false accusations with impunity. With Ikeda such a prominent figure in Japan, they could expect increased sales from supporters and detractors of the Soka Gakkai. After the incident, Eiichi Yamamoto, a lecturer at Gakushuin University uncovered 17 audio recordings from early 1996 of conversations between the Nobuhiras and *Shuhan Shincho* journalists in which the journalist encouraged the Nobuhiras to make their accusations more serious, "to deliver the maximum punch." Even more unnerving is the fact that the recordings include the voices of some lay leaders of Nichiren Shoshu, an anonymous member of Nichiren Shoshu having sent the recordings to Yamamoto outraged at the group's scheming against Ikeda.[62]

The Soka Gakkai successfully took *Shuhan Shincho* to court twice, winning both times. If the cases had taken place in the UK or USA compensation for damages would have been vast, but in Japan it was minimal and the profits made from printing the falsehoods far outweighed any costs paid.

Even Lawrence Carter was not free from attack by *Shuhan Shincho* who pilloried him for his association with Ikeda. In response, Carter wrote a letter to the magazine in protest where he stated:

"'Controversy' is an inevitable partner of greatness. No one who challenges the established order is free of it. Gandhi had his detractors as did Dr King. Dr Ikeda is no exception. Controversy camouflages the intense resistance of entrenched authority to conceding their special status and privilege. 'Insults' are the weapons of the morally weak; 'slander' is the tool of the spiritually bereft. Controversy is testament to the noble work of these three individuals in their respective societies."[63]

In his own book Carter writes:

"I have seen ample evidence of the good work of the SGI, the good hearts of its members, and the caring leadership of its president. My continued commitment to the SGI for nearly two decades has only strengthened my determination to work with them toward global peace."[64]

By 1998, the court proceedings were making it clear that the Nobuhira's charges were patently false. That year, the then Prime Minister of Japan, Ryutaro Hashimoto formally apologised for the Liberal Democratic Party's exploitation of the false allegations in their pamphlets and articles related to the claims.

The perpetuation of false accusations

But sadly, like Nichiren's metaphor of a single crab claw dropped into a pot of lacquer ruining its contents, the false coverage continues to emerge in the internet and even in credible journalism taking secondary sources as factual. For example in November 2003, *The Financial Times* featured the claims with no context or explanation, well after the Supreme Court had ruled all accusations untrue and illegal.[65] On the internet, unregulated and untrammelled, they can regularly still appear, promoted by those who have an interest in undermining SGI. For members who choose to stop practising (and this is absolutely their right to do so), there can be a desire to justify their rejection to themselves by building as negative a

THE EVOLVING BUDDHA

case as they can find on the internet, against Ikeda and SGI. What is empowering for SGI members is that concerted, independent academic research has dissolved these accusations and claims, revealing them as falsehoods.

What will the future hold?

At the time of writing this chapter, Ikeda is 93 years old. His photographed visits to newly-built facilities in Shinanomachi, Tokyo scotch rumours of his passing and affirm that he is still with us, but for how much longer is obviously unknown. It may be that you are reading this chapter after the death of Daisaku Ikeda. What the transition after the mentor's passing is like is also a matter of conjecture at this stage. What seems clear though is that there may be many more presidents of the Soka Gakkai and SGI but at least in the next few decades, there will not be a fourth president in the same spiritual terms. The three presidents have established the bedrock of SGI philosophy and practice. *The New Human Revolution* provides a sutra for our age and the years since the mid-2000s when Ikeda ceased making public appearances have already given the opportunity for the disciples to take the lead. It is likely the mentor-disciple relationship will be nurtured by millions of SGI members even after Ikeda's death. Ikeda himself is a model of this process, only having been with his mentor, Toda, in this lifetime for 10 years, but constantly in dialogue with him in his heart ever since.

I have never met Daisaku Ikeda in person. In fact, I missed my one, slim chance. I was in Japan when he was speaking at a Headquarters Leaders' Meeting at the Makiguchi Memorial Hall in Soka University. I tried to get a ticket for the meeting but was told a large contingent of Soka University of America students had been given the last seats. This should not have stopped me. I had heard of British brothers, who had gatecrashed a similar meeting the year before to meet Sensei. Perhaps my *ichinen*, my inner motivation, was not fully there to meet him, but regardless, I don't regret missing the opportunity. I am, like the vast majority of ordinary SGI members, a disciple who has never met his mentor. Those who have met him will become a vanishingly small minority as the years pass.

Instead, my relationship with Daisaku Ikeda has deepened over the years, as I have believed in him more and put my trust in him. Following his words and behaviour have made me a better person. Following his heart has fulfilled my life and enriched the world and the people around me. As a result, along with so many others, I can call him 'my Sensei' and share his vow for peace.

CONCLUSION

Buddhism is human-made. From its outset, unlike many philosophies and religions, it did not claim to be divinely inspired by a supreme being, but instead was a construct, a road map for maximising human life created by humanity itself.

Is religion really on the wane?

Religion, particularly in the West has had a hard time of it in the last 200 years, primarily because science has undermined the logic and believability of much of the narrative of the Judeo-Christian tradition, such as the creation of the Earth and Jesus' miracles. It may seem that we have entered a secular age without the need for the structure of a philosophy or religion.

And yet, the noted Israeli historian and author of *Sapiens* and *Homo Deus*, Yuval Noah Harari suggests modern society is very different to how we perceive it. He posits that liberalism, capitalism, communism and consumerism are all as much religions as those that are historically and conventionally described as such because they are a system of human norms and values based on a perceived natural law beyond humanity (Theist God centred religions consider God to be the basis of the superhuman order but this is not the case in all religion).[1]

For humanity to effectively work together, it creates cultures grounded on collective myths. But these are not tales of imaginary heroes or gods defeating fabulous monsters. The myths of our time are equally created by the human imagination but gain their power through shared agreement: money, the stock market, nations and even human rights are human constructs which are not absolutes and change over time. Harari states:

"Most people do not wish to accept that the order governing their lives is imaginary, but in fact every person is born into a pre-existing imagined order, and his or her desires are shaped from birth by its dominant myths. Our personal desires thereby become the imagined order's most important defences.

For instance the most cherished desires of present-day Westerners are shaped by romantic, nationalist, capitalist and humanist myths that have been around for centuries."[2]

Makiguchi, the first president of the Soka Gakkai, understood this in creating his Theory of Value which, at its most basic level, looks at all actions through the lens of whether they enhance humanity or diminish the existences of ourselves and others. Makiguchi's Value Creation thereby challenges our passive acceptance of our dominant myths.

CONCLUSION

Soka Gakkai Buddha

This book has been an effort to re-evaluate the constructs of Nichiren Buddhism, to see that, likewise, the framework of practice is not absolute and fixed nor was it in the past. Josei Toda coined the expression 'Soka Gakkai Buddha' to embody the ideal of an organisation of many members all personally transforming themselves through tackling the challenges of their daily lives, and in so doing, revealing their Buddhahood. In this sense, the Soka Gakkai and SGI are also constructs, a flexible framework to afford the realisation of the highest life state for as many as wish to engage with it. Chanting the phrase Nam-myoho-renge-kyo is the absolute, which goes beyond any human myths or order to tap a natural, universal law. But this chanting and its associated teachings find fullest expression within the structures of an organisation. Only through them can the flame of empowerment be passed on, for collective societal myths which cause suffering to humanity and destruction to the planet can then be challenged and reformed.

Hari points out in terms of societal change:

"If I alone were to stop believing in the dollar, in human rights or in the United States, it wouldn't much matter. These imagined orders are inter-subjective, so in order to change them we must simultaneously change the consciousness of billions of people, which is not easy. A change of such magnitude can be accomplished only with the help of a complex organisation."[3]

Hari has made clear, if you feel disempowered by all the awful things in the world or feel you want to make a difference, join an organisation. SGI affords us a means to establish a peaceful society through dialogue, discussion, and action in affirming collective values based on the dignity of all life, the interconnectedness of life and the environment, and respect for individual rights and freedoms.

In contrast, Hari notes how the last two hundred years have also seen how the growth of nation states and markets has resulted in the rise of the concept of individualism. With the state and market taking care of education, health and welfare, the traditional bonds of family and community which were previously relied upon in these areas, were weakened. The liberation of the individual to make his/her own choices in marriage, work or leisure outside of those bonds has resulted in freedoms and opportunities our ancestors could not even dream of.

However, it has come at a cost. Evolutionarily designed to live and think as community members, the increasing isolation of the individual has been to the detriment of our well-being.[4] Our consumer society focused on the individual sees the solution to this loss of well-being in the purchase of goods, experiences, therapies or courses. What I hope this book has also illustrated is that community, spiritual transcendence and finding a meaningful purpose in life are, as the science indicates, a far surer path to happiness. In addition, finding a great mentor in life can most fully facilitate that journey.

A performance that went wrong

As a young man, I was invited to take part in a pan-European SGI event in Milan, Italy. The meeting, held in a large conference hall, would comprise several thousand young Buddhists from all over Europe. I was invited to be part of a

CONCLUSION

choir which would sing 'Ode to Joy' from Beethoven's Symphony No.9. This piece has great significance for SGI, even becoming an important anthem, as it was in December 1990 that the Nichiren Shoshu priesthood criticised the singing of 'Ode to Joy' at an SGI meeting led by Ikeda in the previous month. They claimed it showed support for Christianity and in their minds was therefore a slander of the law. This was one of the pretexts they used to remove Ikeda as head of Nichiren Shoshu lay organisations in January 1991. This was an early point of disagreement which later led to the full separation of the two organisations.

For SGI members, nothing encompasses the difference between the inclusive and outward looking movement they are part of, and an exclusionary and blinkered viewpoint than the rejection of Beethoven's great paean to the highest potential of the human spirit, to inner joy and human freedom. 'Ode to Joy' became an anthem for SGI's own liberation from the shackles of dogmatism and authoritarianism.

Our performance was due in the middle of the event. During an interval, I left my seat to take a rest break but ended up in a long queue for the gift shop. Having finally paid, I heard the opening bars of Ode to Joy as I scrambled to get back to my seat. I felt terrible, unprofessional and completely unprepared for the performance. My head ached and I felt sick in the pit of my stomach. My expectation had been that the performance would be a transcendent moment, singing Beethoven's masterpiece in front of thousands of fellow members. Instead, I felt unnerved by my disorganisation and embarrassed at my late entry. Nonetheless, I stuck with it and sang my heart out. After chanting the next day, I came to a place where I did not feel a failure but felt a sense of appreciation that I had not given up despite the circumstances. This then emboldened me to apply this 'never give up spirit' in my challenges at work.

The Phantom City

The Lotus Sutra describes 'The Parable of the Phantom City'. A group of travellers are journeying to a treasure land, but on their way, they become weary and wish to turn back. At this point, a city appears before them where they rest and regain their spirits, ready to continue their adventure towards their goal. In fact, it is the leader of the group who has magically conjured the phantom city (which vanishes in the morning), to convince his fellow travellers to continue on their quest. The final destination represents our Buddhahood and although the writers of the Lotus Sutra probably had in mind expedient Buddhist teachings, the phantom city can represent any goal we have or activity we partake in on our spiritual journey.

My experience in Milan, can likewise be seen in terms of the phantom city, an experience which was not an end in itself, but something I can take from on my path to reveal my Buddhahood. The preparation and build up towards it was as important as the performance.

The tale of the phantom city resonates with Hari's concept of collective cultural myths but also the evolutionary process of the constructs we have examined in this book. In seeing Nichiren's own journey, his understanding of his mission and his development of the Gohonzon, we see the continuum of his process to access the eternal. Even the Lotus Sutra in its many guises, is a phantom city in and of itself, guiding the traveller towards enlightenment.

CONCLUSION

An all-embracing spirit

Nichiren wrote, "Though the adherents of the non-Buddhist scriptures were unaware of it, the wisdom of such men contained at heart the wisdom of Buddhism." (WND 1, p1122) This is the all-encompassing spirit of Nichiren Buddhism which SGI and Daisaku Ikeda have made a reality. A spirit which can embrace a southern Baptist Christian minister such as Lawrence Carter, who can see the ultimate reality transcending all constructs when he says, "It's very simple. There are many names for that power, that force, that principle, that law which governs the universe."[5] A spirit which equally embraces a communist atheist such as Chinese Premier, Zhou Enlai who insisted on meeting Ikeda despite being in poor health, shortly before he passed away. The scholar Olivier Urbain has used the metaphor of an orchestra to describe Ikeda's universalist approach to engaging in dialogue with those of other faiths:

"There is no music without instruments or human voice. Once a musician has chosen an instrument, the goal is still to play music. Seriously devoting oneself to one specific instrument, for instance the piano, and trying to reach musical excellence, makes it difficult and often impossible to practice several instruments at the same time. This corresponds to Ikeda having chosen Nichiren Buddhism. However the goal of becoming an excellent pianist is not to show the superiority of the piano over all other instruments, but to be able to produce music that will touch the hearts of many listeners, and also to perform in ensembles, bands and orchestras with other musicians playing other instruments. This corresponds to

Ikeda's passion for dialogue and for the promotion of humanism regardless of its spiritual and intellectual sources."[6]

What I hope this book has given you

I hope that this book has afforded the reader the opportunity to reinvigorate their Buddhist practice through a process of reconfiguring the collective constructs at the heart of Buddhism. All the research that I undertook for each of the chapters only affirmed the value of this path to me. Equally, I hope that any reader who has read this book prior to starting to practice Buddhism will be sufficiently inspired by the studies I have presented to see that there is no hidden agenda, no esoteric or unquantifiable mysteries which beggar belief and hold one back from giving chanting the phrase Nam-myoho-renge-kyo a go. Ten minutes in the morning and evening to a blank wall is a great prescription for a beginner with plenty of recordings on YouTube to get the hang of it.

I also hope that the book explodes some of the external criticisms laid upon Nichiren Buddhism. Because most of us live in a free society, we have the liberty to start practising a religion or philosophy of our choice and equally the liberty to stop practising it. Whatever the reasons for someone giving up their Buddhist faith, it is an important right of our society to be able to do so. SGI affirms that right, whilst placing friendship, interpersonal relationships, as the most important priority wherever people are with their faith or lack of it. Nichiren acknowledged the difficulty in sustaining Buddhist practice. He described the unfixed nature of our minds and how easily we are swayed. Whilst exiled on Sado Island and cast as an outlaw he described how 99 out of 100 of his followers left him and ceased to practice for fear of censure from the authorities and due to doubt cast by his criminal status. In his letter, "The Difficulty of Sustaining Faith", he writes, "To accept is easy; to continue is difficult. But Buddhahood lies in continuing faith." (WND 1, p471)

Over my twenty years of practice, I could in no way have predicted those of my friends and fellow members who have continued and those who have given up their Buddhist practice. Some seemingly strong practitioners have suddenly stopped whilst those less active have continued. Nichiren's encouragement to have faith like water, rather than fire, may be of some relevance here. Sometimes, stopping and experiencing life again without the practice can result in a resumption of it with even greater confidence. Nonetheless, steady, consistent efforts are the ideal.

The reasons for stopping can be varied and may sometimes be due to an external conflict, an unresolved life crisis or pressure from family and friends. However, ultimately the cause is internal. To justify their rejection of Buddhism, people can sometimes develop reasons to protect and bolster their choice, even going on the internet to source justifications to undermine SGI, Ikeda and Nichiren. People want to feel vindicated and righteous in the decisions they make. By basing my research on academic studies, my aim was to give a balanced account around these topics.

In the end, it was those supporters of Nichiren who continued in their practice despite tremendous obstacles that we remember to this day: the samurai, Shijo Kingo, who won through despite the envy and rivalry of his fellow retainers and the initial rejection of his lord, or the Ikegami brothers who persisted in following the Lotus Sutra despite the disapprobation of their father, who was eventually won round to practise alongside them.

Spiritual freedom

Although I have not dwelled too long on the subject, I hope that by looking at the research, the contrast between the spirit of SGI and the priestly order of Nichiren Shoshu has been fairly considered. Nichiren Shoshu continues to call itself 'True Buddhism', an inappropriate title for a pluralistic age. It smacks of disrespect to all other faiths. Theirs is a truth which is supported by quasi-magical claims for a supreme Gohonzon, and even a tooth purported to be Nichiren's on which, it is claimed, flesh grows at auspicious times. In separating from priestly authority, SGI has not only been able to reject such medieval thinking outright but to embrace an approach which sees truth in many like-minded philosophies and teachings which elevate the preciousness of life and the desire for world peace. In the main, anybody who makes a choice does so with the opinion that it is right and just.

One chooses a religious path by being confident of the logic and relevance of its teachings and method. Whilst SGI is still firmly convinced of the correctness of its cause, of the elevated nature of its values and the efficacy of its practice, this is not to the exclusion of wider human values that transcend structures and approaches. Our shared humanity and the pulse of life itself supersede all else.

In considering the 1991 split early on in the mid-1990s, Brian

CONCLUSION

Bocking of Bath College predicted that the Japanese members of Soka Gakkai, who were more rooted in tradition, would require a more measured and less radical change to customs and teachings than the overseas members, who would be more prepared for a fuller anti-hierarchical separation from priestly authority.[7] In the end, both Japan and the rest of the SGI have fully unshackled themselves from Nichiren Shoshu but Bocking's point may explain the gradual and measured changes to doctrine which we have seen regarding the Gohonzon and the status of Nichiren. If my conclusions in these areas seem a step further than SGI has officially stated, it is only to inspire debate, allow access to the academic research and contribute to the ongoing development of SGI.

The Buddhism of transformation, not perfection

I must stress that the book should not be used as an excuse to disrupt the precious unity of SGI. Doctrinal evolutions take time and SGI is already open and flexible enough to allow differences of opinion on some matters. As the book has shown, SGI and Nichiren Buddhism have already undergone incredibly rapid change over the last 100 years led by the brilliant innovations of the three presidents whilst ensuring to keep close to Nichiren's true heart and intentions. This book is not an excuse to create counter-narratives or worst of all, conspiracy theories. In fact, by being rooted in University-led academic research, it stands against the sad modern trend on the World Wide Web to sew emotive and paranoid theories. There is a psychological payoff in feeling aggrieved, angry and emboldened by supposed forces or organisations that are seemingly pulling strings in hidden ways. I encourage believers in such theories to question the conspiracy theorists as much as they question the accepted account of things. Are they connected to the alt-right or other movements with their own agenda? Where are their evidential sources and have they been checked? Invariably for SGI members to fall for such claims is because they have neglected their mentor and his teachings in their heart.

Instead, I will be most gratified if this book has empowered you and encouraged you to practise more vibrantly, more confidently and with even greater conviction. The practice of Nichiren Soka Gakkai Buddhism is an amazing tool to direct one's life on a positive trajectory. It has allowed me to create enormous value in mine and others' lives through internal change and decisive external action. As a Vice-President of SGI recently said, this is not the Buddhism of perfection, it is the Buddhism of transformation. This transformation holds as much for the individual as it does for the local district or the whole SGI movement. For it is the flexibility inherent in the SGI movement that has spurred its growth to continue, to renew and transform, and means there is great hope for the furtherance of Nichiren Buddhism. The Soka Gakkai Buddha continues to be an Evolving Buddha.

Additional Information

For more information regarding Soka Gakkai, SGI and Nichiren Buddhism, please visit the site www.sokaglobal.org. Scroll to the bottom to Contact Us/General Enquiries. At the bottom of that page is the Directory of Soka Gakkai Organisations where you can find information on websites and contact details for all SGI organisations across the world. Each website should have a way to connect and find out about local discussion meetings and events in your area. Depending on your country of residence you might prefer to go directly to these websites:

USA	www.sgi-usa.org
UK	www.sgi-uk.org
Canada	www.sgicanada.org
India	www.bharatsokagakkai.org
Australia	www.sgiaust.org.au
Hong Kong	www.hksgi.org
Malaysia	www.sgm.org.my

This is by far a non-exhaustive list as there are 90 constituent organisations across the world.

If you already have a friend who is an SGI member, the easiest way to get connected may be through asking them. Alternatively, your local SGI organisation website may be found through a quick google search of SGI and your country name.

To contact the author regarding the book, please message J.D. Gilbert via Facebook.

GLOSSARY

A

Adi-Buddha First or primordial Buddha giving rise to all others; identified as Universal Worthy or Vairochana in schools influenced by Vajrayana Buddhism. The most common Mahayana Buddhist view is that the Law or Buddha nature, not any particular Buddha, function as the primordial Buddha.

Aizen See Craving-Filled

Amida Buddha of Infinite Light; worshipped by Pure Land Buddhists. A supernatural being that pledged salvation in a paradise after death.

Ananda Prominent disciple of Shakyamuni (Siddhartha Gautama) portrayed as memorizing and reciting many of his teachings, including the Lotus Sutra.

Atsuhara Persecution A series of threats and acts of violence against followers of Nichiren in Atsuhara Village, in Fuji District of Suruga Province, Japan, over a period of three years, beginning in earnest in 1278.

B

Bactria Kingdom in present-day Afghanistan. Closely linked to Buddhist history and, along with Gandhara, a likely birthplace of the Lotus Sutra.

BCE Before Common Era; same as BC ('Before Christ') in older works.

Bodhisattva One who aspires to enlightenment; a life state characterised by taking compassionate action for the sake of others.

GLOSSARY

Bodhisattvas of the Earth Innumerable bodhisattvas who emerge from under the ground in the fifteenth chapter of the Lotus Sutra; they pledge to propagate the sutra after the Buddha's passing.

Brahma Hindu creator deity. Incorporated as protective deity or function in Buddhism.

C

CE Common Era; same as AD (Anno Domini which means 'In the Year of Our Lord') in older works.

Ceremony in the Air Cosmic event described in the Lotus Sutra's chapters eleven through to twenty-two. It begins with the levitation of an earthbound assembly into a gigantic floating treasure tower; as it continues the Bodhisattvas of the Earth emerge from beneath the ground, Shakyamuni reveals the eternal duration of his enlightenment, and the Buddha entrusts the Bodhisattvas of the Earth with transmitting the sutra in the future.

Craving-Filled (Aizen) Figure from the Vajrayana Buddhist tradition; Sanskrit name is Ragaraja. Appears on the Diamond World Mandala; inscribed on the Gohonzon as a Siddham seed character, where he represents the principle that earthly desires equal enlightenment.

D

Dai-Gohonzon A mandala devotional object worshipped by the Nichiren Shoshu branch of Nichiren Buddhism. See Chapter 4 for discussions on its origin and authenticity. Soka Gakkai now describe it as the Gohonzon of the second year of the Koan era.

Daimoku A term used to refer to the chanting of Nam-myoho-renge-kyo.

Daishonin Meaning 'Great Sage'; A title used for Nichiren.

Dengyo (767-822) Founder of Tendai (Chinese T'ien-t'ai) school in Japan; prominent figure in Japanese history. Influenced Nichiren who relied heavily on his interpretations.

Dharma, dharma The Buddha's enlightened teachings and the cosmic or fundamental law indicated in them. Lower-case signifies duty or normative requirements and is used in this sense in Hinduism.

Diamond World Mandala Prominent Vajrayana mandala; represents absolute wisdom.

Dozen-bo Nichiren's teacher at Seicho-ji temple. Although he protected Nichiren at times, he never fully converted to his teachings.

E

Expedient Means Mahayana concept of incremental teaching; the Buddha teaches simpler doctrines first, followed by those that are more profound as disciples gain understanding. Implicit in the concept is the notion that a Buddha or bodhisattva will employ any strategy or technique necessary to bring people to the Buddhist path and lead them to enlightenment. Also, title of the second chapter of the Lotus Sutra.

F

Four Heavenly Deva Kings Deity figures representing natural forces that foster and protect life; characters for them are placed on the corners of the Gohonzon.

Fudo See Immovable

GLOSSARY

G

Gandhara Region located in present-day northern Pakistan and eastern Afghanistan; originally a province in the Persian Achaemenid Empire. Closely linked to Buddhist history and the likely birthplace of the Lotus Sutra.

Gohonzon Mandala or devotional object first inscribed by Nichiren; literally 'supreme object of devotion' or 'honorable object worthy of deepest respect'. The phrase Nam-myoho-renge-kyo is placed prominently in the centre and various figures from the Lotus Sutra are represented in Chinese characters. Other figures and phrases are also included. Considered to embody Nichiren's enlightened life, the Treasure Tower of the Lotus Sutra and the practitioner's Buddha nature.

Gongyo Literally meaning 'assiduous practice'. Recitation of portions from the second and sixteenth chapters of the Lotus Sutra followed by the chanting of Nam-myoho-renge-kyo and a series of silent prayers. Gongyo is the main Buddhist liturgy of Nichiren Buddhism.

H

Hachiman A Japanese divinity of agriculture, fishing, archery and warriors combining elements of Shinto and Buddhism. Considered a protector of the nation.

Human Revolution Transformative process of awakening or inner change. Term first created by Shigeru Nambara in a speech as president of Tokyo University in 1947. Introduced by Josei Toda and used by Soka Gakkai and SGI to describe personal transformation through Buddhist practice but also as a contemporary alternative to the Japanese term for enlightenment.

THE EVOLVING BUDDHA

I

Ichinen Sanzen See Three Thousand Realms in a Single Moment of Life.

Ikeda, Daisaku (1928-) Soka Gakkai's third president, from 1960 to 1979. Founded SGI in 1975 and serves as its founding President. Author of numerous works related to Nichiren Buddhism.

Ikegami Brothers Munenaga and Munenaka. Staunch followers of Nichiren who twice were disowned by their father for following him. By persisting in their faith, in the end, their father converted to Nichiren's teachings in 1278.

Immeasurable Meanings Sutra Considered to be a companion sutra to the Lotus Sutra; introductory sutra of the Threefold Lotus Sutra.

Immovable (Fudo) Figure from the Vajrayana tradition; Sanskrit name is Acala. Appears on the Womb World mandala; inscribed on the Gohonzon as a Siddham seed character, where he represents the principle that the sufferings of birth and death are nirvana.

Indra Indo-Iranian god of war and thunder. Viewed as demonic by Zoroastrians and as a heroic conqueror by Hindus. Became a prominent Buddhist deity, often under the name Shakra Devanam Indra.

J

Jogyo, Bodhisattva Superior Practices First of the four leaders of the Bodhisattvas of the Earth in the Lotus Sutra. He represents 'true self'. Nichiren associated himself with Bodhisattva Superior Practices. Many later followers

GLOSSARY

considered Nichiren to be a reincarnation of Bodhisattva Superior Practices.

K

Kishimojin Both a revered goddess and demon, depending on the Buddhist tradition. In her positive aspects, she is regarded for the protection of children, easy delivery and happy child rearing, while her negative aspects include the belief of her terror towards irresponsible parents and unruly children.

Kosen Rufu Japanese pronunciation of a term from Kumarajiva's Lotus Sutra translation meaning 'to declare and spread widely.' In SGI usage it signifies the creation of a peaceful society by establishing the dignity of life as the spirit of the age; can also refer to the widespread transmission and practice of Nichiren's teachings.

Kumarajiva Buddhist monk and translator from Central Asia; arrived in China's capital in 401 CE. Translated version of the Lotus Sutra relied on by Nichiren, numerous other sutras and texts. He fostered many disciples, developed more accurate renditions of Buddhist terms into Chinese, and clarified a number of poorly understood Mahayana concepts.

Kushan Dynasty/Empire State that included Gandhara and Bactria, ruled by Tocharian-speaking Kushans between the first and third centuries CE. Came to control parts of northern India; attacks by the newly established Sasanian Empire led to its collapse around 250 CE. Important in Buddhist history; the oldest extant Mahayana texts are Chinese translations by Kushan monks.

L

Latter Day of the Law The third of three time periods after Shakyamuni's passing described in various sutras. Associated with the time of Nichiren and to last for 10,000 years and more. It is said to be a muddied age of 'quarrels and disputes' when Shakyamuni's teachings will be 'obscured and lost'.

Lotus Sutra Revered Mahayanan Buddhist text that expounds the eternity and universality of Buddhahood and the dignity of all people. Nichiren employed Kumarajiva's Chinese translation of the Sanskrit text Saddharma-pundarika-sutram, which is known as Myoho-renge-kyo in Japanese.

M

Mahavairocana 'Great Vairocana', an epithet for the Vajrayana Buddha Vairocana. Designation used to indicate the primordial Adi-Buddha of East Asian Buddhism.

Mahayana Form of Buddhism incorporating texts from outside of the Pali canon; literally 'Great Vehicle.' Prominent in East Asia and influential in Tibet. Its diverse sects generally emphasize enlightenment as a goal, the bodhisattva path and concepts such as emptiness and the interconnectedness of all phenomena.

Makiguchi, Tsunesaburo (1871-1944) Co-founder and first president of the Soka Kyoiku Gakkai; developed a value-creating educational philosophy.

Mandala Sacred diagram used in meditation or devotional prayer; often representing the mystical aspect of the cosmos; from the Sanskrit word for circle. Typically includes a circular shape embedded in rectangular panels, populated with images of representative honoured beings and deities. Can be in an enduring form such as on paper, wood or stone, a temporary instantiation such as a sand mandala, or as a visualisation. Found in both Hinduism and Buddhism.

GLOSSARY

Manjushri A bodhisattva associated with insight in Mahayana Buddhism. His name means "Gentle Glory" in Sanskrit.

Mantra Formulaic word or phrase recited to connect with the universe or invoke cosmic or mystical powers; found in Hinduism, Buddhism and early Zoroastrianism.

Many Treasures Buddha Buddha who appears in the eleventh chapter of the Lotus Sutra. He arrives seated inside his Treasure Tower; he had already entered nirvana, but promised to appear with his tower wherever the Lotus Sutra is preached. Thereafter, Shakyamuni sits next to him; both remain in the tower for the duration of the Ceremony in the Air.

Maitreya Futuristic mythical Buddha who will arrive on earth to preach the Buddhist law when Shakyamuni Buddha's teachings have been destroyed.

Megasthenes Seleucid ambassador to the Mauryan court; helped negotiate a treaty between the two empires. Reported on the characteristics of Indian religious sects in Taxila as of 305-304 BCE.

Miao-lo (711-782) Sixth patriarch of Chinese T'ien-t'ai school; wrote treatises clarifying many aspects of T'ien-t'ai's teachings. His disciples taught Dengyo when he visited China.

Minobu Mountain and area in Yamanashi prefecture, Japan where Nichiren spent the final years of his life. The temple complex on the site of his dwellings is now the headquarters of the Nichiren Shu branch of Nichiren Buddhism.

Myoho-renge-kyo Title of Kumarajiva's Lotus Sutra translation, as pronounced in Japanese.

Mystic Law Also, wonderful Law. The ultimate Law, principle, or truth of life and the universe in Nichiren's teachings; the

Law of Nam-myoho-renge-kyo.

N

Nagarjuna Buddhist philosopher from India, dates unknown although assumed to be second to third centuries CE. Viewed as foundational figure by all major forms of Mahayana Buddhism.

Nam-myoho-renge-kyo Mantra advocated as prime Buddhist practice by Nichiren. Literally, 'I devote myself to the Lotus Sutra of the Wonderful Law'. Based on the Sanskrit term *namas* combined with the Japanese pronunciation of the title of Kumarjiva's Chinese Lotus Sutra translation.

Nichikan (1665-1726) 26th Abbot of Taiseki-ji temple and reformer of the Fuji branch of Nichiren Buddhism. Inscribed the Gohonzon Soka Gakkai and SGI members currently use.

Nichigen-nyo (1242–1303) A lay follower of Nichiren and the wife of Shijō Kingo.

Nichiren Daishonin (1222-1282) Reformist Japanese Buddhist teacher; founder of Nichiren Buddhism.

Nichiren Buddhism Form of Mahayana Buddhism advocated by Nichiren and the sects or schools that claim descent from his teachings.

Nichiren Shoshu Japanese Buddhist sect claiming priestly lineage through Nichiren's disciple Nikko; affiliated with the Soka Gakkai until 1991.

Nichiren Shu Japanese Buddhist sect, which prior to World War Two, was the largest Nichiren denomination. Head temple based at Mount Minobu where Nichiren spent his last years.

GLOSSARY

Nichizen, Shosuke-bo (d.1331) A disciple of Nichiren; member of the Yui family of Kawai in the Fuji area, Japan. Originally a priest at Ryūsen-ji temple of the Tendai school in Atsuhara Village of Suruga Province, Nichizen took faith in Nichiren's teachings in 1275. Also known as Sho-bo.

Nikko Shonin (d.1333) Disciple of and secretary to Nichiren; considered founder of a number of schools of Nichiren Buddhism.

Nissho Mitzutani (1879-1957) 64th High Priest of Nichiren Shoshu.

Nirvana Buddhist term defined variously as final extinction, cessation of rebirth, quiet tranquillity or enlightenment.

Nirvana Sutra Any Mahayana sutra describing Shakyamuni's final days and extinction. There are several versions in which key Mahayana doctrines are reiterated. The sutras differ from the Pali Nibbana Sutra.

O

Ongi Kuden See Orally Transmitted Teachings

Orally Transmitted Teachings, The Record of (Ongi Kuden) is a text in Nichiren Buddhism. It is believed by a number of Nichiren schools to be Nichiren's oral teachings (kuden) on the Lotus Sutra, which Nikko Shonin recorded and compiled. The earliest known version dates from a copy made in 1539.

P

Pali Canon Collection of texts in the Pali language considered to be authoritative by Theravada Buddhism.

Pure Land Category of Mahayana Buddhist sect and teachings that encourage aspiration to move to a heavenly realm after death. In general, the world is viewed as too painful and corrupt for Buddhahood to be realised; instead, one calls on the name of the saviour Buddha, Amida or Amitayus for rebirth in a Pure Land.

R

Record of the Orally Transmitted Teachings See Orally Transmitted Teachings.

S

Sanskrit Language of ancient Indo-Aryans; employed in Hindu religious texts and introduced into Buddhism by Mahayana texts and scholars.

Seicho-ji Temple of Japanese Tendai sect, which Nichiren entered as an acolyte in 1233. He took his priestly vows there; he returned to the temple after completing his studies to proclaim his teaching in 1253.

SGI Soka Gakkai International, first established in 1975 in tandem with the International Buddhist League. Global umbrella organisation of Soka Gakkai branches worldwide.

Shakyamuni Also known as Siddhartha Gautama or simply the Buddha. Founded Buddhism in India and probably active during the fifth century BCE.

Shariputra Considered the first of the Buddha's two chief male disciples. He frequently appears in Mahayana sutras, and in some sutras, is used as a counterpoint to represent the Theravada school of Buddhism.

Shijo Kingo (1230-1300) Samurai follower of Nichiren Daishonin who lived in Kamakura, Japan and who is said to have converted to Nichiren's teachings in 1256.

GLOSSARY

Sho-Hondo Temple building funded by Soka Gakkai members' contributions to house the Dai-Gohonzon. Construction was completed in 1972 and it was destroyed in 1999 on the orders of the Nichiren Shoshu priesthood.

Siddham Indic script derived from Brahmi widely used in Vajrayana Buddhist tradition; Siddham seed characters are abbreviated or symbolic representations of Buddhas, bodhisattvas or deities.

Soka Gakkai Buddhist lay organization founded in 1930 in Japan; literally 'Value Creating Society.' Its members practice Nichiren Buddhism; in 2014, it adopted the newly formed stand-alone denomination of Soka Gakkai Nichiren Buddhism.

Soka Gakkai International Global umbrella organisation of Soka Gakkai branches worldwide.

Soka Kyoiku Gakkai Initial name of Soka Gakkai, literally 'Value Creating Educational Society.'

T

Taiseki-ji Head Temple of the Nichiren Shoshu branch of Nichiren Buddhism.

Tatsunokuchi Beach located by Kamakura, Japan, where prisoners were executed. Nichiren was nearly beheaded there in 1271.

Ten Worlds or Ten Life States Buddhist description of the life states experienced by living beings; foundational for T'ien-t'ai's philosophy and theory of three thousand realms in a single moment of life, which Nichiren embraced. Sequentially, the worlds are hell, hunger, animality, anger, humanity or tranquillity, rapture or heaven, learning, self-realisation, bodhisattva and Buddhahood.

Tendai Japanese rendering of the Chinese name T'ien-t'ai; name of the Buddhist school founded in Japan by Dengyo and inspired by T'ien-t'ai's teachings. Nichiren entered the Buddhist priesthood at a Tendai temple.

Theravada Dominant form of Buddhism in Sri Lanka and Southeast Asia, literally 'School of the Elder Monks.' Only complete surviving version of Early Buddhist schools; it relies on the Pali canon.

Three Thousand Realms in a Single Moment of Life (Ichinen Sanzen in Japanese) Buddhist theory first articulated by T'ien-t'ai describing the dynamic potentiality of response in each moment and the interpenetrating nature of life and phenomena.

T'ien-t'ai (538-597) (Personal name - Zhiyi) Chinese Buddhist sage and founder of the T'ien-t'ai school of Buddhism and influential figure in Mahayana philosophy. He drew both from Nagarjuna and from practices based on the Lotus Sutra; he developed the theory of three thousand realms in a single moment of life. T'ien-t'ai greatly influenced Dengyo and Nichiren. Can also refer to the T'ien-t'ai school of Buddhism.

Toda, Josei (1900-1958) Co-founder and second president of the Soka Gakkai; survived imprisonment during World War Two. Renamed, re-established, and powerfully advanced the organisation; recruited and inspired the young Daisaku Ikeda as his successor and disciple.

Toki Jonin One of Nichiren's earliest followers, taking faith in 1254. Nichiren entrusted him with a number of important writings.

GLOSSARY

W

WND Writings of Nichiren Daishonin, in two volumes. Edited by the Gosho Translation Committee.

Womb World Mandala Prominent Vajrayana mandala; represents the true aspect of reality, in its innumerable manifestations, as it develops dynamically.

Y

Yama Hindu and later Buddhist lord of the underworld, similar to Yima in Zoroastrianism.

Yima Zoroastrian lord of the underworld.

Z

Zen Japanese version of Chinese Chan Buddhism which concentrates on attaining enlightenment through direct experience without the use of logical thought or language.

Zoroastrianism One of the world's oldest continuously practiced religions. Centred on a dualistic cosmology of good and evil and an eschatology predicting the ultimate conquest of evil.

TIMELINE

Date	Event
5th Century BCE	Life of **Shakyamuni** - (Siddhartha Gautama, the Buddha) Founder of Buddhism, Northern India
50-200 CE	**Lotus Sutra** likely composed in the kingdoms of Gandhara and Bactria (in the Kushan Empire) between modern day Afghanistan and Pakistan
2nd Century CE	**Nagarjuna** - Patriarch of nearly all Mahayana schools and thirteenth successor of the Buddha, India
344-413	**Kumarajiva**- Monk of Central Asia, translated the Lotus Sutra into Chinese
538-597	**T'ien-t'ai** - Founder of the T'ien-t'ai school, reinterprets the Lotus Sutra, China

TIMELINE

711-782	**Miao-lo** - Sixth patriarch of the T'ien-t'ai school, further systematizes the school's teachings, China
767-822	**Dengyo** - Founder of Japanese Tendai school and proponent of the Lotus Sutra in Japan
Died 1276	**Dozen-bo** - Taught Nichiren at former Tendai temple, Seicho-ji, Awa, Japan
1222	Birth of **Nichiren** - Founder of Nichiren Buddhism in Awa Prefecture, Japan
28th April 1253	**Nichiren** proclaims his teaching and chants Nam-myoho-renge kyo for the first time
16th July 1260	**Nichiren** submits 'On Establishing the Correct Teaching for the Peace of the Land' to the country's most powerful leader

1261-1263	**Nichiren** exiled to Izu Peninsula, present-day Shizuoka Prefecture, Japan
11th November 1264	**Komatsubara Persecution - Nichiren** attacked by Tojo Kagenobu's men
12th September 1271	**Tatsunokuchi Persecution - Nichiren** survives attempted execution
9th October 1271	**Nichiren** inscribes the first recorded rudimentary **Gohonzon** known as 'The Toothpick Gohonzon'
1st November 1271	**Nichiren** arrives at Tsukahara for his second exile on Sado Island off the coast of Western Honshu, Japan.
March 1274	**Nichiren** leaves Sado after being pardoned the previous month
May 1274	**Nichiren** moves to Mount Minobu, Yamanashi Prefecture, Japan

TIMELINE

1278-1281	**Atsuhara Persecution** - A series of threats and acts of violence against followers of **Nichiren** in Atsuhara Village, in Fuji District of Suruga Province, Japan
13th October 1282	**Nichiren** dies aged 61 at the residence of Ikegami Munenaka
1333	Death of **Nikko Shonin**, Nichiren's secretary and disciple
1665-1726	**Nichikan** - 26th Abbot of Taiseki-ji temple and reformer of the Fuji branch of Nichiren Buddhism. Inscribes Gohonzon currently used by SGI members.
1871-1944	**Tsunesaburo Makiguchi** - First president of the Soka Gakkai (then Soka Kyoiku Gakkai); dies in prison during World War Two

1900-1958	**Josei Toda** - Second president of the Soka Gakkai
1928-	**Daisaku Ikeda** – Third president of the Soka Gakkai and founding president of SGI (Soka Gakkai International)
18th November 1930	Founding date of the **Soka Gakkai** - **Tsunesaburo Makiguchi** and **Josei Toda** publish a book on value creating education published by the Soka Kyoiku Gakkai
6th July 1943	**Makiguchi** and **Toda** arrested and imprisoned by the wartime authorities
18th November 1944	**Makiguchi** dies in prison
November 1944	**Toda** has a profound awakening experience in prison
3rd July 1945	**Toda** released from prison and begins to rebuild the Soka Gakkai
14th August 1947	**Ikeda** attends his first Soka Gakkai meeting and encounters Josei Toda

TIMELINE

24th August 1947	**Ikeda** joins the Soka Gakkai
3rd May 1951	**Toda** becomes Soka Gakkai's second president and announces his vow to achieve 750,000 practising member households
2nd April 1958	**Toda** dies aged 58 having achieved his goal of 750,000 member households in December 1957
3rd May 1960	**Ikeda** becomes Soka Gakkai's third president
27th July 1963	**Soka Gakkai** membership reaches 3.6 million member households
28th January 1970	**Soka Gakkai** membership reaches 7.5 million member households
26th January 1975	**Soka Gakkai International** established with **Ikeda** as its president
April 1979	**Ikeda** steps down as Soka Gakkai president

28th November 1991	**SGI Day of Spiritual Independence** – Nichiren Shoshu excommunicate all Soka Gakkai members worldwide
2014	**Soka Gakkai Nichiren Buddhism** established as an independent denomination

SELECTED BIBLIOGRAPHY

Bluck, Robert. *British Buddhism: Teachings, practice and development.* Abingdon, Oxon: Routledge, 2006.

Brannen, Noah S. *Soka Gakkai: Japan's Militant Buddhists.* Richmond, Virginia: John Knox Press, 1968.

Carter SR., Lawrence Edward. *A Baptist Preacher's Buddhist Teacher: How My Interfaith Journey With Daisaku Ikeda Made Me a Better Christian.* Santa Monica, CA: Middleway Press, 2018.

Causton, Richard. *The Buddha in Daily Life: An Introduction to the Buddhism of Nichiren Daishonin.* London: Rider, 1995.

Clarke, Peter B. and Jeffrey Somers eds. *Japanese New Religions in the West.* Folkestone, Kent: Japan Library, 1994.

Cowan, Jim. *The Britain Potential: A politics inspired by a new stage of human consciousness.* Bury St. Edmunds: Arena Books, 2019.

Dator, James Allen. *Soka Gakkai, Builders of the Third Civilization: American and Japanese Members.* Seattle: University of Washington Press, 1969.

Dawkins, Richard. *The God Delusion.* London: Black Swan, 2007.

de Botton, Alain. *Religion for Atheists.* London: Penguin, 2012.

Esfahani Smith, Emily. *The Power of Meaning: The True Route to Happiness.* London: Rider, 2017.

Farias, Miguel and Catherine Wikholm. *The Buddha Pill.* London: Watkins, 2015.

Fenwick, Peter and Elizabeth Fenwick. *The Art of Dying.* London: Bloomsbury, 2008.

Gamble, Adam and Takesato Watanabe. *A Public Betrayed: An Inside Look at Japanese Media Atrocities and Their Warnings to the West.* Washington, DC: Regenery, 2004.

Harari, Yuval Noah. *Sapiens: A Brief History of Humankind.* London: Vintage, 2014.

Ikeda, Daisaku. *Buddhism: The First Millenium.* Santa Monica, CA: Middleway Press, 2009.

———. *Faith Into Action.* Santa Monica, CA: World Tribune Press, 1999.

———. *The Human Revolution.* 12 vols. Revised English Translation. Taplow, Maidenhead: SGI-UK, 1995.

———. *Learning from the Gosho: The Eternal Teachings of Nichiren Daishonin.* Santa Monica, CA: World Tribune Press, 1997.

———. *Life: An Enigma, a Precious Jewel.* New York: Kodansha International, 1982.

BIBLIOGRAPHY

------------------. *The New Human Revolution*. 30 vols. Santa Monica, CA: World Tribune Press, 1995-2020.

------------------. *A Youthful Diary: One Man's Journey from the Beginning of Faith to Worldwide Leadership for Peace.* Santa Monica, CA: World Tribune Press, 2000.

Ikeda, Daisaku with Katsuji Saito, Takanori Endo and Haruo Suda. *The Wisdom of the Lotus Sutra: A discussion.* 6 vols. Santa Monica, CA: World Tribune Press, 2000-03.

Ikeda, Daisaku and Chandra Wickramasinghe. *Space and Eternal Life.* London: Journeyman, 1998.

Lickerman, Alex. *The Undefeated Mind: On the Science of Constructing an Indestructible Self.* Florida: Health Communications Inc, 2012.

Mandara, Ken. *The Journal of Nichiren Buddhist Studies- Issue 03-17: The mandalas of Sokagakkai and Nichiren Shoshu in recent history.* The Nichiren Mandala Study Workshop, 2017.

Mandara, Ken. *The Journal of Nichiren Buddhist Studies- Issue 04-17: How Nichiren's disciples were influenced by the Gohonzon they received and the moji-mandala versus the tridimensional honzon.* The Nichiren Mandala Study Workshop, 2017.

Machacek, David and Bryan Wilson eds. *Global Citizens: The Soka Gakkai Buddhist Movement in the World.* Oxford: Oxford University Press, 2000.

Matsudo, Yukio. *The Instant Enlightenment of Ordinary People: Nichiren Buddhism 2.0 for the 21st Century.* Heidelberg, Germany: DPI Publishing, 2018.

McCarty, Gary. *Daisaku Ikeda: Ambassador of Peace.* Santa Monica, CA: World Tribune Press, 1984.

Montgomery, Daniel B. *The Fire in the Lotus: The Dynamic Buddhism of Nichiren.* London: Mandala, 1991.

Murata, Kiyoaki. *Japan's New Buddhism: An Objective Account of Soka Gakkai.* New York: Weatherhill, 1971.

Nelson, Adrian David. *The Origins of Consciousness: How the search to understand the nature of consciousness is leading to a new view of reality.* Nottingham, England: Metarising Books, 2015.

Nichiren Daishonin – editor/translator The Gosho Translation Committee. *The Writings of Nichiren Daishonin.* Tokyo: Soka Gakkai, 1999.

The Nichiren Mandala Study Workshop. *The mandala in Nichiren Buddhism: Special Edition.* The Nichiren Mandala Study Workshop, 2013.

--. *The mandala in Nichiren Buddhism: Special Feature. The "Honmon Kaidan Daigohonzon" Of Nichiren Shoshu Taiseki-ji.* The Nichiren Mandala Study Workshop, 2015.

Ourvan, Jeff. *The Star Spangled Buddhist: Zen, Tibetan and Soka Gakkai Buddhism and the Quest for Enlightenment in America.* New York: Skyhorse Publishing, 2013.

BIBLIOGRAPHY

Radhakrishnan, N. *Ikeda Sensei: The Triumph of Mentor-Disciple Spirit.* Kuala Lumpur: Soka Gakkai Malaysia, 2007.

Seager, Richard Hughes. *Encountering the Dharma: Daisaku Ikeda, Soka Gakkai, and the Globalization of Buddhist Humanism.* Berkley and Los Angeles, CA: University of California Press, 2006.

Sheldrake, Rupert. *Science and Spiritual Practices: Reconnecting through Direct Experience.* London: Coronet, 2017.

Soka Gakkai Tohoku Youth Division. *March 11, 2011 More than Survival: Messages to the Future.* Tokyo: Daisanbunmei-Sha Inc, 2016.

Stone, Jacqueline I. *Original Enlightenment and the Transformation of Medieval Japanese Buddhism.* Hawaii: University of Hawaii, 1999.

——————————. "Biographical Studies of Nichiren." In *Japanese Journal of Religious Studies 26/3-4,* 1999.

——————————. "By Imperial Edict and Shogunal Decree: Politics and the Issue of the Ordination Platform in Modern Lay Nichiren Buddhism." In *Buddhism in the Modern World: Adaptations of an Ancient Tradition,* edited by Steven Heine and Charles S Prebish. Oxford: Oxford University Press, 2003.

——————————. "Japanese Lotus Millenialism: From Militant Nationalism to Contemporary Peace Movements." In *Millenialism, Persecution and Violence: Historical Cases,* edited by Catherine Wessinger. New York: Syracuse University Press, 2000.

Strand, Clark. *Waking the Buddha: How the Most Dynamic and Empowering Buddhist Movement in History Is Changing Our Concept of Religion.* Santa Monica, CA: Middleway Press, 2014.

Taylor, Steve. *Spiritual Science: Why science needs spirituality to make sense of the world.* London: Watkins, 2018.

Urbain, Olivier. *Daisaku Ikeda's Philosophy of Peace: Dialogue, Transformation and Global Citizenship.* New York: I.B. Tauris, 2010.

Walsh, J.M. *Dial In: Soka Buddhism on the Religious Spectrum.* J.M. Walsh, 2018.

--------------. *Your Enlightened Mind Wants to Know: Mahayana's Origins and the Implications for Buddhism,* J.M. Walsh, 2012.

Watson, Burton transl. *The Lotus Sutra.* New York: Colombia University Press, 1993.

-------------------- transl. *The Record of the Orally Transmitted Teachings.* Tokyo: Soka Gakkai, 2004.

White, James L. *The Sokagakkai and Mass Society.* Stanford, CA: Stanford University Press, 1970.

Wilson, Bryan and Karel Dobbelaere. *A Time to Chant: The Soka Gakkai Buddhists in Britain.* Oxford: Oxford University Press, 1994.

Wilson, Bryan and Jamie Cresswell, ed. *New Religious Movements: Challenge and Response.* London: Routledge, 1999.

BIBLIOGRAPHY

Woollard, William. *A Personal Journey: Ancient Buddhism, modern science, and working out how to make the most of life.* Surrey: Grosvenor House Publishing, 2018.

----------------------. *The Case for Buddhism.* Surrey: Grosvenor House Publishing, 2013.

Yatomi, Shin. *Buddhism in a New Light: Eighteen Essays That Illuminate Our Buddhist Practice.* Santa Monica, CA: World Tribune Press, 2006.

NOTES

Chapter One
The Lotus Sutra

[1] Walsh, 2018, p89
[2] Ikeda, Saito, Endo and Suda, 2000-2003, Vol. 3, pp262-263
[3] Ikeda, 1977, edition 2009, p114
[4] Ikeda, Saito, Endo and Suda, 2000-2003, Vol. 1, p64
[5] Walsh, 2012, p121
[6] Ibid, p172
[7] Yatomi, 2006, edition 2012, pp144-5
[8] Ikeda, 1995-2020, Vol 27, p67
[9] Walsh, 2018, pp220-221
[10] Strand, 2014, p140
[11] Ibid, 2014, p140
[12] Ibid, 2014, pp141-145
[13] Walsh, 2012, p47
[14] Walsh, 2018, pp92-93
[15] Walsh, 2012, p158

Chapter Two
Nichiren

[1] Stone, 1999, p248
[2] Stone, *Japanese Journal of Religious Studies*, 1999, p444
[3] Takagi Yutuka, *Kiyosumi no Nichiren,* Kanazawa Bunko kenkyu, 1966
[4] Stone, *Japanese Journal of Religious Studies*, 1999, p443
[5] Ibid, p444
[6] Stone, 1999, p299
[7] Matsudo, 2018, p127
[8] Ibid, p50
[9] SGI Newsletter 9404, The Basics of Nichiren Buddhism for the New Era of Worldwide Kosen-rufu— Part 3 Worldwide Kosen-rufu and

NOTES

the Soka Gakkai —Chapter 1: The Lineage and Tradition of Buddhist Humanism, Wednesday, 8 June 2016
[10] Ibid, p36
[11] Miyata Koichi, *Some Problems with the Teachings of Nichiu*, 2009
[12] Ikeda, Saito, Endo and Suda, 2000-2003, Vol. 5, pp172-173
[13] Ibid, p167
[14] Ibid, p168
[15] Matsudo, 2018, pp119-120
[16] Showateihon Nichiren Shonin Ibun p10
[17] Stone, 1999, p256
[18] Ibid, pp258-9
[19] Ibid, p261
[20] Yatomi, 2006, pp151-52
[21] Ikeda, 13/8/1996
[22] Yatomi, 2006, p15
[23] Watson transl. *The Record of the Orally Transmitted Teachings*, 2004, p233

Chapter Three
Nam-myoho-renge-kyo

[1] Strand, 2014, p29
[2] Walsh, 2018, pp225-226
[3] Sheldrake, 2017, Ch.6, pp136-161
[4] Ikeda, 1997, p80
[5] Walsh, 2018, p245
[6] Ikeda, 1995-2020, Vol 19, pp197-198
[7] Ikeda from 'Mahayana Buddhism and Twenty-First Century Civilisation,' a speech delivered at Harvard University, 24 September, 1993
[8] Ikeda, 1999, p120
[9] Ikeda, 1997, p80
[10] Strand, 2014, p13
[11] Ikeda, 1995-2020, Vol 16, p158
[12] Makiguchi, quoted in Daibyaku Renge, Oct 2010
[13] Hawking. *A Brief History of Time*, 1988, p174
[14] Taylor, 2018, p6

[15] Damasio, 'How the brain creates the mind'. *Scientific American – The Hidden Mind*, 2002
[16] Taylor, 2018, p72
[17] Ikeda, 1982, p47
[18] Fenwick and Fenwick, 2008, p188
[19] Taylor, 2018, p64
[20] Ibid, p211
[21] The impact of the observer on quantum experiments is further illustrated by an experiment in which two boxes are presented to an observer, one in which there is a photon. By opening in succession the slit in each box to release the photon on to a detector screen, we can ascertain which box has the photon in it because it is detected as a particle point on the screen. However, when the observer opens both boxes simultaneously rather than creating a particle point, the photon creates a wave pattern on the screen, a wave of possibility which stretches out if we put the boxes further and further apart, something impossible if the photon had only been in one of the boxes. Nelson, 2015, Ch.3
[22] Quoted by Nelson, 2015, p51
[23] Ikeda, 1982, p42
[24] Nelson, 2015, Ch.4
[25] A different set of experiments involve a Random Event Generator or REG for short, which uses a random flow of electrons in the same binary way you could flip a coin and on average receive 100 heads to 100 tails. In the REG there are either high counts or low counts. Participants were either requested to focus on creating a high count, a low count or not influencing the instrument at all. Over 800,000 trials, the data showed highly significant statistical changes towards the intended count which hinted at the influence of mind beyond the brain. The REG machine has even been used to monitor 'peak' global moments in collective human experience, such as the dawn of the millennium and the 9/11 terrorist atrocity, when sharp deviation from the standard random pattern appeared. Nelson, 2015, Ch. 5
[26] Ibid, pp95-96
[27] Fenwick and Fenwick, 2008, p101
[28] Nelson, 2015, p102

NOTES

[29] Radin, personal communication with Nelson, 2013 quoted in Nelson, 2015, p107

[30] Ikeda, 1982, pp43-44

[31] Fenwick and Fenwick, 2008

[32] Wickramasinghe and Ikeda, 1998, pp105-106

[33] Fenwick and Fenwick, 2008, p196

[34] Esfahani-Smith, 2017, p131

[35] Taylor, 2018, p130

[36] Ikeda, 1995 Vol.4, p12

[37] Ikeda, Saito, Endo and Suda, 2000-2003, Vol. 1, p25

[38] Farias and Wikholm, 2015, pp143-145

[39] Suzuki Daisetz. *Zen and Japanese Culture*. London: Routledge and Keagan Paul, 1959, p63

[40] Victoria Brian. *Zen at War*. New York: Weatherhill, 1997

[41] Farias and Wikholm, 2015, pp133-135

[42] Ibid, pp124-125

[43] Sheldrake, 2017, p35

[44] Causton, 1995, p74

[45] Wickramasinghe and Ikeda, 1998, p69

[46] Farias and Wikholm, 2015, p135

[47] Ibid, p120

[48] Lynch, Prihodova, Dunne, Carroll, Walsh, McMahon and White, 'Mantra Meditation for Mental Health in the General Population: A Systematic Review'. *European Journal of Integrative Medicine*, 23 September 2018

[49] Gao, Leung, Wu, Skouras and Sik, 'The neurophysiological correlates of religious chanting' in Nature Magazine, 12 March 2019

[50] Perry, Polito and Thompson, 'Chanting Meditation improves mood and social cohesion'. Macquarie University, July 2016

[51] Matsudo-Kiliani and Matsudo. *Change your Brainwaves, Change your Karma: Nichiren Buddhism 3.1*. DPI Publishing, 2017, pp73-78 and pp201-204

[52] Diamond Jared. *Guns, Germs and Steel- 20th anniversary edition*. London: Vintage, 2017, p505

[53] Hunt and Schooler, 'The Easy Part of the Hard Problem: A Resonance Theory of Consciousness' published online in *Frontiers in Human Neuroscience*, 31 October 2019
[54] Hunt, 'The Hippies were right: It's all about vibrations, man! A new theory of consciousness in *Scientific American*, 5 December 2018
[55] Ibid
[56] Walsh, 2012, p240
[57] Nelson, 2015, p171
[58] Ikeda, Saito, Endo and Suda, 2000-2003, Vol. 3, p58
[59] Ibid, pp267-268
[60] Walsh, 2012, p223
[61] Taylor, 2018, p37
[62] *Living Buddhism*, multiple issues, 2004
[63] Toynbee and Ikeda. *Choose Life*. New York: Oxford University Press, 1976, p36

Chapter Four
The Gohonzon
[1] Ikeda quoted in Causton, 1995, pp238-239
[2] Ibid, p230
[3] The Nichiren Mandala Study Workshop, 2013, pp29-32
[4] Ibid, pp137-139
[5] Ibid, see p45 for further details on this Gohonzon
[6] Ibid, p300
[7] Matsudo, 2018, p283
[8] Mandara, 2017, Issue 04, p19
[9] Ibid, Issue 03, p10
[10] Ibid, p10
[11] Matsudo, 2018, pp299-302
[12] Walsh, 2018, p195
[13] For a summary of the research on the Dai Gohonzon see The Nichiren Mandala Study Workshop, 2015
[14] Ibid, p12
[15] Ibid, p8
[16] The Nichiren Mandala Study Workshop, 2013, pp66-67
[17] Yatomi, 2006, p77

NOTES

Chapter Five
The Soka Gakkai and SGI

[1] Brannen, 1968, p23
[2] Ibid, pp162-163
[3] Strand, 2014, p21
[4] Harriet Sherwood in *The Guardian*, 11 July 2019
[5] Frank Newport in *Polling Matters*, 16 July 2019
[6] Esfahani Smith, 2017, p55
[7] Lyubomirski. *The How of Happiness,* 2007, p26
[8] Dutton. *Energize your workplace: How to create and sustain high quality connections at work*, 2003
[9] Dunbar in *The New Scientist* 25 April 2014, p36
[10] Christakis in *The New Scientist*, 3 January 2009, p25
[11] Seligman. *Flourish*, 2011, p20
[12] Sampson in *The New Scientist*, 11 May 2013
[13] Esfahani Smith, 2017
[14] Huta and Ryan. *Pursuing Pleasure or Virtue, Study 4*, 2010
[15] Esfahani Smith, 2017, pp22-23
[16] Baumeister, Vohs, Aaker and Garbinsky in *The Journal of Positive Psychology 8*, no.6 pp505-16
[17] Taylor, 2018, pp13-15
[18] Lieberman and Taylor both referenced in 'Where Belief is Born', Alok Jha in *The Guardian*, 30 June 2005
[19] Farias and Wikholm, 2015, p78
[20] Dawkins, 2006, p59
[21] Ibid, p381
[22] Beckford in Wilson and Creswell (eds), 1999, pp106-108
[23] Barker in Ibid, p29
[24] Beckford in Ibid, p117
[25] Wilson in Ibid, p9
[26] Chryssides in Ibid, p258
[27] Wilson in Ibid, p1
[28] Lilliston and Shepherd in Ibid, p130
[29] Ibid, p128
[30] Wilson in Wilson and Machacek (eds), 2000, p372

[31] Quoted by Nicole Fisher in Forbes.com, 29 March 2019
[32] Hummer, Rogers, Nam and Ellison, 'Religious Involvement and U.S Adult Mortality' in *Demography*
Vol. 36, No. 2, May, 1999, pp273-285
[33] Koenig, King and Carson. *Handbook of Religion and Health*. Oxford University Press, 2012
[34] Quoted by Rachael Rettner, in livescience.com 'God Help Us? How Religion is Good (And Bad) For Mental Health', 23 September, 2015
[35] Inzlicht in *Psychological Science*, Vol 20, No.3, 2009
[36] Taylor, 2018, p26
[37] Rettner, 2015
[38] de Botton, 2012, p12
[39] Ibid, p18
[40] Dawkins, 2006, p27
[41] Ikeda, Vol.19, 1995-2020, p267
[42] Ibid, pp289-291
[43] Whitehead. *Science and the Modern World*. New York, 1925, p189
[44] Strand, 2014, pp58-59
[45] Hurst in Machacek and Wilson (eds), 2000, p86
[46] Strand, 2014, p66
[47] Chappell, 'Racial Diversity in the Soka Gakkai' in *Engaged Buddhism in the West*. Boston, 2000
[48] Hurst in Machacek and Wilson (eds), 2000, p93
[49] Cowan, 2019, p94
[50] Cowan, 2019, pp91-92
[51] Ikeda, Vol.19, 1995-2020, pp218-219
[52] Yatomi, 2006, p106
[53] Machacek in Machacek and Wilson (eds), 2000, p283
[54] Ibid, p295
[55] Seager, 2006, p204
[56] Hurst in Machacek and Wilson (eds), 2000, p70
[57] Seager, 2006, xv
[58] Montgomery, 1991, p207
[59] Ibid, p209
[60] Strand, 2014, p172
[61] Ikeda, 1999, p238

NOTES

Chapter Six
Daisaku Ikeda

[1] Seager, 2006, p124

[2] Gamble and Watanabe, 2004, p220

[3] Ikeda, 1995-2020, Vol 1, xi

[4] Strand, 2014, p111

[5] Esfahani Smith, 2017, p104

[6] Gottschall Jonathan. *The storytelling animal: How stories make us human.* New York: Mariner Books, 2012, p161

[7] For a summary of McAdams research see Esfahani Smith, 2017, pp107-110

[8] Grant Adam and Dutton Jane, 'Beneficiary or Benefactor: Are people more prosocial when they reflect on receiving or giving?' in *Psychological Science 23*, no.9, 2012, pp1033-39

[9] Ikeda, 2000, pp8-9

[10] Ibid, p498 and p500

[11] Carter, 2018, pp56-57

[12] Strand, 2014, p163

[13] Ikeda, 2000, p3

[14] Ibid, p41

[15] Ibid, p183

[16] See Mark Gabor. *Sho Hondo*, 2014 for a first person account of the American movement in 1972-3 where Ikeda is regularly referenced. Also see Yasuji Kirimura. *The Fundamentals of Buddhism*, 1977 pp136-137 for an English language book which explained the concept of 'Master and Disciple' as it was then referred to.

[17] McCarty, 1984, p3

[18] Ikeda, Saito, Endo and Suda, 2000-2003, Vol. 1, p163

[19] Strand, 2014, p116

[20] Stone, 2000

[21] Strand, 2014, pp160-161

[22] 'Orlando Bloom on Buddhism, Nam-myoho-renge-kyo and Daisaku Ikeda', posted by SGI USA on Youtube.com 1 Feb 2019

[23] Carter, 2018, p58

[24] Radhakrishnan, 2007, p21

[25] Ibid, p46

[26] Seager, 2006, p63
[27] Ikeda quoted in Murata, 1971, p173
[28] Ikeda, 1995, Vol 1, Author's Foreword
[29] Tedeschi and Calhoun, 'Posttraumatic Growth: Conceptual Groundings and Empirical Evidence' in *Psychological Inquiry 15*, no.1, 2004 pp1-18
[30] Southwick Steven and Charney Dennis. *Resilience: The Science of Mastering Life's Greatest Challenges.* Cambridge: Cambridge University Press, 2012
[31] Seager, 2006, p142
[32] Urbain, 2010, p6
[33] Ibid, p179
[34] Murata, 1971, p106
[35] Ibid, p106
[36] White, 1970, p232
[37] Ibid, p232
[38] Murata, 1971, p129
[39] Ibid, p176
[40] Seager 2006, p96
[41] Ibid, p98
[42] Machachek in Machachek and Wilson (eds.), 2000, p291
[43] Strand, 2014, p127
[44] McCarty, 1984, p30
[45] Carter, 2018, p19
[46] Ibid, p124
[47] Ibid, p129
[48] Seager, 2006, p175
[49] Strand, 2014, p153
[50] Seager, 2006, p168
[51] White, 1970, p243
[52] Gamble and Watanabe, 2004, p221
[53] White, 1970, p243
[54] Seager, 2005, p62
[55] White, 1970 p84 and p196
[56] Gamble and Watanabe, 2004, p92
[57] Ibid, p107

NOTES

[58] Ibid, p227
[59] Ibid, p228
[60] Ibid, p230
[61] Ibid, p232
[62] Ibid, pp240-241
[63] Ibid, p239
[64] Carter, 2018, p125
[65] Nakamoto Michiyo, 'Japan's LDP Puts Faith in Religious Partner: New Komeito, a Party Backed by Buddhists, Is a Key Element of the Coalition's Re-election Strategy' in *The Financial Times*, Japan Edition. 6 November 2003

Conclusion
[1] Harari, 2014, pp254-256
[2] Ibid, p128
[3] Ibid, p132
[4] Ibid, pp402-403
[5] Carter quoted in Seager, 2006, p177
[6] Urbain, 2010, p42
[7] Bocking in Clarke and Somers (eds.), 1994, pp129-130

Printed in Great Britain
by Amazon